7 FOOT MAN-EATING CHICKEN

By:
Keith Glass

DEDICATION

I' ve reflected many times and in many places how lucky I've been in my life.

When you start off with the two best parents imaginable, that's where the "luck" began! Though they passed away within a year of each other in 2011 and 2012, they are always around me.

My Mom was the one who made me feel "special" every day. She is the one to blame/credit for the stories and the need to tell them that follow here. She encouraged me to express myself daily through story-telling. She always listened, at least I thought she was. As a little boy the main goal of my day was to make her laugh and my stories seemed to accomplish that

It is my Dad though who is more prominently featured in some of these chapters. That's understandable in that we were "partner's" not only in business but in Life.

So this is dedicated to the both of them but especially for you Dad.

I got your back…like you always had all of ours!

Keith

ACKNOWLEDGEMENTS

On first thought, I was going to save my thanks to LARA BURKE for the end of this page. However, I don't want her to get lost in the order since she has been the most supportive and important part of my finishing this book.

Lara not only edited this but she was in reality my collaborator! The reason this book took over a year to write was because it was disjointed. This was the result of writing it at different points in time. Lara focused me in on what I needed to work on and so much more. I can actually still hear her asking me one night:

"What the hell are you trying to say?!"

In short without Lara there is no book. Thank you so much!

My neighbor, Bob Kellner also deserves much thanks. He was always supportive of this effort. Having read my first book, "Taking Shots", he always encouraged me to finish this one as well. Beyond that support, it was Bob who is responsible for the cover illustrating of this book. Flatly, I couldn't have asked for a better version of my vision of what a 7 Foot Man would look like. His talent is obvious to anyone! He has learned to never "volunteer" again!

I also want to thank Scott Spewiak who was the final impetus to getting this actually published and who introduced me to Ryan Spengler at Printopia, who I partnered with to publish this volume. I had been looking for someone to believe in this project and these were the guys. Thanks to both.

Lastly, thanks to all of the "characters" that appear here. Obviously without their uniqueness there would be no stories to tell.

KG

TABLE OF CONTENTS

FOREWARD

I first met Keith Glass in 1979 in Cypress, California. He was a fresh, young law student from New York with the accompanying swagger and confidence. He was also an assistant coach at UCLA and was out recruiting local Southern California talent. Keith showed up at the Cypress Junior College gym to watch me play during my sophomore year. UCLA was having a banner year—they went on to the NCAA Championship Final at the end of that season—and I was definitely interested in playing for them. Keith and I chatted briefly after the game. He was a funny, quirky guy who had a good understanding of the game of basketball. Little did I know that meeting was to be the beginning of an enduring 36-year relationship.

After I signed with the Bruins, we spent a lot of time together. He was assigned to help the new seven-foot-four "project" develop. It was a rough couple of years for me as a player. I didn't get much playing time and constantly dealt with a foreboding sense that my basketball career had run off the rails. Through it all, Keith was there to keep my spirits up and my hope alive. He stayed after practice to work one on one with me, throw me lob passes, and encourage me.

When I left UCLA later the next year, my NBA hopes looked rather dim. I traveled around the country and competed in pay-to-play free agent camps and cold called NBA teams hoping for a shot. I had a couple overseas teams interested in me, but my goal was the NBA.

Fortunately, Coach Frank Layden of the Utah Jazz showed interest after hearing some feedback from a couple of scouts and drafted me in the 4th round of NBA Draft in 1982.

Unfortunately, being drafted is not a guarantee of actually being on an NBA roster. What it meant was I had a chance to audition at training camp in October, and a slim hope of making the team. So I had to entertain other offers. I was seriously considering an offer to play in Israel for $15,000 when Frank came to LA to watch me play in a summer league game a month after the draft. He liked what he saw and suggested we meet at his hotel the next day to discuss my potential future with the Jazz. At that point, I knew I needed a professional assist.

To be blunt, player agents did not have a good reputation in the early 80s. I knew I needed to have someone I trusted walk me through the negotiation process. So I called Keith Glass. As we sat around the pool at the LAX Marriott the following day, I was nervous and in awe as Keith waxed poetically about how I could help the struggling Jazz franchise, even though I had exactly two years of JC experience to back that up! He reminded Coach Layden continually that we were entertaining multiple offers to play overseas.

Agents do not typically like players to be involved in the meetings with a General Manager, but it was my future and I wanted to hear every word. The minimum salary in the NBA that year was $45,000. I watched in amazement as Keith negotiated a $25,000 guarantee for me. Even if the team cut me, I would still make more than if I moved to Tel Aviv. Coach Layden casually mentioned that it might take a couple years for me to improve. Keith turned that comment into an additional $25,000 guarantee added for years two and three as part of a five-year contract. I now had a $75,000 guaranteed contract as an unproven NBA player.

Keith wasn't done either! He created a bonus structure that would pay me if I finished in the top ten in the League in rebounding or blocked shots. My rookie season, I came in third in blocked shots, garnering me an additional $7,000. What I didn't know at the time, was that I was Keith's first client and that was his first negotiation!

By February of my rookie season, the team had traded starting center Danny Schayes to the Nuggets for $300,000 and Rich Kelley, the only other Center on the Jazz, in order to make payroll. I became the de facto starting center and my career began to flourish. I got better and our team got better. In 1985 I broke the NBA record for blocked shots at 5.6 per game and added 11.3 rebounds per contest. Our team was winning! It was time to go back to the negotiation table.

Many agents can write a contract, but don't truly understand the game or take the time to build relationships with owners and General Managers. Keith did all three. Negotiations typically start by the team and agent comparing the salaries and statistics of other players on the team and other players who play the same position, center in my case. I was not a great scorer but our team had that covered in the form of Adrian Dantley and an up-and-coming Karl Malone. I provided a very specific role and defensive benefit to our team. Keith's understanding and knowledge of the game, and the relationship he had with Frank, enabled us to leverage the benefit I brought to the team into a new $2.3 million five-year contract. All guaranteed. Quite a leap from the $15,000 I had considered just a few short years before.

I went on to a twelve-year NBA career with the Utah Jazz that included highlights of a trip to the All-Star game in 1989 and two Defensive Player of the Year awards. I experienced ups and downs and injuries like everyone else. That made for some tough negotiations, saber rattling and heated words exchanged that are all a part of the game. I was privileged to have Keith on my team. He always had my back, stood for what he believed, and kept it real. We had a great run together.

I have always maintained that anyone can represent a first round draft pick. But it takes chutzpah, street smarts and a keen understanding of the game to represent the rest of us. Finding the right team and the right situation for your player is where the real work gets done.

From managing young player's expectations, assuaging families and college coaches, to striking a deal with a team, that is where the best agents shine. That's where Keith shines. Fitting all the pieces together. It's rarely easy, but Keith Glass always gets it done.

Many of the players he represented were not household names. They were solid cast members who contributed to the wins their team achieved in quiet ways. Some played overseas-Italy, Spain, Turkey and other faraway destinations-and had long careers. Basketball is a worldwide game and comes with a wide and diverse variety of personalities. Keith has the incredible skill of relating to all of them!

I have always enjoyed Keith's stories and insights of the people and the situations that make up this game. His negotiation tales with General Managers, team owners and coaches around the globe gave me a great appreciation for the effort to which Keith went to as he took care of his "guys". From screaming matches in Greece to the nuanced conversations with an NBA owner for coffee and a deal, Keith has dealt with and seen it all. And, he has formed a few opinions along the way.

Sports is very galvanizing. We all view it through our own lens and don't usually agree, or even seek to understand, another's point of view. Keith and I have had many a discussion about league management, the Players Association, agents, and many of the intricacies of this game of basketball we love. Keith has never been shy about his take on the current state of affairs. Obviously he is more than willing to share them with others.

Through it all, he has remained fiercely loyal, steadfast, and intensely competitive. I'm not even sure what you and I will read in the pages that follow. Knowing Keith as I do, chances are high that we will be treated to stories well-told. We will laugh and there's bound to be some controversy and mashed toes along the way. Rest assured, it will be a helluva good read and most importantly:

It will all be TRUE!

WHERE WERE WE??

Well apparently like or not, every 10 years I'm writing a book! You have it easy! You can just choose to close the cover and put this sucker away but I had to finish it!

The only question is why?

Many years ago while attending the NBA Combine in Chicago, I ran into Pat Williams, the founder and then President of the Orlando Magic in the lobby of our hotel. Pat and I had crossed paths in the negotiating world of the National Basketball Association (NBA) we once negotiated a $9 million contract for Scott Skiles on a napkin at a Major League Baseball exhibition game. Pat also is a prolific writer. He has written over 20 books. I confess to having only read the first two completely and thought they were very interesting.

I had realized some years earlier that many of my experiences during my travels in the world of professional basketball were somewhat bizarre, so I began writing them down on notepads just to preserve my sanity. I never thought of writing an actual book about them but by the time I ran across Pat in the lobby, I was considering just that. I told Pat what I was thinking and the conversation went something like:

PAT: Well, Keith why would you be writing a book?

KEITH: Not sure, I guess I have something on my mind. Does the reason matter?!

PAT: Absolutely! If you're writing it for money forget it!! If you're writing it for yourself, absolutely do it!!

I took that advice and wrote my first book 10 years ago! I wrote it for myself and it was later published by HarperCollins in New York. I received tremendous encouragement while I was writing that book, which ended up being titled, Taking Shots. This time I've written one in spite of a general lack of encouragement. So this incarnation I'm clearly writing just for myself! If any of you get something out of it or better than that, laugh a little bit that would be terrific.

I fully recognize the reasons for this relative lack of encouragement. The primary one is that my parents were around in 2007 and they supported me in anything I ever wanted to do. They are not physically here now, although as many of us who have lost loved ones understand they are always around us. So my "fan club" is not quite as vocal. For example, if you had the pleasure of let's say riding in an elevator for 90 seconds with my Mom you were probably the recipient of a copy of Taking Shots!

In defense of those close to me who let's say have not been very excited about what might appear in these pages, they probably are concerned about what I might say. After all, they did read the first book. To them I say, relax, it's going to be fine. Look on the bright side, maybe no one will publish it. Although I guess if you're reading this, somebody did. Understand this though, these are MY stories and if you have your own, write them down and see if anybody has an interest in reading them. If not write them anyway; for yourself.

So what's the point?! Why this second venture? Well, I guess I still have some things on my mind. So many of the things I railed against in Taking Shots are still issues today in 2018. There were points I tried to make about the excesses in the NBA and in college athletics. Things like ticket prices, salaries and the attendant bombardment of marketing and branding that I still maintain I was correct about. The reality, however, is that I was completely wrong about these issues actually derailing the growth of professional and collegiate athletics.

On the contrary, the money has increased exponentially to a level that we never dreamed was possible. This economic increase has always selfishly served to benefit my family. I have been an NBA Agent for over 30 years, and I work on commission. Part of me says just keep the money coming. My conundrum with this trend is that I recognize that excesses in any field have a tendency to corrupt and taint the very fabric of an industry. It may not seem like a big deal considering other more important issues we face as a country and a World but when it affects something that has been such a huge part of my life it bothers me. It all apparently causes me to write about it.

I guess it all depends on my motivations in the first place. I fell in love with sports probably before I can even remember. Starting out, it was playing sports but it eventually grew into my actual livelihood as well. Everything we have as a family in some way is due to sports. I have never lost sight of that or stopped being grateful for it. If you truly "love" something and it's going astray, you have to speak up. I did that in 2007 with Taking Shots. People enjoyed the book but nothing really changed in the way things were run. Basically, everybody said:

"Great job Keith! Now leave us alone, we're making
a lot of money!!"
DR. NAISMITH VS P.T. BARNUM

At some point, we need to accurately assess what is going on here. Athletics were created originally just for exercise. Back in 1891 when Dr. James Naismith invented the great game of basketball I suspect he never thought it would become big business. Slowly, things have morphed into areas that had never been considered.

If someone sees an opportunity to make a little cash off something, there's no harm in that. If you put out a product that is interesting enough so that folks will pay to see it, that's terrific. Some of my issues revolve around the disingenuous way these sporting events are being marketed. We can't even tell where the marketing ends and the games begin.

This very nicely brings us to the very title of this book. In 1841, P.T. Barnum, who is possibly the greatest showman in our history, purchased Scudder's American Museum. Located in New York City at the corner of Broadway and Ann Street, it was renamed Barnum's American Museum. He owned and operated it until 1865 when it burnt to the ground in one of the most spectacular fires in New York City history. Barnum filled it with many strange exhibits and educational attractions. There were dioramas, panoramas, scientific instruments, modern appliances, a flea circus, a loom operated by a dog, a rifle range, glass blowers, waxworks, Siamese twins, and on and on.

It cost 25 cents to get in. Barnum realized that people we lingering too long in the Museum and he needed to "turn over" the crowd to get some fresh paying customers through the turnstiles. His solution for this was to post signs saying:

"This way to the Egress!"

Not knowing that "Egress" was another word for "Exit", people followed the signs to what they assumed was just another tremendous exhibit and found themselves outside.

Barnum had another exhibit called the "6 Foot Man Eating Chicken!" No one could even imagine this. First of all, a 6-foot chicken in and of itself is an attraction. Throw the "man-eater" angle in there and you've got to go, especially for 25 cents! When the exhibit opened after three months of advertising the line was around the block. One by one, they filed in. Once inside, they found a 6-foot tall man sitting in a chair....eating chicken! The people had been snookered. They laughed. Most people don't mind laughing at themselves. Barnum got over on them and they would happily come back, especially for only 25 cents.

This anecdote reminded me of how professional sports has been "snookering" the public for some time now. I simply added a foot of height to accommodate for the increased size of an NBA player. Advertise one thing and give 'em something else. The problem is that it's not as funny when the price of taking your family to one of these sporting events no longer costs a quarter and you went expecting to see an actual sporting event.

So what's my problem? While I admire the accomplishments of P. T. Barnum, I also realize that he came as advertised: A Showman. He never claimed to be a coach/teacher or an administrator or anything else associated with athletics. When he "snookered" you, he was doing what he warned you he was going to do. That's honest. What professional sports are doing to some degree is not. They are advertising one thing and giving us something else. I think they call this a "bait and switch." Fine at a used car lot but...

Maybe the best way for me to explain this is through the example of the Harlem Globetrotters. The "Trotters" to millions of people around the world are extremely entertaining. You know exactly what you're signing up for and they deliver the "show" you were anticipating. They market themselves as purely entertainment. They don't pretend that you're about to witness an actual basketball game or contest. It is fun and kids and some adults eat it up. That is in stark contrast to what we are witnessing in professional sports. They promise us an athletic competition and only after we get in our seats do they attempt to disguise what we are seeing as something else.

Simply put, I'm tired of having sports hijacked by people who just view it as just another "show," which it wasn't intended to be. I'm all in favor of making an easy buck. I've made that easy buck myself. I've been able to rationalize this as just recognizing an opportunity that presented itself. Today's players are in a similar situation. They clearly are not to blame for any of this. In fact, today's professional athletes are better trained, work harder, and are trying to perfect their craft 12-months a year. This makes for more talented players who have honed their abilities through this often extraordinary hard work. Whether those individual efforts have translated into better overall players, teams, and the subsequent product we see on the court is open to debate.

I am not begrudging the NBA's success. On some level, I greatly admire what they've done business-wise. Beginning with the leadership of former basketball commissioner, David Stern and continuing now under Adam Silver, one would be hard-pressed to point to another industry that has been run more efficiently or better in a purely business sense. This has never been my concern. What has worried me in the past what continues to concern me today is the effect that this financial and marketing "success" has had on the game itself and the lure that it has created for corruption.

Certainly, I'm not alone in this concern. "Dinosaurs" like myself look at the current state of play and can't quite equate the quality of the game to the amount of money being paid out. Revenues that are being generated are certainly not consistently merit-based. Rather the players in the league today are the beneficiaries of a record television contract, which took effect in the 2016-17 season. The contract lasts for nine years and is worth $24,000,000,000. That's not a typo - that is 24 billion dollars. ESPN & Turner will combine to pay the NBA $2.6 billion per season through the 2024-25 season. Under the previous deal, which was signed in the year Taking Shots was published in

2007, ESPN & Turner paid the league $930 million per year. This new contract represents a 180% increase. Not bad!

My warnings about the NBA, the NCAA, and what I perceived to be corruption in the Agent community have not only been ignored but also have been basically dismissed as some kind of raving. The corruption has not only continued in my specific field of agenting but those who perpetrate it are thriving! My concerns have always been that there is too much of everything in sports. However, it just keeps growing, with salaries, ticket prices, the cost of a hot dog, etc., etc.

Even though my point of view is seemingly archaic, it doesn't make it wrong! The more money that surrounds any industry the stronger the urge becomes for people to get in on the action. The more people who are in on the action the greater the probability that some of them will do whatever it takes, legal or otherwise, to get involved. This is not the exclusive modus operandi of professional sports. In 2018 corruption seems to be the accepted way of things. In business, in politics, in society, it often seems that corruption is the ONLY way to success. I don't think the sports culture invented this corruption.

We're just trying to keep up!

CHAPTER ONE

RAZZLE-DAZZLE 'EM

"How can they hear the truth above the roar?"
CHICAGO

I don't remember the exact date but I do recall when I finally recognized that something was out of whack in our country. Don't be alarmed I'm not talking politics… at least not yet. I'm referring to the unrelenting commercialization of all things American.

One of my clients was in Florida playing a couple of exhibition games against some NBA teams. His name was Nikos Zisis and he was born and raised in Thessaloniki, Greece. I've been there several times and it is a beautiful place. At this point in time, Nikos was under contract with CSKA Moscow, the biggest team in Russia. I went to Orlando to visit with him and watch the games. It was his first visit to the United States and naturally, I was curious about his initial reaction:

> **NIKOS**: I was in my hotel room and I had the TV on. Keith, they are constantly selling things. Doesn't it bother you?!

I was expecting something more along the lines of how beautiful it was here in Orlando. After thinking this through I realized how different a culture we have here than in Europe. I have been to many parts of Europe over the years and Nikos was 100% correct. While it's true that we have more of everything here, we also have more marketing, branding, billboards, commercials, etc. than anywhere else I've been. On his initial foray into American life another European basketball star, Vlade Divac was flown into Los Angeles after being drafted in the 1st round of the 1989 NBA Draft. Innocently he went to the supermarket looking for chocolate. His overriding impression was disbelief over how many varieties of chocolate he was faced with. He settled on a cookie and went home. Instead of the Grand Canyon or the Statue of Liberty or Griffith Park, it was the overwhelming display of "stuff" that colored their first impression of us.

I never thought the hype and non-stop marketing and influence of money would go this far into the area of sports. I am still hopeful that at some point some sanity will creep back into all this. We as participants, fans, and consumers have for whatever reason bought into arbitrary definitions of what Sport actually is and is not. There has been a blurring of the lines between sports or athletics in general and other parts of American life.

Let's start with the now almost totally accepted idea that:

"Sports is just another Business"

This notion actually started creeping into discussions not so long ago. I would sit at Union meetings with the National Basketball Players Association (NBPA) and this theory would be propagated. I understood that the NBA was created back in 1946 and there was certainly some "business" component to it. The founders of the league certainly didn't establish the NBA so they could jointly go broke. The product was put out there and if people didn't show up (and many times they didn't) they tried marketing their product in a different way. There were certainly changes made to their game in order to make it more appealing but the sport itself remained basically the same. While elements were added or subtracted from the game, those were mostly done in the interest of improving the sport being played. Widening the lane, the addition of the shot clock, cleaning up the grabbing and fouling, etc. were not done in the primary interest of "business" but to benefit the quality of the sport overall.

I realize that we are never going back to the "old days." Hopefully, the people who have clearly benefited from the idea that sport is ONLY a "business," don't forget that there is an actual game being played down there on the floor. When and if that product goes further into the toilet, they may be watching their "business" go with it. This is the area where I was proven "wrong" 10 years ago, in my first book. The "business" may be thriving. The game is struggling.

THE BIG 3

While we're on the subject of the game itself, here's another platitude that we have all swallowed whole:

> *The only way you can win a Championship in the NBA is to assemble a "BIG 3!"*

Really?! Where did that come from?! I'm finding out that if you say something false over and over again there are a lot of people who will believe it. This is becoming clearer by the day in more important areas of society. Here are some facts. There are 12 guys on a roster, with five of them starting. You mean to tell me that all this time we only needed three?! This is going to come as quite a shock to the old Boston Celtics, the 76ers of the 60s, the Portland Trailblazers of 1977, the "Bad Boy" Pistons, and the New York Knicks of 1970 and '73. I think I know when and why this one was perpetrated.

In the "old days" they actually had something called TEAMS. These were entities that were built to win, sometimes even grow together and to last. With the advent of free agency, it became much more difficult to "last" and thereby "grow" as a unit. Players were on the move and "teams" were broken up. This was great for the players because the overriding, if not the only reason they would leave a good team was to get paid. It was not so great for the team they left though. It wasn't so great for the fans either or for the quality of the game itself.

When you couple free agency with expansion things really start to dissipate. When the owners are faced with the decision to increase the number of teams in the league it's not a tough call for them to make. Their choice breaks down to whether they want to receive a lot of money by merely letting new owners pay them for the privilege of joining their club. It is very rare that an owner will reject that premise.

In 1989, we all looked on with some degree of wonder at the fact that the NBA was expanding to four new markets: Orlando, Minnesota, Charlotte, & Miami. The cost of that "buy-in" was around $36 million. Crazy, insane! What is wrong with these people? In 2015 in the midst of an embarrassing development between the owner of the Los Angeles Clippers and a woman who was not his wife, the Clippers went for $2 BILLION. This was accomplished through a "forced sale." Imagine what it could have gone for if they could have really taken their time.

Teams were forced to "expose" players 9 through 12 on their roster to an expansion draft. In order to fill out the rosters for these 4 new teams, the player's had to come from somewhere. While it was true that a team could only lose one of those unprotected players to an expansion franchise, it is impossible to explain how this process improved either of those teams as far as the actual product on the floor was concerned. Obviously, it hurt the depth of every team that lost a player in that fashion. There is another side to that coin. What kind of a team are you putting out there and simultaneously claiming are of NBA caliber, when supporting role players are now your starters?! Save that argument for someone else. There is no convincing case you can make that this improved the level of play in the NBA.

When I first started watching the NBA, I believe there were 12 teams. 12 x 12 is 144. That was the talent pool in the 1960s. Today, there are 30 teams and roster size has been recently increased to 15 and even to 17 players if you want to count the new "2-way contracts." I'm not a math major, in fact, I don't remember majoring in anything, but I think that makes 450 or so. We have tripled the players at a time when some will argue that the instruction and therefore productivity of modern players is down.

So what is a league to do? Privately, they know they are very successfully marketing a product that is inferior and is less competitive across the board. How about this! We won't market "TEAMS" anymore. Just the "Big 3!!!" That's it. 3 x 30 is only 90 players. The league is even greater than before when we had 7, 8, 9 guys that were really good solid pros on EVERY team in the league. This is perfect! In an age where we want everything to be easy, simple, and immediate, this makes total sense. We're just tapping into a National movement! Thus, the glorification of "Average" took control and remains firmly in place!

Let's deal with some specifics. To begin with, I guess there were "Big 3's" before. We just didn't know it because it wasn't rammed down our throats. If you doubt me, take a look at some of these trios:

Wilt Chamberlain, Jerry West, & Elgin Baylor
Willis Reed, Walt Frazier, & Earl Monroe
Elvin Hayes, Wes Unseld, & Phil Chenier
Bill Russell, John Havlicek, & Sam Jones

But let's bring things a bit more current for those with shorter memories:

Isiah Thomas, Joe Dumars, & Bill Laimbeer
Michael Jordan, Scottie Pippen, & Horace Grant
Michael Jordan, Scottie Pippen, & Dennis Rodman
Kareem Abdul Jabbar, Magic Johnson, & James Worthy

I think you get the point. I don't ever recall hearing one reference to any of these combinations as being the "Big 3". You want to know why?! Because they all played on TEAMS! Bird, Parrish & McHale had a tremendous backcourt of Dennis Johnson and Danny Ainge. Yes, the same Danny Ainge who put together what I think launched this current "Big 3" bull crap in the first place in Boston consisting of Paul Pierce, Kevin Garnett & Ray Allen. This very talented group actually won one NBA title. The Russell Celtics won 11. Those Celtics teams with Bird won three. Those players that I have referenced here would be the first ones to tell you that they won those titles because they were on tremendous "teams!" Many of those teams have players who are not in the "Big 3" that reside in the Hall of Fame.

That Knick threesome I mentioned above rounded out their starting five with a couple of "rummies" named Bradley & Debusschere. In 1996, Dave Debusschere was named as one of the top 50 players in NBA history. This in spite of the fact that he was never part of a "Big 3"! They also brought in Cazzie Russell, Dave Stallworth, & Phil Jackson off the bench. Today, those bench guys outside their teams "Big 3" would have had statues built in their honor!

What is even more amusing is that the "need" to fill up your team's "Big 3" is so important today that even if you can't find three great players, we just make them appear great. Why…we can even create "Stars". That process is self-defeating at best to the sport:

"The main ingredient of stardom
is the rest of the team."
JOHN WOODEN

Let's look around. You want Westbrook, Paul George, & Carmelo, I'll give it to ya. But please don't try and sell me on some of the others. I don't want to denigrate today's players. They work their asses off and are tremendous athletes and many of them are really good players. It's the dispersing of talent over 30 cities coupled with the system in which many of them were brought up in that has conspired to dilute the game we see today.

I know that this is the opening part of this book. Some of you may be saying; "Why should I listen to this guy? He sounds a bit jaded and old-fashioned!" OK, how about Michael Jordan? Not the Michael Jordan who is arguably the greatest player in the history of the NBA. I'm referring to the owner of the Charlotte Hornets. As an owner, I think he has a vested interest in promoting the league in which he owns a team. This is his quote from October 12, 2017, in Cigar Aficionado Magazine. In discussing the overall effect of "Big 3's" on the balance and quality of "teams" in his league:

"I think it's going to hurt the overall aspect of the
league from a competitive standpoint. You are going
to have one or two teams that are going to be great,
and another 28 teams that are going to be garbage."
MICHAEL JORDAN 2017

Even I didn't go that far. Michael's comments were in reaction more to the creation of "Super Teams." This is the fairly recent practice of players congregating on one team instead of building through the draft or heaven forbid learning to play as a cohesive unit. Some say this starts in the AAU environment that many of today's players grew up in. You don't like the coach or your team, leave it, and go to another one. You lose an AAU game in the morning? There are two more games later that day. There is quite of bit of synergy between what Michael is talking about and what I have described as the dilution of talent in the league.

"COACH"

I have at least five children. Other than being called "Dad," for me the most flattering thing anyone has called me is "Coach." And I've been called a lot of things! As a young man, I learned to coach in the mountains of Pennsylvania. From there, I went on to coach for two seasons at the University of California Los Angeles (UCLA) as an assistant. I then spent 16 seasons as the head coach at three different high schools on both sides of the country. As I wrote that last sentence I realize that I need to do a little explaining. The question of HOW I even ended up on the bench at UCLA fresh out of law school requires a bit more history.

The irony is that growing up on Long Island, my brother Brent and I really hated UCLA. Hate is a little strong but I think resentful and jealous would certainly apply. Think about it, beginning in 1964, when I was 13, the UCLA Bruins won all the time! They won 10 National Championships in 12 years. (Read that again) We would watch those games religiously just praying for them to lose somehow, someway. I should also point out that we didn't get to see college basketball games the way we do today. There weren't 475 channels that streamed sports 24 hours a day, seven days a week. We only got to see for the most part the NCAA tournament. A fellow assistant coach of mine at UCLA, Larry Farmer told me that as a player they referred to the NCAA Tournament as "The UCLA Invitational." That's really annoying! What was equally annoying was that "Farms" consistently reminded me that as a player with the Bruins his record was:

"89 and 1, and I had no help!!"

Their coach John Wooden was a guy who, to us, looked like one of our teachers at school. The whole thing was just unbearable with the only exception maybe being the cheerleaders! With his black-framed glasses and rolled up program in hand, he seemed to never lose a game! He managed to win with every type of roster. He earned his first two championships primarily due to the play of two guards: Walt Hazard for the first title and Gail Goodrich for both of them. They then gave us a break, for ONE season, while a freshman center was biding his time on the freshman team. In those ancient times, freshman were not eligible to play until they were sophomores. Incredible since that meant that really good college basketball players basically needed to attend a University for more than 10 months. Insanity! After this "break" UCLA, with Lew Alcindor (soon to change his name to Kareem Abdul Jabbar), won three consecutive National Championships.

We were looking forward to that group graduating. Coach Wooden and his Bruins won the next two after Kareem & Co. graduated. This time they did it with primarily with two forwards: Sidney Wicks & Curtis Rowe. That made seven titles in eight years! Don't hold your breath to see that happen again.

At least now, they were done. In those days high school recruits were not covered and certainly not hyped to the extent we see today.

They were a lot more under the radar except for those in the basketball community (No Big Baller Brands in the 1970s). Just as we were trying to figure out who now could legitimately win a Championship other than UCLA, the "Walton Gang" arrived in Westwood.

This group may have been the best of them all. This was the team that won 88 straight games and two more titles under Coach Wooden. They were upset in the Final Four by North Carolina State and the great David Thompson in a classic game at the 1974 Final Four in Bill Walton's final game. Whether this version of the Bruins was the best ever or whether it was Kareem's teams doesn't matter. The fact that they remain two of the most dominant college basketball groups in history is enough.

The "Walton Gang" left after that "disappointing" 1974 season. If you asked any other coach in the country how they would feel about losing in double overtime at the Final Four, they would be ecstatic and immediately be hiring someone like me to get them an extension. In Westwood, this was an abject failure.

Nobody knew it at the time and I don't even think Coach Wooden knew at the beginning of that year, but that following 1975 season would be his last. By that time, I was living in a trailer 20 minutes north of the UCLA campus. As such, I got to see every game that year, at least on a black and white 12-inch screen in my trailer. The Bruins were not supposed to be contenders but they had some very good players in David Meyers, Richard Washington, and Marques Johnson.

They won it all again!!

_____

Years before that remarkable run of success had begun, events took place in my own family that would ultimately lead me to that spot on the UCLA bench. My brother Brent went to camp in Pennsylvania.

While that was not a newsworthy event, his counselor happened to be a 16-year old basketball player named Larry Brown. A bond developed between them that actually led to my parents basically adopting Larry into our family. This relationship between Larry and my parents, Brent, my sister Jodi, and myself lasted over 50 years! (I'll discuss this in detail later).

It was through Larry and my dad that in 1975 while a 1st-year law student living in California, and in fairly desperate need of money, that I found myself working at various basketball camps in Southern California. Six weeks of that summer were to be spent at John Wooden's Camp. I was 24 by then and my feelings of animosity had long since given way to astonishment and admiration for what those UCLA teams and their bespectacled coach had accomplished.

My first week there I was hired as a coach. My salary was $150 a week and I needed it! During that week, I noticed that Coach Wooden was spending an inordinate amount of time with a certain counselor. They were always together and I was curious about what that guy's job actually was.

As the week was ending I approached the director, Rick:

> **KEITH**: What's up with that guy? Why does he get to spend so much time with Coach Wooden?!

> **RICK**: Oh, he's the Commissioner. His main job is to drive Coach Wooden back and forth to his house.

> **KEITH**: How much does he make?!

> **RICK**: $75 a week.

> **KEITH**: Can I get that job?!

Cost me $75 per week for those last five weeks to drive Coach around. I've invested heavily in Apple since those days but that $75 per week was the best investment I ever made. Years later I did ask Coach Wooden to reimburse me for that $75 but that went nowhere.

I would pick Coach Wooden up in my Chevy Vega station wagon, with the simulated wood on the sides, at 5:30 each morning. Coach had already walked his five miles when I got there. Some of those mornings, I was just coming in from the night before. I have little doubt that he knew this as well so he would always be extra cheerful when he saw that I was not in the mood for chit-chat! Thankfully, the ride from his condo in Encino was 45 minutes, which enabled us to really talk. We talked about everything. I knew this was the opportunity of a lifetime to spend this kind of time alone with John Wooden. We argued as well which I think Coach enjoyed tremendously. I've never been one to "yes" people to death and after about 20 minutes of our initial trip, I felt comfortable enough to be myself.

When I asked him questions about basketball which I did often, after he answered he would always add:

> **COACH**: But Keith, that's how I liked to do it. That's doesn't mean you need to do it the same way.

After the 5th time he said that I couldn't resist:

> **KEITH**: You know Coach, as soon as I win my 11th Championship I'll do it MY way! For now, I'm gonna steal everything I can from you! Now, let's go over that 2-2-1 zone press again!!

Those five weeks flew by much too quickly. Coach Wooden, outside of my father, was the most incredible man I've ever been around.

It wasn't just basketball but it was his essence that has stayed with me all these years. Unassuming doesn't cover Coach Wooden. Humble doesn't make it either. At 6:30 in the morning if we passed a water fountain at camp he would calmly go into the nearest bathroom, grab some papers towels and pick out all the chewed gum the kids had deposited there. Then he would polish the fountain. While doing this, he never said a word. It was no big deal. That was just him.

> **COACH**: I always try to leave a place a little cleaner than when I got there. (Man, I hope a couple of my sons read this).

I could never begin to duplicate the confluence of events that specifically put me on the UCLA coaching staff. When young people today ask me to describe how I ended up where I am my initial thought is I hope you're not going to use my path like some sort of guide. In 1979, with me living those 20 minutes north of the UCLA campus, my "brother," Larry Brown, was offered the head coaching job at UCLA. Two days later I was an assistant at the most successful basketball school in the country! If you were to advocate that as a career path to coaching, they'd lock you up!

Obviously, coaching has been a tremendous part of my life. As such, I didn't need the FBI to let me know that something was wrong with the coaching or coaches at the highest levels of college basketball. I've seen and voiced my concern for 20 years. I know it would be really "sexy" for me at this juncture to spill the beans on all the ways that agents, shoe companies, universities, and coaches pay the top recruits in the nation. The subtle truth is: I don't know any of the details. I specifically never wanted to know. This FBI investigation is still supposedly in its early stages and I'm very happy to say that I'm learning just like you. It has never been our modus operandi to cheat and believe me that has cost us. But maybe the pendulum is now starting to swing. Maybe this truly is the tipping point. I wouldn't bet on it though.

Thankfully my only connection to this FBI probe is that currently the only agent specifically under investigation is the one agent I had filed an arbitration against years before. (***For those interested in the actual Arbitration decision see the APPENDIX at the end of the book***).

Whatever happens with this FBI probe there is no question that today's coaches have become very different than coaches from the recent past. For the most part, they look better than the "old guard" but only on the outside. On the inside what was truly motivating them seemed to have changed in recent years. Having been brought up and later having the pleasure of interacting and becoming friends with that "old guard" spoiled me.

Is it just me or don't you get a different feeling from watching a Jud Heathcote of Michigan State or a Lou Carnesecca from St. John's or a John Thompson of Georgetown or Gene Keady from Purdue or my late good friend Ben Jobe or Don Haskins or John Chaney or Bob McKillop et. al, than you do with some of today's versions of what a "successful" coach is. A feeling of "corporateness" permeates many of today's programs. Several of the top coaches seemed to be in it for themselves. Recruiting became paramount in many instances over actual coaching and teaching. As the money grew, things only got worse.

I had grown up watching the NCAA Final Four as a kid but the nation became obsessed when Michigan State, with my friend, the late Jud Heathcote at the helm, beat an undefeated Indiana State in that 1979 Final. Indeed there was plenty of hype surrounding that game. I don't recall the exact marketing plan for that game or for the one I would be involved in the following year but I'm sure there was one in place.

Truly great events usually happen fairly naturally. Once they do "naturally" take off someone always has a plan to get rich on it. Hello Brackets!! Today, every conceivable mechanism is employed to cash in on the NCAA Tournament. I could go into excruciating detail but let's just cite one example, which I think makes the point.

All of us (and that means millions) who watch the NCAAs are familiar with the "cutting down of the nets" after the Championship is decided. It's a nice tradition. Whether it's historically accurate or not, most people give credit to Coach Everett Case of North Carolina State University. He was so excited after his team won the Southern Conference title in 1947 that he wanted a souvenir as a remembrance. Sweet! His team hoisted him up on their shoulders and he cut down the nets! I've researched this and have found no evidence that any money changed hands during this spontaneous celebration.

When I coached at UCLA in 1980, we beat Clemson to advance to the Final Four. My favorite person that I met at UCLA was our trainer "Ducky" Drake. Mr. Drake had been at UCLA as both the trainer and track coach for over 50 years. The track stadium was named in his honor. He was Coach Wooden's trainer for all of those 10 champion-ship runs. "Ducky" had seen a few things. When our players in their excitement tried to cut down the nets to celebrate going to the Final Four, "Ducky" would have none of it:

"At UCLA, we only cut down the LAST nets!!"

Compare and contrast. For the past several NCAA Tournaments, Werner Ladder has sponsored a formal net-cutting ceremony. So now, a spontaneous and real emotion has been converted into a stage show complete with financial incentives. What began as an innocent expression of a coach's joy is now simply reduced to a commercial opportunity. When you parlay this over the almost total marketing of the NCAA tournament the picture becomes very clear. The current President of the NCAA, Mark Emmert himself is on record as saying, "I'm uncomfortable with the commercialization of the NCAA."

What Mark Emmert and the NCAA became even more "uncomfortable" with occurred in September of 2017. That was the day that the Federal Bureau of Investigation, aka the FBI, charged 10 individuals in a wide-ranging indictment. The indictment centered on corruption within collegiate basketball. The individuals named included four assistant coaches as well as "runners", financial "advisers" and sneaker company executives who were working with agents.

I have no idea where this will lead. Thankfully I have never been involved with the seedy side of my business although I don't claim to be Pollyanna either. As I write today there have already been guilty pleas entered in conjunction with this investigation. Additionally, the University of Louisville has been rocked to its core and had its Hall of Fame coach ousted in disgrace. There are other schools implicated but so far that's been the extent of things. It's hard for me to believe however that the FBI has spent this much money and man-hours in order to get rid of Rick Pitino.

The charges in this investigation center on a conspiracy developed between shoe companies, agents or their henchman and Universities. In very simplistic terms, an agent or someone working on his behalf contacts a particular school through its coaching staff. They convince at least one member of the staff that they "control" a particular highly rated prospect that the staff covets. The agent negotiates a financial number that will convince that player or his family that this is the place of higher learning that he should attend. The shoe company foots the bill. The quid pro quo is that it is understood that when the player leaves the University he will be steered to sign with the agent and the shoe company. Beautiful!

Although the FBI investigation seems to suggest a prima facie case for hypocrisy there is still remains a major distinction to be made between the "business" that is the NBA and that of college basketball. While one can certainly try to argue that the originators of the NBA were merely 11 men whose goal and vision was to run a multi-billion sport, no one can reasonably put forth the notion that College Basketball was created for the same purposes.

Justifying the costs of the NBA today by claiming it's not a sport but a "business" is one thing but to extend that same rationale to collegiate sports is a bridge too far! Clearly, the commercialization of college football and basketball was never the intent. As recently as the 1980s when I was at UCLA, things were exciting and riveting but looking back on it comparatively understated. The year before we got to the NCAA Championship game Magic Johnson & Larry Bird sent "March Madness" to a new level.

"ARE YOU NOT ENTERTAINED"

-GLADIATOR 2000

Let's get back to some bitching! I've saved my biggest complaint and probably most of my sarcasm for my favorite bit of nonsense:

"Sports is merely Entertainment".

"The Entertainment industry is part of the tertiary sector of the economy and includes a large number of sub-industries…. It applies to every aspect of entertainment including cinema, television, radio, theatre, and music."

-GOOGLE DEFINITION OF ENTERTAINMENT

No mention of basketball or football or for that matter any other competitive sport. When did these athletic competitions become ENTERTAINMENT?! I would estimate right around the time that the front office was trying to justify how they can get away with convincing the public to pay such extravagant prices. In other words, make fans believe they are getting their money's worth.

Once the product suffered, the preening and the smoke screens arrived on the scene. If the game is boring let's pipe in some annoyingly loud music, maybe they won't notice. Players don't really know how to play together as a unit, which is difficult to achieve, so how about some dancing-girls. Too many turnovers from lack of fundamentals, here - have some fireworks! This way maybe they won't be able to see what's actually going on down there through the smoke!

Throughout all the decades that professional sports have been on the scene, we already had "entertainers." Real ones on stage and screen and in concerts halls. Although, you can say that professional sports are the first and truly the only "Reality TV". But even though sports may have an antagonist and a protagonist and provides drama, comedy, suspense, and thrills, the difference is the word "REAL". Entertainment is scripted, choreographed and performed. Sports itself is as real as it gets. Calling it "entertainment" does it a great injustice but does justify a higher price tag.

I also love being "entertained." We all do. Some of the greatest experiences I've had have been in a theatre or at a concert or just at home watching a good show on my TV. "Entertainment" is a developed, rehearsed event. The ending may still be a mystery but the outcome has already been written. The allure of a sporting event is that we are actually watching something where the outcome is unfolding before our eyes. That's dramatic to me. That is part of what separates sport from entertainment. It doesn't make one better than the other.

Sports just gives us another experience entirely, so why conflate the two? The idea of men and women facing off against each other with the goal of beating the other team is a terrific invention.

My theory on this revolves around the fact that it's hard to win!! Athletics discourages shortcuts; at least it used to. Put in the work and good things will happen. When they don't you're faced with two distinct choices. Work harder or make excuses. The shift to label sports as "entertainment" is simply a shortcut. No more no less.

At the same time in our history when Willie Davis was terrorizing quarterbacks for the Green Bay Packers, Sammy Davis was already "entertaining" in a multitude of ways. Willie would have added little to the act. In the same decade that Michael Jackson was dominating the world of "entertainment", I don't recall Bo Jackson being summoned to enhance the music. With Crosby's such as David and Bing shouldn't Mason Crosby stick to kicking field goals?!

When NFL players Merlin Olsen and Bernie Casey retired from playing professional football they wanted to become "entertainers." It was not DURING their playing days though. They wanted a second career in acting. There's nothing wrong with that but it is a whole separate thing. They studied acting and they made a buck too. Merlin had a hit TV show and I loved Bernie Casey in "Brian's Song!" They were "entertaining" and they were honest about their intentions. They didn't try and turn the LA Coliseum into the Hollywood Bowl. Those are separate venues. Just as I don't need to see DeNiro carrying the ball on 3rd and 3, I don't want to see Dwyane Wade doing "Shakespeare in the Park."

The point is that Sports were an attempt to get us to a higher or at least a different place. The idea of forming teams to work together is not a frivolous undertaking. I firmly believe that the discord that we are experiencing in 2018 in this country, especially along racial lines could never have festered if every citizen had been on a team. Any team for that matter! Teams promote many things. There is a sacrifice for the betterment of the group over your own selfishness.

There is also, if you're lucky, the added advantage to living and working together with people who are not from your own narrow background. Once you have the opportunity to play with teammates from different social, economic, and ethnic backgrounds, it becomes evident that we are all at our core basically the same. Once you all strive for the same goals and rely on each other to meet them, the idea of hate out of pure ignorance of others vanishes. Don't get me wrong I have disliked teammates from all races and backgrounds but not because of those differences.

> *"If you want to go fast go alone. If you want to go far, you need a team"*
> JOHN WOODEN-UCLA

When I first moved to New Jersey from California, I was named the head coach at Mater Dei High School. I was the token "Jew!" We had great success at Mater Dei. Our main defense was a straight man-to-man, which we taught and practiced for at least an hour a day. The kids worked their asses off. No shortcuts! The signal to institute this defense was when I raised a clenched fist.

In my second season, we were on the road somewhere and we had the game pretty much under control. I happened to glance over at the opposing coach to see if he was about to clear his bench. He was frantically waving a clenched fist in the air signaling for something. His team never reacted. They didn't have a defense that correlated to the signal. This coach thought that he didn't need to actually practice or implement the defense. In his mind, if he just clenched his fist in the air he would get the same results as we did. The difference was our kids had done the work. I made a conscious effort to schedule that school as often as I could.

The point the story underlines is that it seems to be emblematic of today's culture where everything is style over substance. The preference is to gain something immediately without putting in the work. Extending this to an NBA game if you accept my overall premise (and you might not) that the players of today are better athletically but not as accomplished technically or fundamentally, then you need to distract the public from that very problematic fact.

People are paying a lot of money to go to these games. If you cannot make a shot, then how about having a half-court shooting contest? If you have no discernible offense other than a pick and roll, what's wrong with a little laser show beamed at the crowd! Can't make a foul shot? Fire a bazooka-like weapon filled with T-shirts into the crowd. Actually, the bazooka is only brought out after they have changed the rules to enable bad foul shooters to escape unscathed.

Here is a question: Why is there a one and one free throw regulation in all of basketball except when you get to the NBA? These are allegedly the greatest athletes on the planet. They average $9 million plus per season in salary and yet THEY get the relief from the "pressure" of having to stand up in the guts of a game and make the first foul shot in order to earn the second. We can't have that. People may realize the product is not as great as advertised. So instead of going back to the gym for however long it may take to improve this flaw the league changes the rules to disguise this. You "give" that player two foul shots. The kid in high school has to deal with it but not Dwight Howard. I mean how can you expect poor Dwight to work on his foul shooting for only $24 million a year?

This automatic 2-shots, however, was not enough protection for some of the NBA's "Star" players. This is an actual quote from the Sports Illustrated Wire of July 12, 2016:

"The NBA has announced rule changes meant to discourage teams from intentionally fouling poor free throw shooters." Known as 'hack a fouls,' teams often employ the intentional fouls on struggling free throw shooters by grabbing them away from the ball...with many complaining the hacks significantly reduce the entertainment value of the game."

Honestly, the actual "rules" themselves are irrelevant to me and should be to you. The concept that they are necessary or even remotely considered a good idea is the issue.

10 years ago when I wrote Taking Shots, I made some suggestions to help the game. They were generally ignored but the league is starting to come around. For example, my complaints and suggestions regarding "time-outs" are now being addressed. Unlike our current President, I'm not taking credit for the change but I'm glad they are doing something to make the flow of the game better. The stock market, however, is all me!

This morning I realized that I'm right again on this foul shooting "enabling." theme. I hope you get it that when I criticize a Dwight Howard or another poor free-throw shooter it is done with the understanding that if he worked on anything he could conquer it. That's how great I think these players could be. There is really nothing athletically beyond them.

Andre Drummond, the center for the Detroit Pistons, was possibly the worst foul shooter of them all. It was literally painful to watch him shoot free throws. If they really cared about the fans, the league should have issued special glasses to shield their customers when Andre was attempting a free throw. As recently as last season he was constantly intentionally fouled away from the ball just to put him at the foul line. He was shooting free throws at a 38% clip. His coach,

Stan Van Gundy, wanted to play him for his obvious other contributions. But he did have to at least consider taking Andre out at the end of games to prevent him from being fouled. This, in spite of the fact that the Detroit Pistons had recently invested well over $100,000,000 in Andre to actually PLAY in the games.

This is the exact dilemma that the NBA faced when it came up with the "brilliant" idea of enabling or hiding this problem. Don't improve the sport; hide the flaws so the people keep coming without realizing that they are watching an inferior product. Well thankfully at least, for now, Andre Drummond didn't want to be enabled. Apparently, he wanted to get better. Andre was asked about his 6 for 6 start coupled with his 75% free throw shooting during the preseason. He said that during the summer of 2017 he worked on his weakness. He spent:

> *"Many, many, many weeks and thousands of hours developing a repeatable free throw. For me, it's like running now. I put the work in. I put the time in. I've done what I was supposed to do this summer."*
> ANDRE DRUMMOND

Good for you Andre! While the league was busy devising rules to allow you to cover up your inadequacies, you were working to get better. Wow, what a concept!

The behavior that further causes me concern is the actions of the players in the actual game. Some have bought into the notion that they are "entertainers." I mean they've been told they are. They can read the advertisements just like the rest of us. The preening, the flexing, the screaming if they make a lay-up, the celebration of the most mundane accomplishment is all part of what I think will eventually turn off a lot of fans.

It's amazing that a Bruce Smith or a Walter Payton or a Tim Duncan could somehow have accomplished the things they did on fields and courts without celebrating each and every tackle or lay-up. It's all too much and the saying, "act like you've been there before," is simply an overused meaningless refrain spouted out by guys like me yearning for a way of conducting oneself with class, which may never return.

There is no desire by NBA nor other professional sports teams across the board to hide what they're doing anymore. There is an actual cottage industry for all of these distractions and gimmicks. They call it "In-Game Entertainment." The NBA proudly has a highly successful division called NBA Entertainment. The NBA assigns a game presentation manager to all 30 teams in the league. This person's job is to help and then evaluate their "in-game" performance. Not of the players but rather of the "entertainment". So much for the spontaneous joy they attempt to project. It's all part of the act. It's a show. A couple of years ago, the Orlando Magic employed 9 "entertainment" teams to deal with their "in-game" presentation. This included dancers, face painters, jugglers, and balloon artists. They finished that season with 27 wins and 55 losses. Jugglers are fun but maybe they should have hired a real point guard instead!

Just so no one mistakes my feelings here. I like jugglers. I've got nothing against face painters. I'm not a big bearded lady guy but that's just me. I love the circus. I just don't need it breaking out at a basketball game. That does presuppose that the basketball game is as advertised. That it is a legitimate competitive sporting event. If not, then "here come the elephants!"

None of this is new with me. I know its "old school". I know it's corny but it is true! The part that riles me the most is when these coaches who are making incredible sums of money through salary, endorsements, camps, etc. pontificate about "our game" and the lessons of the great coaches who influenced them. I wonder what those "mentors" would really say about how some of today's coaches have hijacked the sport for their own purposes.

I think it's fairly pompous to quote yourself but this is what I wrote in Taking Shots in 2007.

> *"I have seen this coming for a long time. I have been the guy tilting at the windmills of the NBA for 23 years (now it is 33). I have had issues with the league itself, the players, the player's union, the fans, all the way down to my fellow agents. What follows in these pages will attempt to show how we got to this point. I'm not a great philosopher. I'm not an investigative journalist. I'm a storyteller. I will not preach. I would rather have you think about something after I get you to laugh. I'm going to tell my stories and then leave it to you to figure out if there is some meaning. (I can't do all the work)."*

I wasn't exactly hiding my opinions 10 years ago when I wrote that. It's on PAGE TWO!! I wasn't wrong either!

I guess the kid in me has never left. The feeling I got when my Dad and Mom took me to sporting events has stayed with me. I even made a career out of it. You grow up in New York and you get to go to Yankee Stadium. You sit at the Polo Grounds before it was reduced to just another apartment complex. My friends and I got to "sneak" into Shea Stadium after the fourth inning, although I suspect the ushers simply closed their eyes and let us in!

I remember taking the train or the subway or driving in the family car through all that traffic and concrete and buildings and being overwhelmed by the throngs of people. After all those intimidating and mostly gray surroundings, you entered the portal which led to your seats. Suddenly there it was! GREEN!! The grass on that field was so out-of-place and so beautiful! It's a feeling I'll always remember and I want it back!

And then if you really got lucky you got to go to the "The Garden!"

CHAPTER TWO

THE RIGHT WAY???

The ironic part is that being born in Brooklyn, raised on Long Island, and kind of into basketball a bit I was always a huge New York Knick fan. So what happened?

My earliest memory of Madison Square Garden centers on the very 1st game I ever saw there. My dad and I went to a Knicks game at the invitation of my Great Uncle Benny. It was the late 1950s and I was somewhere in the neighborhood of eight years old. Just walking into the "Garden" was awe-inspiring. The sights, the sounds, even the smells were unique. The fact that I couldn't really make out the actual players on the floor due to the thickness of the cigar and cigarette smoke I figured was just part of the charm of the old place. This was the "Old Garden" and predated any smoking guidelines or political correctness.

My Uncle Benny was not a man to just gloss over in an opening paragraph of a chapter. Uncle Benny was the part of the family that people didn't really openly talk about, back then or I suppose not now either. He was in some businesses that respectable families would just as well avoid discussing. Uncle Benny who was my paternal grandfather's brother, was a loan shark who also owned pornographic bookstores in Times Square and other parts of the City. This was as sinister a profession as our family would be involved in until I became an NBA agent. This agent thing established a new low for the Glass family.

I didn't really know about any of Uncle Benny's exploits, nor did I care. He was a Damon Runyon type character, and it was fascinating to me just being around him. It also wasn't always that easy to get around him. There was for instance a period of several years where we couldn't directly contact Uncle Benny. We had to go through his attorney who would then relay the message to Uncle Benny. Maybe he was shy.

Or maybe the above-mentioned businesses weren't the only ones he participated in. I have no facts, just rumors and innuendo but a couple of anecdotes will give you a glimpse into my Great Uncle.

Many years after this game at Madison Square Garden my brother Brent was getting married. The wedding was in a beautiful part of Connecticut, which was where my future sister-in-law Bobbie grew up. Uncle Benny naturally was invited along with a "plus one." Benny's "plus one" turned out to be a very nice woman who was alleged to have at one time been affiliated in some way with the world's oldest profession. She was 42 or so and Uncle Benny was 74.

Uncle Benny lived on Park Ave in Manhattan and didn't drive as I don't believe he even had a driver's license. So Brent arranged to have one of his closest friends pick the couple up and drive them to Connecticut. Uncle Benny dressed immaculately. His girlfriend wore a black mini-skirt. I was 19 and I do recall it being a very nice mini-skirt.

They made the pick-up. No problem. Things became a bit dicier when you add in the fact that Brent's friend was Greek, which in and of itself should not be a problem. However, it should not be a surprise that being from Greece it followed that he had a Greek name. Again to the average person, this would not be an issue. The introductions began:

UNCLE BENNY: So what's your name?

CONSTANTINE: I am Constantine Varvitsoulous.

UNCLE BENNY: You know nobody likes a wise-ass!! I asked you your name!!

CONSTANTINE: No, no Mr. Glass, I am from Athens and my name is

Constantine Varvitsoulous.

UNCLE BENNY: Yeah, well for this trip, you're going to be "Bill!"

The rest of the day Constantine was Bill.

UNCLE BENNY: So Bill what did you major in college?!

At the wedding all day, we would hear

UNCLE BENNY: Hey Bill, you need a drink?

Back at the Garden, the Knicks were losing. They were down 5 with about a minute and a half left in the game. We were in Benny's box and a very nice gentleman from two boxes over yelled over to Benny:

> **GUY FROM 2 BOXES OVER**: Hey Ben! Looks like the Knicks are dead!

Uncle Benny apparently disagreed:

> **UNCLE BENNY**: That ain't necessarily so!"

Uncle Benny's loyalty to the Knicks was not only commendable but also elicited a response,

> **GUY FROM 2 BOXES OVER**: I've got 5 that says it is so!"

Uncle Benny ended the conversation:

> **UNCLE BENNY**: 4-to-1 and you're on!

Wow I thought, Uncle Benny just bet $5 dollars on the Knicks. He must really like them. My dad explained what 4-to-1 actually meant which, would not be the last math lesson I got from my father.

30 seconds left and the Knicks are still down 3 and it's not looking good for the home team. Uncle Benny got up, walked through the lobby of the "Old Garden" and came back with a fist full of cash to pay off his loss. I should note that this was 50 years before ATM's, thereby creating some suspicion about where the cash came from. However, being eight at the time that issue never occurred to me.

Unbeknownst to Uncle Benny, the Knicks rallied to win. I was ecstatic. Thanks to my quick math lesson, Benny had won 20 bucks figuring in his odds. I jumped on Uncle Benny. He calmly brushed off his overcoat like he was shooing a fly,

UNCLE BENNY: Ain't that something? Let's go eat.

It was 15 years until my dad told me the actual wager and it wasn't $5.

A couple of years after Brent's wedding my friends and I were playing poker with my dad at his house on Long Island. My dad was winning the majority of the pots by "getting the shoe clerks out." A little after midnight the phone rang. It was Uncle Benny's girlfriend.

Uncle Benny has just passed away. Being that this was Uncle Benny that wasn't the end of the story. When it came to Benny, you always had to expect a bit more chaos. Before my dad could even process his Uncle's death, his girlfriend had some additional information to share.

According to her, Uncle Benny had managed to put away over $1,000,000 in cash in 10's and 20's. This money was residing in seven safety deposit boxes scattered across the five boroughs of New York City. She went on to explain that she had the keys and the locations, but she also knew that not being family she couldn't get to the cash. My dad naturally asked what she had in mind and was informed that she wanted to be cut in. My father being a most reasonable man and more importantly a man who 10 minutes earlier had no clue that there was any cash, agreed to the request.

Not having been part of any of the negotiations surrounding the safety deposit box saga, I really don't know the specifics of what transpired. Apparently though, my dad was the only truly reasonable person among the rest of the family. They wouldn't cut her in and as far as

I know nobody in the family ever received a dime! I do however recall being at the service for Uncle Benny and there did seem to be an awful lot of arguing for a funeral. Chaos reigned! I had a vision of Uncle Benny looking down with a big smile on his face thinking to himself:

PERFECT!!!

KEEYUMAH

Like a lot of kids in the New York area at that time, our parents shipped off to the mountains of Pennsylvania every summer for Camp. In 1960, I was nine years old. That was my first and almost last summer at Camp Keeyumah in Orson, Pa. It rained for the entire first week I was there. I was miserable and began a campaign of "fake news" that would have been the envy of today's White House!

The purpose of these letters and postcards was in general to move my mom in the direction of a nervous breakdown. This would then prompt both of my parents to rescue me from this awful fate. The initial five writings home were beauties and were clearly having an effect. My parents decided to give it one more day. Day six was my "coup de grâce." The beatings I was subjected to, the wild animals in the bunks, etc. painted a picture of horror previously unknown in camping lore! They immediately jumped in the car and started on the five and a half hour trek to Orson.

Unbeknownst to them, the sun had made an appearance and when they arrived as my saviors I was at shortstop on the main diamond, fielding grounds balls. I had no time for them. Not now. I did wave. I stayed at Keeyumah for the next 14 summers.

A lot of people I run into rave about their own experiences at camp whenever I talk about Keeyumah (which is often). With all due respect, I just don't think they get it. Keeyumah was a special place. Not the physical layout. We actually had some of the worst facilities in the mountains. But the people were special.

Without even going in to the extraordinary owners and people who ran the place, it seemed like every group had a counselor or three that could play or teach you what you needed to learn. My counselor for five years was Mike Brandeis who played at C. W. Post on Long Island, where he held scoring records for decades. Mike was a monster. As I mentioned earlier, Brent's counselor two bunks away was Larry Brown, whom I'm fairly certain will appear again later in these pages. Larry's brother Herb, who himself would go on to coach in the NBA and around the world, but who's career highlight was coaching me as an assistant at C.W. Post College, was in another bunk. It went on and on.

One year, we got a new counselor from C. W. Post named Richie Scheinblum, who played basketball and a little baseball at Post. Richie was a great guy and a terrific athlete. 1972 was my final year at Keeyumah. By this time I was wrapping up my seventh summer working there. There were no TVs at Keeyumah with the one exception being a little black and white job that one of the camp owners had. At the end of July that year, we were treated to a special night when we all got to watch the Major League Baseball All-Star game. Batting third for the American League was Richie.

Keeyumah was not like other places!!

Every summer a contingent of Knick players actually came to Keeyumah! Coach Red Holzman himself would bring up three or four of his current players to put on a clinic for us and then play a game against our counselor team at night. I remember "Jumpin' Johnny" Green, Paul Hogue, George Blaney, Phil Jackson, Dave Stallworth, and Emmett Bryant, who I got to play against when I was 15, all coming to Keeyumah. Coach Holzman couldn't have been more gracious and down to earth. He was a role model for all of us. One of those years, our counselor team BEAT the Knicks! Before anyone asks, no Derek Fisher was not coaching the Knicks at that time.

Coach Holzman arranged to have a group from Keeyumah play at halftime of a Knicks game. I got to play twice at the "Old Garden." My New York Knick fandom was out of control and growing.

If I could concoct a team to emulate from all my years of watching and/or being peripherally involved in the NBA, it would come down to the 1977 Portland Trail Blazers led by Bill Walton and Maurice Lucas or the Knick teams of the late 60's and early 70's.

Those Knick teams, with the "Captain" Willis Reed along with Walt Frazier, Bill Bradley, Dick Barnett, and capped off by the trade that brought Dave DeBusschere from Detroit (in exchange for Walt Bellamy), were a joy to watch. Earl Monroe and Jerry Lucas, who were instrumental in their 2nd NBA Championship later joined that core. These teams along with the later additions of Magic Johnson and Larry Bird are in fact primarily responsible for why many of us can't get through a full NBA game today.

Imagine if you will, the ball being passed sometimes three times in one possession to an open man on a regular basis. It sounds like a fantasy but it happened every night during those seasons. It was the way we were taught to play in those mountains during the summers. Like a team! As strange as this may sound, I just recently found out that a Keeyumahite was the first one to suggest acquiring DeBusschere. Coach Holzman himself through various sources verified the story. However, in the interests of full disclosure, the "Keeyumah Proposal" called for Walt Bellamy to remain and Willis Reed to be traded. That little wrinkle would have resulted in two fewer NBA titles, which would have left the Knicks with none. The idea of winning those 2 Championships without Willis Reed is not a plausible outcome.

Nobody needs me to breakdown those great teams. Holzman coached them beautifully, and they exhibited a tremendous blend of talent and personality both on and off the court. They were a joy to behold, and they won! I mention them only because this ended my fan phase with the Knicks. It has been strictly business for me ever since.

AN EMBRYO AGENT

I went on to finish college and then embarked on a 3,000-mile search for a Law School that would consider accepting me. I finally found one that would even entertain the very idea of having me on their campus. It was a little school in the San Fernando Valley in California. It was cleverly named the University of San Fernando Valley-College of Law. I'm sure you've seen our t-shirts! It didn't even have a campus! To be fair though, there was patio in the back with a table and six plastic chairs. The law school was located on Sepulveda Blvd. wedged between an apartment complex and an Earl Scheib auto painting plant.

The school was accredited but only in California. It was state accredited, not nationally accredited but even THEY put conditions on my acceptance. I was provisionally accepted and could only take a limited load the first semester. I weighed my options, quickly realized I didn't have any and loaded up that Chevy Vega station wagon, the same one that would eventually be picking up Coach Wooden in for camp and headed 3,000 miles west. I spent nine years in Los Angeles, eventually graduating from Law School and somehow passing the California Bar Exam, which to all my friends in New Jersey is a hell of a lot harder than the New Jersey Bar.

I enjoyed my years in Los Angeles. I spent my first 5 years living in a trailer in Northridge Park with the first of my countless wives. We had Samantha (aka Sami), my first child there. I would have stayed in that trailer park for the whole 9 years but as every new parent knows, those brats take up quite a bit of space. Playpens, clothes, diapers, a place to change them and then they expect a place to sleep. Between Sami's stuff and the increasing evidence of the impending arrival of another one, Tyler, we had to get out.

I met and became friends with some terrific people in my time in California. I got to coach some great kids in the park system at Northridge Park, and I set myself up as a sole practitioner of the law. Wills, trusts, and thankfully divorce cases, which would prove invaluable to me later in my own personal life.

If it seems like I'm racing through this portion of my travels, you are correct. I already went through this with many of you people in my first book, *Taking Shots* and also to some degree in the preceding Chapter. So two things are possible here. Either you did not truly study my life closely enough and have forgotten it, or worse, you didn't read it in the first place. Either way, this annoys me, and it may be too late to correct the problem as I believe *Taking Shots* is sold out, certainly the hardcover edition. I know this because my mom bought most of the copies available.

> **SO THE DEAL IS:** This is a new book and sad as it is, events and relationships have changed dramatically since the publishing of that book in 2007, as you will discover only if you pay close attention.

By 1981, my coaching days at UCLA were over. Many of my former players at UCLA beginning with our 7'5" backup center Mark Eaton were looking at their professional possibilities in basketball. I had absolutely no desire to become a professional sports agent. I specifically enrolled in law school to try and represent the American Indians. I am aware that in 2018 that is not the politically correct term. Today they are "Native Americans" and I respect that but in 1977 they were "American Indians." I'm sorry but keeping up with the proper vernacular gets complicated. I was understandably caught off-guard when Mark called:

MARK: Coach (that's me) I need you!

KG: What happened?!

MARK: I just got drafted!!

KG: Mark, that's impossible the Army has a 6'6" height restriction.

MARK: Dummy. I got drafted in the NBA! You are the only lawyer I trust.

KG: I'm the only lawyer you know!

Maybe some background here will help. Mark Eaton, whose jersey number 53 is actually retired by the Utah Jazz, was a player for us at UCLA. Well, "player is a bit of an exaggeration, but he was there with us. I saw him on the bus. He had trouble getting on the court because he had a tendency to "walk" when we threw him the ball in the post or anywhere else. Walking is not a good thing in basketball as it results in giving the opposing team the ball. Mark would be the first one to admit this. But Mark and I became friends and as such I would throw him 300 lobs passes a day after practice to try and help with this affliction. Nobody worked harder than Mark and those sessions brought two results. Mark no longer "walked" and I am still the best lob passer in the United States!

Even the way Mark began playing basketball was bizarre. Mark's size made him an obvious candidate to play basketball. I don't know about any of you people but I cannot remember any 7'5" kids in my high school. Furthermore, being that the center on our high school team was 6'5", Mark would have been urged to join us. There was only one problem with that obvious route, Mark hated basketball. The reasons for this are complicated. Often when someone is expected to do something automatically, they repel from it. In Mark's case, I think that plus the feeling that he wasn't good at basketball were the main problems.

In addition, Mark had other interests. He wanted to be an auto mechanic. He studied up and did indeed become the world's largest auto mechanic. He went to work at a Mark C. Bloome Auto Center in Orange County, California. On a now fateful day an assistant basketball coach, Tom Lubin from nearby Cypress Junior College, was driving in the area and got lost. As we all do, he looked around for a gas station or something similar to get directions.

Auto mechanics many times have to work on the underbelly of cars. To do this, they roll under the cars on those little "creepers." Mark had done this five minutes before Tom Lubin pulled up. Coach Lubin looked under the car and saw feet. He then walked around to the other end and saw a head. Naturally he figured this was two individual people. He began asking the guy with the head for directions being that it is very difficult to get directions from feet.

Suddenly, Tom Lubin got the feeling that this might actually be one person and demanded that Mark roll out from under the car. Mark obliged and when he finally unfolded one can only imagine the reaction of a lost assistant basketball coach at discovering what could be his starting center.

After some introductions, Mark let Tom Lubin know that he had no intentions of leaving his current job to enroll at Cypress Junior College. Thankfully, for Mark, Tom, Cypress, and my entire family,

Coach Lubin kept returning to that service center every week until Mark succumbed.

Mark became a major factor at Cypress and as such many Division 1 programs were now recruiting him. UCLA had interest but when it came time for awarding scholarships the staff came to the conclusion that we were not going to continue Mark's recruitment. We even had a meeting with Mark in our offices where we encouraged him to accept a scholarship to Pepperdine University in Malibu.

Mark being extremely perceptive realized at that meeting that we were basically not going to recruit him anymore so he decided to recruit us:

> **MARK**: You know guys; nothing has ever come easy for
> me but no one will work harder than I will.

Larry offered him a full scholarship right after that sentence. Mark spent two seasons at UCLA and played a total of 61 minutes in 60 games. You can easily now see why I thought it was the Army, not the NBA that had drafted him. However, we need to also understand that this was a different time in the NBA. First of all, when Mark was drafted, there were seven rounds! A big difference compared to today's two-round format. Additionally, those were the days when every team in the league had three centers on their roster and for whatever reason most of the back-ups were white.

I took the job as Mark's "agent" and scheduled a meeting with the Coach and General Manager of the Utah Jazz, Frank Layden. Frank and I are friends today but back then we had never met. Frank was not only in that position of power but was also acknowledged as the biggest character in the NBA. He is a 300 pound coaching comedian, who when asked why he only carried 11 players on the Jazz roster when the rest of the league was carrying the allowed 12 said:

FRANK: Even Jesus had trouble with 12!

The truth was he was saving money on salaries and travel, so heading in to this meeting I had to be prepared. My goal was to get Mark a guaranteed contract of some sort. I felt this way because even though Mark had made tremendous strides in his game, he would require an extended look from an NBA team in order to impress them thereby enabling him to keep improving his game. Without any guarantee, it would be too easy to simply release him.

Frank and I sat down at the pool at the Marriott at the LAX Airport. That alone was a sight to see. I didn't lie to Frank, but I may have made an insinuation that we had a deal in Spain. It was a long time ago and to quote Attorney General Jeff Sessions:

> *"I don't know/ I can't recall/ I'm not sure/ I can't remember,"* etc.

Frank's reaction to my requesting a guaranteed contract was understandable

> **FRANK:** Let me get this straight. You want us to guarantee this guy?! You were on the coaching staff at UCLA, and YOU wouldn't play him!!! Why the hell should we?!

> **KG:** We couldn't play him, Frank. Every time we threw it to him he walked and every time we went down the defensive end he fouled. In the NBA they let you walk and they let you foul. He's perfect!!

We got two years guaranteed. That was the first, last and only guaranteed contract in the history of the 4th round of the NBA

Draft. Since there is no more 4th round, I feel secure in stating that is something not likely to occur again. Mark went on to lead the league in blocks, become an NBA All-Star, and was even the defensive player of the year in the NBA. Mark Eaton's #53 jersey is now retired by the Utah Jazz and hangs in the rafters of their arena in between the jerseys of two other guys named Stockton and Malone, whoever they are!

People mistakenly felt that I had something to do with all this, so many of the other guys that I had coached signed with me as well: Mike Holton, Mike Sanders, Rod Foster, Darren Daye, Cliff Pruitt, Stuart Gray, Brad Wright, Ralph Jackson, et al. Players from other schools started signing with me also.

Suddenly I had a business. Goodbye Wills and Trusts!

GLASS & FATHER

As my client list was growing, I realized that I didn't want my "guys" to wind up as financial cautionary tales. I had heard quite a few stories of athletes going broke after their careers were over and had zero interest in that happening to my players. I needed someone to advise them and manage their finances. Somebody they could trust. There was only one guy for that job, and I called him. It wasn't hard to find him; I always could reach my dad.

He had dabbled in this area over the years. Mainly, he had become the unofficial agent for Larry Brown. As you will see below that became an almost full-time albeit "unpaid" position, at least for a while. Additionally, whenever Larry would encounter a troubled player on his roster, he would reach out to my father to help him. This happened on two or three occasions. So while we had some degree of experience in this burgeoning area, it wasn't until I left UCLA that it really morphed into an actual business entity.

This is how the firm "Glass & Father" began and although there were some bumps in the road I think we did right for our clients and ourselves over the past 30 years or so. We placed 110 players in the NBA and an equal number overseas in that time period and we're still at it.

Naturally with this amount of NBA players, I had occasions to sign contracts with the Knicks. While I was no longer really a "fan" like I was when I was a kid, the Knicks were in the NBA and they had money. I have never been known to discriminate when a team had money.

There were several interesting negotiations throughout the years but one stands out as a harbinger of things to come financially, not for me but for the sport in general. I was trying to get one of my clients, Greg Grant, a deal with the Knicks. A good friend of mine, Al Bianchi, was the Knicks General Manager at that time. Greg was a 5'6" point guard out of Trenton State (now known as The College of New Jersey). He had somehow been drafted by the Phoenix Suns in the 2nd round a few years earlier and now was a free agent.

This occurred during the beginning period of the Salary Cap. The "Cap" was designed mostly to protect NBA owners from themselves. It has since become a birthright of the owners. The "Cap" was supposed to be the way the NBA could get control of the rising salaries in the league. You can see how well that has worked. Around that time, I was fighting to get players like Greg $200,000 to $300,000 a year. I understand that's good money, especially back in the 1990s but remember we are talking about professional sports here.

One of the offshoots of the Salary Cap was that it created Salary Slots. These "Slots" became more valuable than many of the players. If your team established a particular slot, they would want to keep it in order to possibly use it to go over the "Cap" in the future. This enables the team to overpay the next player. I know it's a bit complicated and I'm not doing a great job of explaining it but this isn't a textbook and

I don't feel like breaking it all down at this time. If you really want to get the details, call me.

So I'm trying to get Greg Grant a deal with the Knicks. Greg's value at that time is around $275,000 or so, based on his production and potential. So naturally I asked for $350,000 thereby giving us a little room to move that number down. Al Bianchi's response was:

AL: Would you take $375,000?!

The Knicks had a $375,000 "Slot" they wanted to preserve! This is where my brilliance as an agent kicked into high gear:

ME: OK!

So Greg Grant became a New York Knick. An interesting aside for Knick fans is that the day before the roster was to be trimmed down to 12 I received a call from Greg. He was updating me on the management moves that day, since it was cut-down day. A player who was scheduled to be released that morning had suddenly come down with a suspicious ankle injury.

Since you couldn't waive an injured player, the Knicks were forced to put that guy on their injured reserve list and therefore pay him until he healed. That's how John Starks made the Knicks!

There were probably 10 or more instances where we signed players with the Knicks but they really weren't a "go-to" franchise for me in terms of signings. That just happens in this business. What also happens in this business is that an agent loses his "fandom" quickly. It's all about your clients and their best interests. You become a Jazz fan or a Bulls fan, etc. if that's where your guys are playing.

That impartiality changed.

CHAPTER THREE

BIG JOE & LARRY

To fully understand my dad's relationship with Larry Brown would take a volume in and of itself. I'm going to try and give the "Cliff Notes" version of that relationship and in doing so concentrate mostly on the business side of things. Their personal interaction could not be described in words anyway. Certainly not by me. You'd need a real writer for that.

The NBA believes that my father was Larry's agent. While that description has some merit, there was a lot more to it than that. In short, my dad was Larry's surrogate father. Every life event or decision that Larry made was run through Joe Glass. The amount of time spent on Larry's various stops and starts was staggering.

As mentioned earlier, Larry came to our family through my brother Brent. Larry was 17 years old and Brent's favorite counselor. After they returned home from the mountains, Brent missed Larry and since Larry lived in Long Beach, which was 15 minutes from Lynbrook where we lived, my parents said Brent could invite Larry over for dinner. He never left, and I ended up on a cot. I didn't even know we had a cot! I was six and having Larry around was like having two older brothers instead of one.

At Keeyumah, Larry had reached near legendary status as a basketball player and role model for most of the campers. He was clearly the best player Keeyumah had ever seen. Even then though, he was demanding that his campers did things "the right way!" This wasn't just for sports but extended to everything they did.

While everybody in camp seemed to do whatever Larry suggested, I didn't. I think it was basically because to me Larry truly seemed like my brother. I didn't do everything Brent said and I always respected Brent more than Larry, so what's the big deal about Larry?

But Larry WAS a big deal! As such, there was a "right way" for everything. There was obviously a "right way" to play, but there was a "right way" to behave as well, exhibited by his code of conduct that continued all throughout his various playing and coaching stops.

At each of these stops, my dad was there, negotiating Larry in to contracts and invariably getting him out of them when Larry's whims or excuses would surface. In my father's eyes, Larry was never wrong. This wasn't a business move on my father's part, although many team executives and college athletic directors did not and probably still don't buy that. The truth is that as with all of his children my father simply loved us, believed in us, and would do anything to protect us. Lucky for Larry this extended to him for over 50 years.

This included many different negotiations as Larry continued his sojourn around college and professional basketball. Here is the unabridged list:

TEAM	YEARS	REPRESENTATIVE
Davidson College	1969	Joe Glass
Carolina Cougars-ABA	1972-74	Joe Glass
Denver Rockets-ABA	1974-79	Joe Glass
UCLA	1979-81	Joe Glass
New Jersey Nets-NBA	1981-83	Joe Glass

Kansas Univ.	1983-88	Joe Glass
San Antonio Spurs-NBA	1988-92	Joe Glass
LA Clippers-NBA	1991-93	Joe Glass
Indiana Pacers-NBA	1993-97	Joe Glass
Philadelphia 76ers-NBA.	1997-03	Joe Glass
Detroit Pistons-NBA	2003-05	Joe Glass
New York Knicks-NBA	2005-06	Joe Glass
Charlotte Hornets-NBA	2008-11	Joe Glass/Tyler Glass
SMU	2012-16	Joe Glass/Tyler Glass

Keep in mind that this above list only deals with Larry's coaching stops. My dad's involvement in guiding him through his career began much earlier, during his playing days. It was during his playing career that Dad first got into things involving Larry's finances.

I think it began (and I can't be sure about this) at our dining room table on Long Island. Larry had brought his best friend at the time, Doug Moe, to the house for the night. Doug and Larry were playing for the New Orleans Buccaneers. They had a game against the New Jersey Americans of the newly formed ABA (American Basketball Association) the following night. This was the league that tried to compete with the NBA and would later have four of its teams merge with the NBA. Interestingly. Larry would coach all four of those entries!

Doug Moe was a great player in his time, but what I remember mostly about him was that he was FUN! He took no crap from anyone on or off the court as both a player and later as a Coach for Denver and San Antonio. Doug was also the only one who seemed to tell Larry the truth and not care about the consequences.

There are many stories about Doug but one that illustrates my point is that after Doug became Larry's assistant with the Carolina Cougars of the ABA, he simply walked away from the job after

Larry didn't support him in front of the players. It took several trips and quite a bit of groveling by Larry and the general manager of the Cougars to get Doug to reluctantly return. Nobody else did that with Larry.

One of my favorite Doug stories is that during his time with Larry in Carolina, they had an excellent backcourt consisting of Mack Calvin & Steve Jones. Both were great guys but Steve was more calculating than Mack. Steve went to Larry and told him he couldn't play with Mack anymore and they needed to trade Mack! Larry then went to Doug:

> **LARRY** We have a problem!
>
> **DOUG**: What is it?!
>
> **LARRY**: Steve says he can't play with Mack, and we should trade Mack. What do we do?
>
> **DOUG**: TRADE STEVE!

They did just that!

So the family is sitting down to eat. My sister Jodi and my Mom were there. I think Brent was away at College. My dad had recently negotiated the contracts for Larry and Doug to play for the Buccaneers for the astounding sum of somewhere in the neighborhood of $30,000. Doug got a bit more I think. I was 15 when all of this was going on so forgive me if I get any of the details slightly wrong. These are my recollections, and they had to have come from somewhere! I can't imagine being creative enough to conjure this up out of nowhere.

Larry's middle name is Harvey and he didn't like it. So Doug naturally referred to him only as "Harve":

DOUG: Hey Harve, why don't you tell Joe about the cattle deal?

LARRY: Not now Doug.

DAD: What cattle deal?!

Apparently, Doug and Larry had been snookered into some kind of phony cattle deal in New Mexico. They lost a couple of grand or something. My memory is clear however on the fact that my dad took Larry upstairs and from that day forward all of Larry's checks came to Woodmere, NY. This lasted for over 40 years.

Doug and Larry's playing careers took them on a wild ride! They played for the Buccaneers then went on to the Oakland Oaks, where they teamed with the great Rick Barry. Larry told me that during the 1st quarter of a game Rick had missed his first eight shots. He went immediately up to Larry and was very excited:

RICK: Get it to me now Larry!!

LARRY: Rick, you're 0 for 8!!

RICK: I know, but I'm a 50% shooter. My next eight are going in!!

I tell all my clients and players that I coach or represent that anecdote as it serves as a perfect illustration of how one's mental approach can often be the difference between good and great!!

From Oakland, Larry moved on to the Washington Caps for the 1969-70 season. Then he went to the Virginia Squires for the 1970-71 campaign and finally landed as a player with the Denver Rockets from 1971 to 1972. At every stop, my dad was by his side trying to get him what he could in a fledgling league. Teams in the ABA were constantly financially challenged throughout the leagues existence. Players' and coaches' checks would bounce the same height as the multi-colored balls the league introduced.

There was no financial benefit to my dad's efforts on Larry's behalf. It was for the most part a labor of love for my dad. In fact, I don't believe there was any commission arrangement between them until many years later when the money and his time became more of an undertaking than in these early years.

My dad was always working but remember when you were in grade school and they asked you what your father did for a living? I never could answer that one. It was too confusing for me. He worked when I was very young in lower Manhattan in the garment industry along with my grandfather and other family members. Later on he became a developer of some sort where he built discount stores and would then lease out the various departments. After I became a lawyer and my dad and I joined forces, I was often asked if he was a lawyer as well. He wasn't but he thought he was and I didn't have the heart to tell him.

The ABA was a terrific idea and the basketball played in that league was really exciting. I was basically raised on that brand of ball, from the 3-point shot to the colored ball and mostly to the individuality that separated the ABA completely from the NBA of those times. The stories about the ABA are legendary and could fill a book on its own. In fact, it already does. Terry Pluto's excellent *Loose Balls* published years ago is a superb accounting of those times and characters. There is no reason for me to give a 2nd best history of that remarkable league. Terry nailed it pretty well.

Despite all the stops that my dad helped steer Larry through, their relationship really never totally morphed into a pure agent/client relationship. This, I'm sure comes as a surprise to some especially those in the National Basketball Players Association (NBPA). The people in power at the Union at that time actually suspended and decertified my dad only on the grounds that he was representing Larry.

This occurred after Larry had become the coach of the Knicks. Things became too public in the New York media. It was ironic because my dad had always chosen to avoid contact with the media for the most part for 40 years. It wasn't out of any interest to hide his activities; it was rather that he felt coaches and players salaries, etc. were private matters. If one of our clients wanted to discuss his salary that was his business. It wasn't going to come from him. Obviously, the business has changed dramatically since then. In today's NBA, details of contracts I negotiate are in the public space within an hour and that information still doesn't emanate from us.

Technically, the reason for his decertification was that he was representing Larry and that the regulations of the NBPA forbid a certified agent from representing players and coaches at the same time. The fact that my dad hadn't represented a player in the 10 years prior to Larry signing with the Knicks apparently was not deemed relevant. Compared to some of the shenanigans that agents in the NBA have been involved with, this decertification or suspension was and is laughable but it is what happened.

As far as my own personal involvement in Larry's adventures, things really didn't concern me until Larry offered me that assistant coaching job with him at UCLA. After turning the opportunity down several times due to my reluctance to leave practicing law before I really even started, I accepted the position. My acceptance came after a pointed discussion with my father where he told me that I could always return to practicing law but I would never be asked to coach at UCLA again!

Eight months after I arrived on campus, we found ourselves playing for the National Championship. Considering that UCLA had never experienced such heights, it was obvious that bringing me on board was an historic move for that previously undistinguished University!

We lost to the University of Louisville in the National Championship game. We were up by 3 points with four minutes left and never scored again. I still haven't watched the tape of that game. We had a banquet in LA after the season with some 2,000 people in attendance. That Championship loss was still fresh in everyone's mind especially the fact that we never scored again in the last four minutes. I was asked to address the crowd and since I didn't know how many people knew who Keith Glass even was I began this way:

> *"For those of you who don't know me, I coached the*
> *first 36 minutes of the Louisville game!!"*

Everyone in the place laughed! Well not "everyone." Larry didn't seem to have quite the same reaction to my humor.

During our second year at UCLA, Larry started with his rumblings about wanting to leave. I didn't quite understand his complaints. Personally, I was having a ball. UCLA was a fantastic place, especially to play or coach. Specifically regarding coaching, you went to work at Pauley Pavilion and had no classes! For me, it was similar to what I thought heaven would be like. As with the banquet joke, Larry didn't share my view of nirvana.

He started complaining that the University wouldn't paint his office. Little things like this didn't seem significant enough to leave such a place. But I was new to all this and didn't have Larry's reputation or accomplishments so all I did was inform my dad to get ready to bail Larry out if things got ugly.

They did! My dad had to fly out to LA to meet with UCLA's legendary Athletic Director, J.D. Morgan. The LA Times daily reported on

Larry's "issues" with the University and of my dad's impending arrival and meeting with Mr. Morgan. I was asked to attend even though I was in an awkward spot being family with Larry but also being an employee of the University. After some pleasantries the meeting began:

> **JHG**: Well, JD, we have a problem!

> **JD**: You know Joe, I'm an old submarine pilot from World War II and my philosophy is as long as they're not shooting at me; I don't have a problem!!

> **JHG**: What division?!

For the next hour and 45 minutes I was treated to an in-depth discussion by two World War II veterans, comparing their experiences. It was fascinating and believe me a lot more interesting and relevant then the painting of Larry's office!

Larry ultimately left UCLA. I literally laughed when I read his reason for it. According to him, he only left because J.D. had passed away during our stay there. Since Mr. Morgan was the guy who signed him, Larry claimed that it wasn't the same. This, of course, was nonsense! That simply was not true, but it does make for a great cover. Larry had decided months before Mr. Morgan's passing that he needed an excuse for whatever reason to leave UCLA. I realized then and there that Larry was a guy who made up his mind first and then looked for reasons to justify it later!! This wouldn't be the last time Larry would use someone's passing as a way out of something!!

So "Big Joe" kept getting Larry in and out of things. I marveled at how no matter what the reason or supposed reason was, my dad never wavered. He honestly believed Larry was always right. I remember being in a hotel room in Manhattan with them when I was in college. Larry had been fined by the NBA for throwing a ball at a ref:

LARRY: Joe, I didn't do what they said.

JHG: It says here that you threw a ball at a ref!!

LARRY: He caught it!

To my Dad, that was always enough. To me if the ref "caught it" then Larry "threw it." But that was my dad, and Larry knew that he had a guy who would always have his back.

From UCLA, Larry next signed with the New Jersey Nets. And guess what? More drama. The Nets owner, Joe Taub, a guy that my dad really liked, became irate when it was discovered that either Larry or someone on his behalf had been making contacts and advances to the University of Kansas. People do get a bit testy when their coach who is under contract starts making plans to go somewhere else. Throw in the additional twist of doing so DURING the season, and you have a situation. My dad didn't make those contacts; he was however the one who cleaned up the mess. The Nets relieved Larry of his duties! Dad did the deal with Kansas. Just standard operating procedure!

This pattern continued almost uninterruptedly for decades. In 1988, Kansas won the National Championship. Larry coached the whole 40 minutes that night and by the way did in my opinion the greatest job of coaching that I have seen to date. I know he had the best player in Danny Manning but sitting courtside, I felt that Larry literally took the game over in the last five minutes.

My Mom, Dad, & I celebrated in Larry's hotel suite with him. We talked about what he had just accomplished and how much he loved Kansas. The next morning while we were leaving for the airport, we got a report that Larry was IN Los Angeles talking with UCLA; can't make this up!!

My dad smiled, shook his head, and started thinking about how to deal with this one. In this case Larry either wasn't offered the job or turned it down. I don't have any first-hand knowledge, as I wasn't there. He returned to Kansas for a press conference where he dramatically announced, in front of adoring students that he was staying at Kansas.

6 weeks later he signed with the San Antonio Spurs.

In San Antonio, it was a similar exit, but there was a slightly new wrinkle. This time, I believe my dad had already lined up the LA Clippers as a place to go in the event Larry soured on the Spurs. Dad was learning!

Dad learned very well, thank you. He got the hang of things and learned also to anticipate Larry's moves rather than get surprised by them. This kept them in much better position than in some of their previous encounters. But rather than have me go through each stop and the attendant "reasons" for leaving, I again call on an author far better than myself to provide some insight.

Mitch Albom, the author of *Tuesdays with Morrie* and *The 5 People You Meet in Heaven*, wrote a piece for the Detroit Free Press in 2009, which I include below. It deals with the time period only when Dad was navigating Larry through the Detroit Pistons/Cleveland Cavaliers/New York Knick portion of their travels.

Trust me, it is not lost on me that this article is not totally flattering to my dad. It is satirical and extremely "tongue in cheek." It does however on a different level clearly demonstrate what my dad did for Larry and just as importantly, how good he was at doing so!

"MILLIONS OF REASONS TO LOVE LARRY'S AGENT"

By <u>Mitch Albom</u> | Feb 25, 2009 | <u>Detroit Free Press</u> |

To: Mr. Joe Glass, Larry Brown's agent

Dear Mr. Glass,

I would like you to represent me.

Before you say yes or no, may I say how much I admire your work? I have watched you take Larry Brown from Denver to New Jersey to San Antonio to L.A. to Indiana to Philadelphia to Detroit to New York City. Wow! Where I come from, you only move that much if the cops are chasing you. Any agent who can find that much work is my kind of guy!

I also admire how you stand up for your client. The way you insist Larry is seriously ill even when everyone else around him is scratching their heads and saying, "He seems fine." That's the loyalty I need!

And the way you insisted the Pistons say they "fired" Larry even though it was clear he wanted out? Brilliant!

And – ooh, I love this one – the way you complain how Larry is being "disrespected," even when Larry was the one letting Cleveland woo him last year, and Larry is the one this year being accused by the Knicks of calling teams on his own to suggest trades?

And LARRY is being disrespected?

Smashing! Genius! You're the guy I want!

Don't say yes or no yet.

Show me the money!

First, let me add my admiration for your numbers. We all know this is a money business, brother, and brother, is money ever your business!

Just take your last few years. You got Larry a five-year, $25-million deal with Detroit – after escaping from Allen Iverson's insanity in Philly. Personally, I would have kissed you for that!

But no, after two years, you managed to wiggle out of Detroit, go to New York for double the money, $50 million for five years, AND you got the Pistons to give you $7 million in walk-away money. I love that! Walk-away money! Personally, when money walks away from me, I never see it again.

But you get Larry paid EVEN WHEN HE DOES NOTHING!

In fact, last year, with the $7 million from the Pistons and the $10 million from the Knicks, Larry made around $17 million FOR WINNING 23 GAMES! That's almost $740,000 per win. Now that's what I'm talking about.

Still, this current deal may be your masterpiece. When you brought Larry "home" to New York, and you made it seem like it was all about the basketball, even though he was leaving a championship-caliber team to take over an asylum? That was amazing spin.

But now, after one year, after Larry's complaining about players he knew he was getting, after debating those players in the press, after lamenting how he was a "dead man walking" even though dead men don't make $10 million a year unless they're named Elvis – now Larry has managed to get fired again, and you are going for the whole $40 million in owed money. Forty million to NOT work.

Joe. Buddy. I take my hat off. I put it in my hand. Hat in hand. Take me on. Please?

It's all about me. I need your tenacity. I need your myopia. I need your ability to always portray me, your client, as the victim, to rush to my defense, to tell the world that I am misunderstood, that I'm a good guy, that I only want to do what I do best – all the while trying to figure out how rich we can get.

I need that magic. I need that touch.

I hear you're even considering a new move, to Charlotte, where Larry could be united with another former NBA guard, Michael Jordan. The way I see it, if he signs fast, Larry could be cashing checks from three teams in 13 months.

Please! You gotta rep me! I'm a good guy. Just ask me. I'm a victim. Just ask me. I'm misunderstood. Just ask me. Say yes. I'll pay you whatever Larry is paying you. The way I see it, given the players I'm dealing with, I may need one of his get-out-of-town deals really fast.

Your biggest fan, Isiah Thomas

(https://www.mitchalbom.com/millions-of-reasons-to-love-larrys-agent/)

The years rolled by and so did Larry's jobs. As the above article indicates, my dad and Larry ended up back "Home" in New York. Larry was the coach of the New York Knicks. Unreal. The marquee at Madison Square Garden, not Uncle Benny's Garden but the Garden just the same, proclaimed Larry's return:

"WELCOME HOME LARRY!"

As usual my father had negotiated Larry's contract with the Knicks, five years for $50,000,000.00. (I just had to check that for zeros.) The largest coaching contract in the history of United States sports! Not bad! And to make things even sweeter, my dad had started to actually receive a commission for his efforts. I'm not even sure when this began, but I think it was around their time in Philadelphia with the 76ers. I never asked so I can't be certain.

Don't get me wrong; Larry had reciprocated in the past with my dad. Hell, my job at UCLA was probably part of that reciprocity. Larry had my father run his basketball camps in Denver, which Dad parlayed into other camps as well with Dan Issel, David Thompson, and Bobby Jones among others. Larry also on occasion would give my dad a gift. Not little ones either. I remember a BMW 7 series that my father was subsequently car-jacked in! Larry immediately replaced it saying he didn't want "Dad" driving in the same vehicle he was car-jacked in. Bad karma. Larry was legitimately upset about the incident. You see what makes what follows in these pages even worse than it will appear is that I do believe that Larry truly loved my father.

So now the family is courtside at Garden! Everything is great. Then the season began. Not so good. After 24 games, the once-proud Knicks of my youth were 6 and 18. Nobody needs or wants my personal analysis of why. It has been well documented in the press at the time and thankfully I wasn't involved in it.

I was however representing a member of the Knicks at that time named Jackie Butler, who played center. Isaiah Thomas, the Knicks general manager had orchestrated bringing Larry to the Knicks and had made the contract with my dad. Isaiah and I had brought Jackie to the Knicks a year earlier after Jackie had become my client. Jackie was playing on a minimum contract, which at the time was probably around $500,000. Isaiah had signed Jerome James, who also was a center the year before for $30,000,000 over six years ($5,000,000 per year). Larry and Isaiah then followed that brainstorm up with a sign and trade for Eddy Curry, another center, from Chicago for $50,000,000 over five years ($10,000,000 per year).

Despite both of these highly inflated salaries, Jackie became the Knicks starting center. So what you had was the franchise paying $15,500,000 a year for their centers but the guy actually playing was making $500,000. Some people claimed that Larry was doing that because I was representing Jackie. That was not the case and if anything as you will later see, I believe the opposite would have been true. Larry would never favor any of my players. One thing about him was that Larry not always played the "best" players. He preferred the ones that played the hardest and smartest. You know, played "The Right Way." Jackie Butler listened, played hard, and had what they call a very high basketball IQ. If coincidentally this was a way to embarrass Isaiah' decision making on Jerome James and Eddy Curry, all the better. Even though the Curry signing was done not only with Larry's blessings but at his insistence.

To put it mildly, things began to get a bit strained between Larry and Isaiah. I was at the Knicks facility late that season when Isaiah approached. I've always liked and respected him and I think we had and still have a pretty decent relationship. All he said was:

ISIAH: All I'd like to do is take your 'brother' outside!!

It didn't sound like he was interested in a picnic lunch.

Being a genius, I immediately figured out that things were deteriorating rapidly. The chaos that ensued is well documented. Where there was Larry inspired chaos, there was my father. Larry got himself fired this time, no arguments. For a myriad of reasons, the Knicks had had enough. The problem for our side was that there were $40,000,000 left on the contract and the Knicks claimed that he was fired "for cause!" If that was the case, then the $40,000,000 would be gone. Well not gone but back in the hands of the Garden.

This was something that neither my dad nor Larry had a huge interest in seeing happen. During the initial negotiation with the Knicks, Dad had put in a clause, which named the Commissioner of the NBA, David Stern as the official arbitrator if a dispute ever arose. This was an unusual clause to be put in any contract and was due to the fact that he did not totally trust the entire situation.

The league had very little interest in having a potential public dispute unfold in the media capital of the country. David Stern would have a strong interest in seeing that did not occur. The fact that the arbitration clause was in there I believe helped get the whole matter settled in a less costly and drawn out process. On November 8, 2006, The New York Times,' (the "Failing" New York Times) Howard Beck wrote the following:

"$18.5 Million for Brown in Knicks' Settlement"
BY HOWARD BECK NOV. 8, 2006

Larry Brown once called coaching the Knicks his "dream job." He was owed $41 million when he was fired. Credit: Barton Silverman/ The New York Times

DENVER, Nov. 8 — Larry Brown's chaotic 331-day term as coach of the Knicks netted him $28.5 million — or $1.24 million for each of the 23 victories he posted last season — after he was awarded $18.5 million in a settlement with the team.

The figures came to light Wednesday afternoon, when Brown's contract settlement was included in Cablevision's third-quarter filing with the Securities and Exchange Commission. According to the filing, the Knicks agreed to pay Brown $18.5 million to resolve their dispute — significantly less than the $53 million Brown sought through arbitration.

Brown had $41 million and four years left on his contract when the Knicks fired him in June. In challenging the Knicks' decision to withhold that sum, Brown also asked for $12.5 million in liquidated damages.

Brown was paid $10 million last season, so he walked away with $28.5 million for less than a year's work. The settlement was announced Oct. 30 by Commissioner David Stern, who was serving as arbitrator in the dispute. The two sides reached the agreement before Stern could render a decision. Stern also ordered all parties not to comment publicly. A Madison Square Garden spokesman cited that order Wednesday in declining to comment on the settlement figure.

James L. Dolan, the Garden chairman and Cablevision president, indicated in June that he did not intend to address the issue publicly again.

Although the settlement was deemed confidential when it was announced, the amount became a matter of public record because of Cablevision's status as a publicly traded company.

It has been an expensive two months of housecleaning for the Knicks. On the same day that the Brown settlement was reached, the Knicks bought out the contract of the veteran forward Jalen Rose for about $15 million. On Sept. 29, they bought out the contract of Maurice Taylor for about $7 million. The Knicks will pay an equal amount in luxury-tax penalties on the two players' contracts.

The Knicks failed spectacularly under Brown, despite his Hall of Fame credentials and a well-earned reputation as a reclamation artist. Brown clashed with his superiors over personnel issues, openly feuded with Stephon Marbury and alienated nearly all of his players.

After dismissing Brown, Dolan said he was fired "for cause" and detailed a long list of grievances that he said constituted a breach of contract. Among the allegations were that Brown undermined the team's president, Isiah Thomas, by trying to negotiate trades and that Brown violated team rules about dealing with the news media.

Based on the fraction of the contract that Brown received in the settlement, it appears that the Knicks had a strong case when it went to Stern for arbitration hearings on Sept. 29 and Oct. 3.

In contrast to Brown's results elsewhere, the Knicks underachieved with him as coach. Despite an N.B.A.-high $120 million payroll, they finished with a franchise-record 59 losses. Brown, a Brooklyn native who grew up on Long Island, departed with the worst record of any coach in Knicks history. He has since moved back to Philadelphia, where he coached for six seasons.

This is the second straight job that Brown has left under adverse circumstances. In July 2005, he agreed to a $7 million buyout with the Detroit Pistons. He had three years and $21 million left on that contract when the relationship soured. Over his last two seasons of coaching, Brown has earned a staggering $42.5 million in salary and contract buyouts. Brown has kept a low profile since his dismissal. His agent, Joe Glass, declined comment Wednesday afternoon, saying, "I think Commissioner Stern's message speaks for itself."

It has fallen to Brown's extensive circle of friends to provide insight into his plans. They have generally been reluctant to say much.

"He's doing good," said Doug Moe, a Denver Nuggets assistant coach and a former college and pro teammate of Brown's. "To get out of a situation that's really bad for you for some pocket change is pretty good."

Concerning Brown's tumultuous season with the Knicks, a position Brown once called his "dream job," Moe said: "He's probably thrilled that it's over. And you go on with your life and New York goes on with their life. It didn't work out."

A consummate gym rat, Brown has kept busy despite being unemployed for the first time since 1972. He has spent time with the University of Memphis team, coached by his friend John Calipari. In the N.B.A., he has standing invitations from Mike Woodson of Atlanta, Gregg Popovich of San Antonio and George Karl of Denver to visit their teams.

"How can you bring him here? His schedule is already filled," Moe said, laughing. "I said, 'Larry, when am I going to see you?' He said, 'I'm free in July of '09.' "

Asked if the 66-year-old Brown missed basketball, Moe said, "How can you miss it if you're around it every day?"

(http://www.nytimes.com/2006/11/08/sports/
basketball/09brown.html)

As the article states, Larry and my dad had successfully (at least from a business standpoint) "earned" $42,500,000 for just the past 2 seasons. This obviously had never been done in the history of sports coaching. But that wasn't all.

What has never been discussed but was a main point for Dad and I on the way out the door of the arbitration was the "Offset" provision in the Knick contract. As with many coaches' and players' contracts there is a clause, which enables the team to "offset" any salary owed under the existing contract to be reduced by a percentage of any new contract the player or coach may sign in the future. The range of "offset" can be from 50% to 100%.

Let's give an example (no charge)! Let's say a coach/player has a 100% "offset" in his contract and gets fired or is released. Let's also say he is owed $1,000,000. If he were to sign a contract with another team for $1,000,000, his former team would owe him nothing. If he were to receive $500,000 from the new team, his former team would only pay the remaining salary above the $500,000. Long story short it's good for the team to have an "offset."

Larry's contract had a 100% "offset." Sometimes, you have to give a little to get $50,000,000. I wasn't at the arbitration, but Dad kept calling me for either advice or just to commiserate. I had thought that being able to arbitrate under the circumstances Larry had placed him in and get $28,500,000 for 10 months and 23 wins was a pretty good job. But he wanted something else. So on the way out he got the Knicks to "waive" or eliminate the "offset." In full! I guess the Knicks feeling was nobody was going to hire Larry after this debacle.

Two years later, Dad did Larry's contract in Charlotte with Michael Jordan. The deal was for $5,000,000 per year for 4 years, another $20,000,000. The elimination of the "offset" saved Larry an additional $5,000,000 for the first 2 years of his contract with Charlotte. If that "offset" wasn't removed the Knicks could have recovered $10,000,000 through the "offset" provision.

Overall then, the Knicks arbitration yielded not only the $28,500,000 for 10 months of work but additionally freed Larry up to sign with another team, which led to him being able to secure $10,000,000 more. I plead guilty to being partial, but I don't think it's a stretch to say that Joe Glass did a terrific job again!!

As hard as this may seem to understand, I actually think the Knicks did well in that arbitration as well. Forgetting for a second the obvious disaster that occurred that season, the Knicks still potentially had a contract with Larry that had $40,000,000 left on it. Even though it was true that Larry received an exorbitant amount of money for little results, the Knicks in essence paid $18,500,000 on the $40,000,000 they "owed." The issue in any arbitration is that neither side truly knows what the arbitrator will rule. David Stern also did a very good job of having both sides thinking they might lose totally. That's how you settle cases.

CHAPTER FOUR

THERE REALLY ARE MORE HORSES ASSES THAN HORSES!

As I have previously spoken about here, Larry did on occasion recommend that certain players or coaches talk to my dad about representing them. The usual common denominator with these prospective clients was that they were having some sort of an issue and therefore needed his guidance and/or negotiating skills. It could be personal matter or that they felt they were not being treated fairly by management. It was that way for example with Charlie Scott and Anthony Roberts two of Larry's early players in Denver.

An interesting sidebar to all of these negotiations that my dad did for Larry was that in most of these stops Larry had my dad negotiate the contracts for his assistants as well. Guys like Maurice Cheeks, Garfield Heard, Phil Ford, Dave Hanners, John Kuester, Bill Blair, Ed Manning, Alvin Gentry, and probably a dozen more all benefitted from my father's efforts on their behalf and at Larry's request. Many of them to this day aren't even aware of this and as such my dad was never compensated. He viewed these efforts as helping Larry to be successful, so that was alright with him.

Another one of these assistants was Mike Woodson. I really don't even know when my dad started to represent Woodson. Woodson had served on Larry's staff in Philadelphia from 2001-03 and later in Detroit for the 2003-04 season, which culminated in an NBA title. I do know that they were together throughout Woodson's tenure as the head coach of the Atlanta Hawks from 2004-2011.

I would discuss Woodson's prospects with Dad during that time but I was never involved in any of the negotiations. Again I was basically there to bounce ideas around. However, after being swept out of the play-offs at the end of the 2011 season, the Hawks declined to enter into any talks about Woodson remaining as their head coach.

In September of 2011, my dad was having shortness of breath issues. By the time he actually went to the hospital, they said he had a 95 % blockage in 3 of the 4 blood vessels leading to his heart. I'm not a doctor but that doesn't sound so good. I drove out to Long Island to his hospital room. It was just my dad, my Mom and me! He was scheduled for quadruple bypass surgery the next morning.

When I went to get him some water there was a gurney outside his room with his name on the side. I asked the two orderlies standing beside the gurney what was going on. They informed me that the surgery had been moved up due to the seriousness of his condition. I forgot about the water and went back to tell my parents about the new plans:

MOM: No way!!!

DAD: Good, let's go!!!

He made it through the surgery but when we met with his doctor he informed us that the next 24 to 48 hours were critical because that was when strokes are most likely to occur. He told us to watch carefully for any signs of slowness of speech or generally not being as sharp as he normally was. The only thing my Mom heard from that entire conversation was the word "stroke" and she proceeded to drive me to point where I literally threatened to take her to the roof of the hospital and throw her off.

Thankfully, it never came to that. By this time the rest of the family had already arrived. My brother and sister, my five kids, Larry, and some members of his crew were there as well. As serious as the surgery was, there was another issue my dad was apparently more concerned about. It was fantasy football season. We had our annual family draft the weekend before this all happened. My dad had a team with my youngest son, Luke as his general manager. The buy-in for each team was $300. My dad had mistakenly sent me a check for $200. No big deal. I knew where he lived.

As they were placing him on the gurney for the trip to the operating room he suddenly demanded that my Mom give him his envelope full of cash. I won't go into the exact amount of cash that he took to the hospital because you probably wouldn't believe me:

> **MOM**: What do need cash for Joe, they're taking you for quadruple bypass surgery?!

> **DAD**: It's my money give me $100.

> **MOM**: What are you tipping the nurses?!

> **DAD**: Here Keith, we're even for the fantasy league.

What a relief! More than anything that hundred was my concern. With that money now safely in my pocket and Dad in recovery, we all gathered around his bed. He was in and out for a bit but we were all watching closely to see if there were any signs of mental issues.

Tubes everywhere made it a scary scene. I got an idea on how we could check him out:

KEITH: Dad its Keith.

DAD: Give me a kiss.

KEITH: This may not be the best time but you owe me $100 for the fantasy football league.

DAD: Go F____ yourself Keith, I paid you yesterday!!

He was fine! He would get tired but that was expected during a recovery. It was during this recovery period that he asked Tyler and me to help out with Woodson's career until he was back to himself. He was still in complete control of this situation but Tyler mainly would do some of the leg work for him if necessary.

We had two options with Woodson, the Lakers were offering the head assistants position while the other interest came from the Knicks who offered the same job just less money. I spoke with Woodson several times and felt that the Knick situation was the better opportunity. My reasoning was that there was always some type of turmoil with the Knicks. I viewed this as a positive since it could lead to Woodson moving up or over 18 inches to become the Head Coach. Mike D'Antoni was the current coach of the Knicks and he was a terrific guy and a very good coach. I also knew Mike to be a guy who would not be very comfortable in a situation where there was a lot of strife especially in a very public setting. Mike was and is a very competitive guy. He was as a player and this remained the case as a Coach. To me, this all added up to a potentially volatile situation. Volatile could equal opportunity for Mike Woodson.

LINSANITY

That 2011-12 season saw the phenomenon of Jeremy Lin hit New York. "Linsanity" took over Manhattan!! It was especially interesting to us in that my sons, Tyler and Luke, and I had met with Jeremy and his family the year before, trying to sign him out of Harvard. I always liked him as a player but no one expected him to explode the way he did for the Knicks that season.

His capture of New York and therefore the New York media didn't thrill everyone, especially some in his own locker room. In particular, the rumors were rampant that Carmelo Anthony was not too pleased with the ceding of his role as the "Star" of the Knicks. Shocking since NBA "Stars" usually have limited egos and require very little attention!

Whatever the truth was, the Knicks were winning games and for a change were exciting to watch. Incredibly the ball actually moved. Like back in their Championship years, the Knicks sometimes had more than one player physically touch the ball on a given possession. This was unheard of and it needed to stop. It was so bad that the locker room allegedly split apart. On March 14, 2012, Mike D'Antoni decided that he had enough and resigned. He has really suffered ever since, having made a stop with the Lakers and is now the reigning Coach of the Year with the Houston Rockets. His resignation led the Knicks to offer the interim Head Coaching position of my boyhood team to Mike Woodson. Here we go again!

That same day in March, I was asked by Woodson to go to White Plains, New York, which is where the Knicks practice facility is located. I went with Tyler. The president of the Knicks at this time was Glen Grunwald. Glen was a former teammate of Woodson's at the University of Indiana. While Woodson became a high 1st round draft choice, coincidentally with the Knicks, Glen took the management path to the league.

Glen is a terrific guy, who I always enjoyed talking with and even negotiating against. He was one of these guys that you could have a back and forth with but it never got personal or nasty. It was Glen with whom we had negotiated Woodson's assistant contract with New York just a few months earlier. Now, we were to discuss an interim head coaching contract.

First stop on our White Plains tour was to visit with Woodson to gauge his feelings and most importantly his expectations. That doesn't mean wins and losses but rather any increase in salary. This is normal. Obviously when you are assuming a much more prominent role in the organization a bump in salary is fair and appropriate.

Like most coaches and players, Woodson had started asking friends and colleagues about what they thought his increase should be. That's fine with me except there have been many times where one of my clients have asked "friends" what they were making only to have those "friends" greatly distort those numbers. This may seem harmless or even comical on some level but if your client buys into fake numbers you can have a real problem. I've had players turn down significant offers based on the faulty research they did with their "friends".

In Mike Woodson's case, he asked Tyler and me if we thought we could get him an additional $300,000 for the remainder of that season. He had heard that was the number Randy Wittman (another Indiana grad) had received from the Washington Wizards that same year. The only significant difference was that Wittman was promoted much earlier in that season. We said we would try.

We got him $600,000.

With Mike Woodson at the helm and Jeremy Lin at point guard the Knicks continued to win. Over their final 24 games they went 18 and 6. That would be good even in San Antonio, where they are used to winning. But with the Knicks?! Wow!! They even made the play-offs. Woodson had done a very good job and was in prime negotiating position.

On May 3, 2012, I was at the Garden with Tyler for the Knicks playoff game against the Miami Heat. In case you haven't had the pleasure, there is no place in sports that is as electric, as the Garden when the Knicks are at least playing in a meaningful game. No matter what has happened over the recent history of failure and waste, the fans of the Knicks have stayed incredibly loyal, vocal, and almost irrationally supportive.

We sat in the first row at half court with Glen Grunwald. We had been having preliminary discussions about a new contract for Woodson. In fact, after the Knick/Clipper regular season game on April 25th Glen had escorted us down to Woodson's office in the Garden to discuss a contract. When the playoff game ended on May 3rd there was no question that the Knicks were going to sign him. The only issue left was for how much and for how long.

Glen and I left the Garden with a general understanding that we were going to insist on getting Woodson in the neighborhood of $18,000,000 over a 4-year period. I informed Glen however that my dad was still running the show as far as Woodson was concerned, so I was going to run things by him the next day. I didn't get the chance.

14 hours after I left the Garden I got a call from Woodson. He was stumbling around but he finally got to the point:

WOODSON: I'm in a tough spot!

KG: Talk to me.

WOODSON: They want to continue talking about the contract but they will not deal with the Glass family. The situation with Larry won't allow it.

In 29 years of dealing with the NBA and all forms of European and Asian Clubs as well, this was a first. Teams and agents always have their battles but they usually end in some form of actual mutual respect. Both sides fight the fight, dust themselves off, and move on.

I think back to 1992. I filed an arbitration proceeding against the Houston Rockets. It was over my client Chuck Nevitt and was told by everybody that we couldn't win because it involved an obscure point regarding Chuck's weight (Chapter Six in *Taking Shots*). I was also told not to "piss off" the Rockets. They might not deal with me ever again. I didn't represent the Rockets, I represented Chuck.

We won the arbitration. Six days later, the Houston Rockets drafted my client, Robert Horry in the lottery, 11th overall! Not exactly the Hatfield's and McCoy's. It's called business. Mike Woodson needed to peddle that story elsewhere.

I was upset with the phone call, but worse I had to go tell Dad about it. Obviously complicating matters from an emotional view was the fact that my mom had passed away about 7 months earlier but they had only been married for a brief period...67 years so it wasn't like he missed her or anything.

We had moved my parents about 15 minutes from our place in New Jersey, so that someone from the family could be there almost daily. Luckily when I got there, my oldest, Sami, was already there playing a poor game of gin rummy with him. Dad has just recently finished negotiating Larry's latest move, this time to SMU! He was extremely happy and proud with the job he had done for Larry and as soon I arrived:

> **DAD**: You need to finish up Larry's deal for me and then all we have to worry about it is Mike!!

I filled him in. He wasn't happy! He didn't say anything but after 20 seconds he calmly picked up his phone and dialed. It was Woodson on the other end:

DAD: Keith filled me in. The job is already yours. Your choice is do you coach with or without BALLS?!

They never spoke again. Woodson paid his fee and moved on. Let's get a couple of things straight because it's starting to sound a bit whiny and also can be construed as painting my dad or myself for that matter, as victims. My dad was never a victim of anything. Was this and some future incidents disturbing, troubling and upsetting to him? Of course, they were but we always seemed to survive them even if they were hurtful at the time. The line between business and personal can get blurry at times. In this case it definitely did. My dad thought that he and Woodson had a personal relationship as well. Obviously, that was not the case so it did sting.

Another thing should be cleared up in regards to Woodson. While I understand that to a normal ethical person the eight years my dad spent helping put Woodson into this position to cash in with the Knicks, should have elicited something resembling loyalty, but loyalty wasn't legally required. Legislating loyalty is not easy or even possible.

Dad and Woodson had never even signed a contract. My dad relied on Woodson's word and their relationship to cover him. To be frank, he never even considered that Woodson would screw him in the end. But again legally Woodson owed us nothing except to pay my father, which he did. Like it or not, that is the business we are in. Trust me, there have been other occasions where the shoe has been on the other foot. We have had players switch to our side and I'm sure the agents they left don't have a great feel for them or us. The only difference in the Woodson example was the alleged interference by the Garden and the fact that my father had in essence already done the bulk of the work for him.

As awful as the actions of Woodson were, what I found the most troubling was the reaction to all this from Larry. Let's examine this for a second. If you are to believe the initial Woodson version of why he was changing agents, someone in the Knick organization initiated the agent change. If you want to go to the next step, the reason for the Garden's "demand" to change agents stemmed from the fact that my dad had done too good of a job on behalf of Larry.

You therefore would have clearly expected Larry to have some guilt about this turn of events. You would expect him to side with the "family" but that's not what happened! I spoke to him privately as I didn't want my dad more upset than he already was. I had some choice words and language for Woodson on that phone call to Larry. I don't remember all of them but I do recall "punk, coward, disloyal…." being tossed around.

Larry's reaction stunned me. He completely defended Woodson:

> **LARRY**: Keith, "Woody" had no choice.

> **KEITH**: Really? I was negotiating last night with Glen Grunwald at the Garden! There is no issue with the family. If Mike wants to switch agents tell him to be a man and try telling Dad the truth. The truth is bad enough.

> **LARRY**: "Woody" said he would make this up to you guys!

> **KEITH**: Bull Shit Larry!

That was the end of that call. I was kind of listening for something like:

> *"Gee Keith I can't believe that I caused all of this.*
> *I'm so sorry for putting Dad through this crap." But*
> *no, his main concern was "Woody!"*

Just so we are all on the same page, these are the facts:

1. Dad represents Woodson through good times and bad for some eight years.
2. Woodson, with my father doing his negotiations and offering advice along the way, ends up getting a contract offer from the New York Knicks.
3. On May 4th, he calls me to tell me his "story."
4. Nineteen days later he signs his contract with the Knicks after making a switch to a "Big Time" agency doing the "representing."

While we're on the subject, let's take a specific look at the contract that Woodson ultimately signed and the circumstances surrounding that signing. The agency that Woodson switched to had actually been hired in the past by the Garden to do certain commercial events there. Conflict anybody?!

Moving past that little nugget, remember we also had initiated preliminary talks with Glen Grunwald regarding the Woodson contract. These discussions centered on a four year deal for approximately $18,000,000 all guaranteed. Would we have gotten that? History shows that we would have gotten real close and that was my feeling after these conversations with Glen. Dad would have to ultimately negotiate the contract but these were the indications at least.

By switching to the "Big-Time", Woodson signed a widely reported 3-year deal worth $10,000,000 total. However only the first two years of that contract were guaranteed. The third year was the Knicks option. Sounds like Woodson's move to the "Big-Time" cost him some money. One can only hope.

The media in New York ate this little story up! Accounts were in the papers every day. Many of the reporters raked Woodson over the coals not only for his obvious disloyalty towards my dad but also his apparent lack of courage in standing up to management especially factoring in his perceived position of strength.

Woodson's seeming hypocrisy centered on his constant public preaching about "accountability" and "teamwork" etc. You know doing things "The Right Way." Lawyer friends of mine were pushing us to consider a lawsuit perhaps even against the Garden for interference type of stuff. My father left those decisions totally in my hands. We met with some people about it but at the end of the day the reason I didn't pursue any claims may surprise people.

We didn't sue because I don't think "interference" ever happened. I think Woodson did this on his own. Do I think that some at the Garden felt it would be an easier negotiation financially if they could deal with Woodson's new agency instead of my father? Possibly. But you're not going to prove that in a court of law. I've tried to make it a practice that I never file a lawsuit unless I KNOW I'm going to win. Whether or not the new agency was actively recruiting Woodson behind my families back is also unknown. More importantly it would be a very difficult thing to prove.

No, the only thing we know for sure is that Woodson lied. We just don't know when. Remember the phone call on May 3rd when Woodson tells me that someone in management talked with him about us? Then compare that "story" with multiple media accounts from him on the day of his press conference announcing his signing with the Knicks. This was in response to him getting a bit testy regarding answering repeated questions about what went down "agent-wise". This is part of an article from ESPN:

> "Woodson wanted to set the record straight regarding his agent. 'I have no contract with the Glass'. I paid for my services and I elected to move on. Mr. Dolan had nothing to do with me making this deci-

sion. This was Mike Woodson's decision. I had every
right to make that decision..."

Nobody said he didn't. In fact, nobody but you mentioned James Dolan or anyone else in Knick management. Woodson obviously lied to someone due to his conflicting "tales" but I wasn't going to waste any more time on his nonsense. Let him and his diminished contract move along and we did the same. Woodson was fired by the Knicks after the 2014 season. I was very upset for him.

See.... I can lie too!!

My Mom passed in November 2011 and my dad followed her almost exactly a year later. That was his plan as he explained to Brent and me over some more gin games. Since Mom's passing, while he was as sharp as ever, he had seemed distracted. He would look up to the sky and take a deep breath every so often. I think 67 years of loving and fighting with someone on a daily basis makes you do that. They fought over nothing at least four times daily but I still have never met two people more in love.

> **BRENT:** What's the matter?
>
> **DAD:** What am I still doing here? Mom's gone and I'm a burden to Keith and his kids. They come here almost every day!!
>
> **KG:** You're not a burden Dad. We love coming here and I'm finally starting to beat you at gin!
>
> **BRENT:** So what are you going to do?

DAD: Well, next week is the anniversary of Mom's death. I'd like to go then.

KG: Well good luck with that!

Ten minutes passed:

DAD: I would like to stick around for the election. I want to make sure Obama gets re-elected!!

A bunch of us were at his apartment election night. We left around 10 pm. It was the week after Superstorm Sandy had devastated most of the Jersey Shore where we live. My house in Rumson was without power for 13 days but Tyler and my daughter-in-law Blair had theirs restored after day five. I went to their place to watch the election returns.

As soon as I sat down, my sister called and said we better get back to his apartment. Even though it was only a 15 minute drive by the time we got back he was gone. His nurse Joan swore to me that ABC News projected Obama as the winner and my Dad passed. I don't doubt that for a second. He always liked to do things on his own schedule and in his own way.

When my Mom was failing, Tyler and I were in Europe on business. There is no doubt that with my Dad and Mom's failing health I had to back off things business-wise. I started to cancel out- of-town recruiting trips and there really weren't too many NBA players hanging around in Rumson, New Jersey.

My Mom liked to do things her way as well. She never wanted to get old. It just wasn't her thing. She had been predicting her death since she was in her 30's. Now she was 84 and it was starting to take on a more realistic and ominous tone. Her constant reference to her imminent demise was so prevalent that my dad had bought her a cemetery plot for her 40th birthday! The following year he didn't get her anything for her 41st and when she asked where his gift was:

DAD: You didn't use the gift I got you last year!

The guy waited two years just to say that line!!

My mom and I argued every day about her taking better care of herself. When I finally took that trip to Europe, no one will ever convince me that she didn't figure this is my chance to go with Keith off my ass!

We landed in Paris and as I got off the plane my daughter Sami was on the phone:

"When are you coming home Dad?! Grandma is not good."

My sister Jodi was there and told me that everything could wait until I got home. The last time I spoke with my Mom I was in Rome. I called her from our favorite place, the Piazza Navona where we had spent great times together:

KEITH: Mom, what's going on?

MOM: Honey, if you knew how I felt you wouldn't fight me anymore.

KEITH: I'm changing my flight then to tonight.

MOM: When are you scheduled to leave?

KEITH: Tomorrow morning.

MOM: (Laughing) Don't worry I'm not going to be that lucky. I'll still be around when you get home.

She wasn't. She passed as we landed at Newark airport.

My sister and my other four children, Sami, Alex, Maggie, and Lucas were at the apartment. (Tyler was with me in Europe). Larry was there as well. No matter what has occurred since that day, I won't forget how Larry dealt with Luke. Luke is the youngest and wasn't handling this too well. They told me later that Luke was near collapse when Larry took over and got Luke calmed down. How much was Larry a part of our family? Sum it up like this: In both Death Notices of my parents, Larry is simply listed as their son. Enough said.

I have absolutely no idea why I just wrote all of that but to tell you the truth, it was cathartic! That just saved me $2,500 in therapy! I may leave it in here. If I did you'll be the first to know!

Maybe I'm also avoiding writing the final chapter concerning my dad and Larry and trust me this will be the hardest one to write.

CHAPTER FIVE

FADE TO "BROWN"

As previously discussed, in April of 2006, Larry and the Knicks parted ways. We've dealt with all that. For the next two seasons, Larry was out of coaching. It was obvious to anyone who knew him that he was miserable. He basically haunted every gym he could just to be around the game.

He visited his "tree" of coaches, guys that he knows or has hired along the way. It's an impressive list too. John Calipari at Kentucky, Bill Self at Kansas, Mark Turgeon at Maryland, and the place he frequents the most, Villanova and their coach Jay Wright. This was because Larry and his family still maintained a house in Bryn Mawr, Pa., which lucky for Jay was 10 minutes from Villanova's campus. ("Lucky" may be a bit sarcastic)

Finally or mercifully in 2008, Michael Jordan and the Charlotte Bobcats (Hornets) came calling. As usual my dad did the deal with Michael and off Larry went again. This was his 9th coaching job in the NBA.

Predictably Larry made a difference on the court for the better. Charlotte even made the playoffs but as the 2010 season began, some familiar tendencies began to crop up. The Bobcats/Hornets began the season 9 and 19. Larry was complaining about the roster. He didn't like some of the moves Michael had made. If any of this sounds familiar, that's because it was the same script.

One of Larry's closet friends who he had worked with in various incarnations was Donnie Walsh. When Larry was coaching the Indiana Pacers, Donnie was the President of the Club. Donnie and Larry played together in the same backcourt for the University of North Carolina over a half century earlier. Donnie knows Larry well. In response to a question regarding Larry's penchant for getting rid of players:

> **DONNIE**: If you listen to Larry you would trade your entire roster and re-acquire them the same season.

Not surprisingly, Larry was again either fired or resigned from Charlotte depending on whom you were listening to. My dad always preferred firing to resigning because you got paid if you were fired.

COACH LARRY BROWN, BOBCATS PART WAYS

ESPN.com news services
Dec. 22, 2010

CHARLOTTE, N.C.—After a miserable start to the season in which he took shots at his players and himself, Larry Brown is out as coach of the Charlotte Bobcats in another messy exit in his well-traveled career.

The team announced later Wednesday that former Charlotte Hornets coach Paul Silas, who lives in the Charlotte area, will take over on an interim basis.

"This has been a dream for me for a while," Silas told ESPN.com's Brian Windhorst. "... I've been through a lot over the last couple of years. But I'm healthy now, my weight is down and I'm ready to go."

Owner Michael Jordan announced Brown's departure in a news release a day after the Bobcats were outscored 31-12 in the fourth quarter in their fourth straight loss.

The 70-year-old Brown had been upset with the makeup and effort of his team for weeks. The Bobcats (9-19) had lost three games by 31 or more points in 10 days before Tuesday's fourth-quarter meltdown against Oklahoma City.

"I met with Coach Brown two weeks ago about the team's performance and what we could do to improve it," Jordan said. "We met again this morning after practice. The team has clearly not lived up to either of our expectations and we both agreed that a change was necessary."

News of Brown's departure hit close to home with many other coaches around the NBA, including Philadelphia's Doug Collins and Boston's Doc Rivers.

"Larry's one of the all-time great coaches. The guy has won an NBA championship, an NCAA championship, he was a great point guard at [North] Carolina, he won an Olympic championship and was an Olympic coach. I mean, he's done it all," Collins said to ESPN Boston's Chris Forsberg. "He opened a lot of doors for coaches like myself, because any time former players stepped in and did well, it gave other former players the chance to do the same thing. It sounds, from what I'm hearing, that Michael [Jordan will] keep him on in advisory capacity. It will be interesting to see what happens."

"It's disturbing," said Rivers, a close confidante of Brown. "I have a great relationship with Larry. It's just tough. He's a great coach, you know — it's tough. It's our business, as we've learned way too much."

The 70-year-old Brown, a Hall of Fame coach who was in the third season of his 13th professional and college head coaching job, had been upset with the makeup and effort of his team for weeks.

Brown, whose contract runs through the end of the 2011-12 season, didn't immediately return a message on his cell phone seeking comment. But his agent, Joe Glass, said Brown will be back on the bench soon.

"Larry is going to coach again," Glass said. "He's got plenty of strength and energy."

Glass declined to discuss details of any buyout or if Brown will be paid through the end of his original four-year contract.

Brown leaves with an 88-108 mark with the Bobcats. His 1,327 victories in the ABA and NBA are nine shy of supplanting Don Nelson for the most all-time.

"This was a difficult decision for both of us, but one that needed to be made," Jordan said. "I want to thank Larry for everything he has done for our team. He has played a key role in this organization's development including coaching us to our first-ever playoff appearance last season.

"Larry will continue to be a valuable advisor to me regarding the team."

Higgins said they didn't contact the 67-year-old Silas until late Wednesday afternoon and "both sides were OK" with Silas getting an interim label.

"It allows us an opportunity to see how Paul does and see how he can get our team to a certain level," Higgins said. "Paul has been out of it for a while."

Silas, who was a popular figure when he coached the Hornets through their departure to New Orleans in 2002, was busy working to put together a staff before Thursday's practice.

Silas' staff will include Jordan's former teammate and longtime friend Charles Oakley as the lead assistant, a league source confirmed to ESPN The Magazine senior writer Ric Bucher Wednesday night.

The Bobcats are off until Monday when they host Detroit.

Silas will take over a team that's in disarray, but yet sat only 2½ games out of the final playoff spot in the Eastern Conference before Wednesday's games.

"Could I be naive? Maybe, but I firmly believe that this team has an opportunity to get back on track," Higgins said.

It won't be with Brown, who has followed a familiar script in a career that includes quick turnarounds and then usually ugly divorces.

The only coach to win NBA and NCAA titles had been out of coaching for two years following his dismissal after going 23-59 in his only season in New York in 2005-06 when Jordan hired him to replace Sam Vincent in 2008.

Brown immediately demanded changes and Jordan and general manager Rod Higgins responded with a number of trades that completely rebuilt the team. Behind Gerald Wallace and Stephen Jackson, the Bobcats went 44-38 last season and secured the franchise's first playoff berth.

But after getting swept by Orlando in the first round, Brown started having reservations about returning. He lamented about being away from his wife and young children in suburban Philadelphia. He stressed that he would only coach for Jordan, and eventually agreed to come back.

But the offseason included point guard Raymond Felton's departure to New York in free agency and the trade of center Tyson Chandler to Dallas in what amounted to a salary dump to get under the luxury tax threshold.

A day before training camp opened, Brown said, 'I died' when Felton left, then questioned his team's front line. That stood in contrast to Jordan, who was bullish on the team just before the start of the season.

"I think we're going to be a better off team than we were last year," Jordan said. "We're together, we're coming off some success from last year. Granted, Raymond's not here. But when you think about, Tyson came off the bench.

"At the minimum, we should make the playoffs."

Instead, the Bobcats have struggled all season under a barrage of turnovers and a stagnant offense, with Brown getting increasingly critical of his team and himself in recent weeks.

"I never thought I'd have to be in a position where I'd have to beg guys to play hard," Brown said before Tuesday's game. "Then if you look down the bench I don't know if guys on the bench are playing any harder. Again, it's my responsibility. We look so disorganized.

"I just feel bad if anybody who really enjoys the game would watch our team play. They'd look at me and say, 'That coach is not doing his job.' That's the thing I feel most bad about."

Brown was similarly despondent after Charlotte missed its first 11 shots of the fourth quarter to go with five turnovers against the Thunder, turning a one-point lead into another one-sided loss.

Brown was at the practice on Wednesday morning, working with mostly the second unit before he met with Jordan.

It leaves Jordan in a tough position after he bought the team outright from Bob Johnson earlier this year. Jordan has been in charge of the basketball operations of the club since 2006.

Jordan has made several questionable moves that included taking <u>Adam Morrison</u> with No. 3 overall pick in the draft and hiring the inexperienced Vincent, who was fired after one season.

Information from The Associated Press was used in this report.

(http://www.espn.com/nba/news/story?id=5947959)

Naturally, there was a dispute over money. Did Larry quit or was he fired? There's that recurring theme again! My dad and now me to a minor degree dealt with the Charlotte saga as he had with all the others. Somehow, he never got tired of it. I think it actually energized him in some ways. He always loved a good fight! And throughout it all, Larry was never in the wrong according to my dad.

Some might think that I would be envious of that loyalty and devotion he showed to Larry but I didn't have to be. He showed that to all of us. It was simply who he was. Both Mom and Dad always thought we were right. If and when they found out we weren't they dealt with us privately and pointedly.

SMU- THE FINALE

After quite a bit of negotiating and several lawyers getting involved on both sides, things were settling down with Charlotte. While some issues lingered it wasn't nearly the fiasco that had occurred in New York. With Charlotte in the rear view mirror, Larry headed back to the gyms of his friends. His "tree" was still in full bloom and they were having great success.

Another North Carolina alum, Matt Doherty was the coach at SMU. At the end of his 6th year there Matt was fired with one year left on his contract. Larry clearly wanted the job. At this point in his career Larry wanted ANY job! SMU at that time was not what you would call a basketball powerhouse. It was however, the type of place Larry could build into one. There was one significant problem; they had no interest in Larry. Maybe it was the constant moving around or maybe it was the fact that both of the colleges he coached at, UCLA and Kansas, ended up on probation after he left them. Not great on your resume.

Larry had called the Athletic Director, a gentleman by the name of Steve Orsini, whom my dad and I would get to know fairly well. He didn't even return Larry's calls. This did not discourage Larry's "tree" from basically bombarding poor Mr. Orsini. They kept calling on his behalf. Maybe some of them wanted to get Larry out of their gym.

The real reason is closer to the fact that whatever else he's done or how he's done it, Larry Brown is a tremendous basketball coach; one of the best. This cannot be denied. Despite all of this firepower however, it was really the interference of the SMU football coach, June Jones, which provided the impetus to get things moving in Larry's direction. Apparently and for whatever reason, Coach Jones spoke to the Athletic Director and convinced him to at least give Larry a shot.

They granted Larry an interview. When he went into that room, the word was he was their 5th choice. When he left the room, he was the new Head Coach at SMU, pending the successful completion of contract negotiations.

As I mentioned, SMU was no basketball elite. As such, they didn't exactly pay like one. Coupling that fact with Larry being their 5th choice, you get the atmosphere surrounding the negotiation that my father was entering into this time. He had his work cut out for him. Just the way he liked it.

Matt Doherty was set to make $500,000 in his 7th season at SMU. Normally, a franchise or in this case a University will start their negotiations for a new coach based on what they were paying their former one. My personal thoughts were that due to Larry's reputation as a coach, maybe my dad could get him up to say $800,000 or $900,000 to start and then build in some incentives.

When he was finished with SMU and Steve Orsini, he had the basics of a 5-year contract with an annual salary of $2,100,000. Honestly, I couldn't believe it and neither could Mr. Orsini. I was sent in at the very end of these negotiations to simply dot some I's and cross some T's. My dad was really still recovering and while I had never been directly involved with Larry's stuff, I did wrap this one up.

The first thing that Steve Orsini said to me was:

STEVE: Keith, how old is your father?!

KG: 86

STEVE: You've got to be kidding me!! I have never been put through anything like that in my life!!

Dad could be a bit, let's say, tenacious in his dealings. But Steve's reaction was not one of animosity but rather respect and some amazement.

The $2,100,000 per year was not the total either. As I reviewed the proposed agreement, I noticed a bonus package as well with some of it being standard stuff like making the NCAA tournament, winning their league, etc. etc. But then I noticed that Dad had put in what was referred to as a "retention" bonus. Specifically, it looked like in spite of the bloated salary SMU had concerns about Larry's reputation for leaving places. Instead of treating that as a negative, Dad turned it into more money for Larry.

This little beauty "allowed" SMU to pay Larry for staying! If he stayed three years, he would receive an extra $1,500,000! Basically this was an additional $500,000 per year that was totally in Larry's control to receive. If he stayed the fourth year it was another $500,000 and so on. And he did indeed receive it! That brought his total to $2,600,000.00 per year.

My dad and I have done some things in this business but this deal under the circumstances was arguably his best! I say this because of the circumstances of that negotiation. To go into that room with a client who the other side didn't initially want, and come out with a deal worth more than five times what the previous coach was receiving was truly a remarkable accomplishment.

The contract was for five years and initially the total salary would be $10,500,000. When you add in the "retention" bonus, Larry was poised to make upwards of $13,000,000. However only the first three years were guaranteed! My dad sat Tyler and myself down for a talk about how he wanted to handle the fee due from Larry. His feeling was that Larry should not be charged for the non-guaranteed years, only for the first three that were guaranteed. He also said it should be a flat fee of $100,000 per year for 3 years. He didn't care about percentages of the total package. He thought this was fair.

If you do the math, the percentages totally worked in Larry's favor. In a normal situation, an agent would charge 3-4% of this deal and that would be on anything he directly negotiated. Eliminating all the extras that my dad put in there besides the salary and the "retention" bonus, the total was 2,600,000 per year. A fee of $100,000 per year equates to less than 4%. Also consider that the fee on the final two years which was also payable at $2,100,000 per year was to be zero. Summing things up, Larry received $13,000,000. The fee charged was $100,000 per year for 3 years or $300,000. That computes to a fee percentage of under 2.5%.

This arrangement was very specific and well thought out. We are talking about a man who for my brother's Bar Mitzvah had realized that he was probably going to be inebriated at the end of the night but would still have some things to wrap up. For example, the band would have to paid - the band was charging by the half hour. Their fee was based on what time they finished playing. Made sense. We went late that night and my dad's best friend approached:

UNCLE DICK: Joe the band is exhausted. They want to leave.

JHG: They were good, weren't they?!

UNCLE DICK: Yes they were Joe.

JHG: What time is it?!

UNCLE DICK: It's 1 o'clock Joe.

My dad proceeded to reach into his tuxedo pocket and pulled out 7 envelopes. Each envelope only had a time written on the outside. It started at 11, then 11:30 and so on. He had written out 7 checks and put them in each corresponding envelope. Since he realized he would probably be drunk so he wanted the checks already made out.

> **JHG:** Oh what the hell, they were good, give them the 2 o'clock envelope!!

My dad was an organized man. He didn't leave things dangling. He left nothing for anyone to figure out. He wrote it down or at least told you 10 to 20 times what the deal was. If there ever arose a situation where there was any lack of understanding regarding any transaction, I sided with my dad.

At crap tables in Vegas and Atlantic City the pit crews asked HIM to calculate the odds on payouts. We never saw him make a mistake. All this is common knowledge to anyone who knew him or negotiated with him. This only serves to make the way the relationship with Larry ended so puzzling and hurtful. What follows are facts and if there is anyone who would dispute them I have the proof.

The deal agreed upon with SMU was sent to my father on April 18, 2012. There was a sheet of deal points, which had been agreed to by my dad and Larry. On top of that my father had specific conversations with Larry regarding his fee arrangement.

As usual, my dad always tried to get Larry more. I don't even know if Larry always knew how hard he tried. Although I had no involvement in it I remember hearing that even though Larry had a very healthy salary when he was with the 76ers, my dad negotiated into his deal a significant amount of Comcast stock, which was fairly low at that time. Lord knows what that's worth today!

On the day after the terms were agreed to, Dad told Tyler and me that he was going to make an attempt to get SMU to even pay Larry's fee directly to my dad. This apparently was Steve Orsini's red-line:

STEVE: Joe, we are a University, we can't pay an agent!!

JHG: Ok then why don't we just add the fee to Larry's base? Then he can pay directly but it really doesn't cost him anything!

STEVE: Deal.

Mr. Orsini and SMU sent an amended "term sheet" reflecting that arrangement the following day: April 19, 2012. It would be obvious to anyone who bothered to look at it that the only revision to that "term sheet" is that Larry's salary is raised $100,000 to $2,200,000. This was the fee due to my dad. Even though Larry would physically pay it, it wouldn't cost him a penny. This is not really disputable. I quote that legal scholar Chris Rock when discussing Bill Clinton's lying about his affair with Monica Lewinsky:

"Do we need the Supreme Court for this one?! Judge Judy could knock this out in 15 minutes with commercials!!"

In point of fact, Larry did pay the first fee as he agreed to do for year one of the contract. When we didn't receive the fee for year two, I was unfortunately placed in the awkward position of calling Larry to remind him that he owed Dad for the 2nd year. I say unfortunately because not only was it awkward asking your "brother" for a payment due but more importantly this payment was due to Dad's Estate since he had passed 11 months earlier.

To be honest, it didn't initially shock me that Larry said he had no idea what I was talking about. Since my dad handled so much for Larry for so many years there were times where he didn't specifically remember business details. He didn't have to since there was a total faith and trust in my father. In these latter years, Larry's wife, Shelley, would take care of certain bills etc. as they had accepted more and more responsibility for their finances. I'm sure this was because my dad was indeed getting older and to be honest my mother was pushing him to relinquish some of these responsibilities surrounding Larry. To my Mom enough was enough. Dad was 80 at that time.

So to be accurate it was Shelley who sent the fee to Dad for year one. Obviously, Larry should have known since he was the one who made the arrangement but as I said that would not be the first time or apparently the last that Larry would be mistaken about a business matter. All great coaches are not Warren Buffett.

Larry said he would talk with Shelley regarding this but oddly his attitude was much more defensive than I thought appropriate. It was a bit testy between us. It was almost like he was waiting for this call. You know, you're "brothers" for 55 years so the discussion should have gone something like: "Gee Keith, I don't remember that but...." It wasn't like that at all. Strange! He did say that he would talk with Shelley about it. To me, there was nothing to discuss.

When we never heard from Shelley, I was ready to just drop it but Tyler wasn't. It was frankly too emotional and awkward for me to discuss this issue directly with anyone, especially Larry. I didn't deserve to be put in that position. The fact that Larry had denied the existence of ANY arrangement with Dad was more than troubling. Infuriating was a more apt description of my feelings.

Tyler finally spoke with Shelley and told me that she too had no recollection of this agreement. When Tyler asked why she had sent the initial check for $100,000 her story changed. Now she remembered. That payment was now suddenly the total owed. Interesting. Shelley's new version was, yes there was a commission due but the first check covered it all! So my dad according to them charged a fee of $100,000 based on earnings for Larry of approximately $13,000,000. That would come out to roughly 0.7%.

I leave to your judgment after reading these pages whether that sounds like something my father would have agreed to. To those of you not in this business that's what we call an insult! If my father had been confronted with this proposal by Larry and Shelley that he was worth less than 1%, he would have sent that 0.7% back before the postman had left his office!.

Let's cut the crap! They used the fact that my father had passed away to get out of paying his estate $200,000. Unfortunately, there is no other side to this. I agree that it's strange after all the business dealings they had together. To me it was even stranger due to their personal relationship.

If this strikes you as greedy it's actually even worse if that's possible. Remember those 2 two "terms sheets" which were changed solely to add in Larry's fee? Since that was specifically what was done, there was an extra $100,000 per year added to Larry's salary. He paid year one which cost him zero!! But when he refused to pay the rest he pocketed an extra $100,000 per year for the rest of his contract. By the way, I still have those "term sheets"!

In my opinion their actions established the price of what "the family" was worth to them. This was 4 years ago. I haven't spoken with either of them since. That is MY choice! To me, they have disrespected my father. After everything that he did for them for over 50 years. In the end this was his was version of "The Right Way"!

SUMMARY

I also would like to add some perspective, which will make this situation even more confusing. For the overwhelming amount of years that Larry was truly part of my family, he was always a very generous person. When I was growing up and especially all through my law school days, he would and literally did give me the shirt(s) off his back. He gave me his clothes when I really needed them. Boxes of them.

During my last year of law school, my then wife and I went food shopping. We suddenly realized that between the two of us we had $17 to our name. We needed to ask for help for the first time. I knew Larry would have given me whatever I asked. The only reason I didn't ask him was because I knew he wouldn't let me pay him back. I ended up borrowing the money from Brent. He not only let me pay him back, he charged me 7% interest. There are plenty more instances where Larry was more than generous as well.

So what happened here? To this day, it still puzzles me and believe it or not I worry about what happened to Larry. It didn't and still doesn't make sense. The real shame of this is that if my dad were still here, this conversation would have lasted about 10 seconds. Dad would have told Shelley to put the check in the mail and that would be that. I totally understand that. I was never Larry's representative and therefore didn't have the sway over him that my dad did. But I also reflect on Larry's defense of Mike Woodson over my father. The combination of these two incidents is really what prompted me to reveal all this in the first place.

Mike Woodson & Larry in the end felt that my father didn't really matter that much. He was treated as collateral damage. Well, to me nothing can be further from the truth. My dad was someone to reckon with and to his family he remains so. He was someone who worked his ass off for both of these people. He didn't deserve to be summarily dismissed. And he wasn't worth 0.7%!

I've been asked by those people close to me, some in own family, why I'm writing about this?! One reason is a practical one. I'm not a famous person. I have however worked in this business of the NBA for 34 years. As such, I am fairly well known. People throughout the industry I work in clearly know of my family's history with Larry. It's difficult to be in this business my sons and I are in and not discuss our relationship with Larry. People innocently ask how Larry is doing. It's a natural thing to ask. I have up until recently chosen to not explain or give any inkling that there was even a problem between us. But I now realize that like my dad, I was protecting Larry from his own actions. That's over now! I don't have anything to explain. HE does!

I certainly didn't write this for the money that they screwed my father's estate out of. The money that was owed is long gone and apparently they needed it a lot more than we did. This story also has little to do with me. I was an incidental character here. This is all about my dad and he is not here to tell his story. The idea that he could simply be dismissed or ignored doesn't sit too well with me. To be honest, it shouldn't sit too well with some of the people asking why I'm writing this either!

Do me a favor if someone treats me like this at the end of my life, and you truly cared about me, don't just slink into the night and take it! Find the highest spot you can, set up a sound system, and go to work!

As most of you reading this probably could predict, Larry's SMU career ended very similarly too many of his other coaching stops.

LARRY BROWN LEAVES SMU IN THE MOST LARRY BROWN WAY POSSIBLE

Larry Brown created NCAA issues and then resigned abruptly — just like he did at UCLA and Kansas
By: Gary Parrish July 8th 2016

NORTH AUGUSTA, S.C. — In the end, it was all so predictable — first the winning, then the NCAA scandal and, finally, the abrupt resignation that leaves a basketball program in an awkward spot.

Larry Brown followed the Larry Brown model step-by-step. Bravo, sir.

I'd say you outdid yourself but you really just did yourself.

A source told CBS Sports that Larry Brown texted the parents of SMU players early Friday to inform them that <u>he's resigning after four seasons as the school's men's basketball coach</u>. According to the source, Brown said he'd been in negotiations for a contract extension "for 20 months" but could not reach a deal and thus felt he had no choice but to resign. He apologized, the source said, and insisted this was never his plan. And Brown probably believes that. But this was always the way most figured his time at SMU would come to a close, if only because Brown has been leaving jobs abruptly after short stints literally since before I was born. And I'm 39 years old.

This is, after all, the way Brown's career began — considering his first head-coaching job was the Davidson job that he only kept for a few months and left before ever even coaching a game. And this will also be the way Brown's career likely ends — unless somebody is interested in hiring a 75 year-old who just quit on his team during the worst possible time (i.e., the July Evaluation Period) for a college coach to quit. But this was always the most likely time that he'd quit.

Larry Brown is leaving another program sooner than expected.

Brown famously hates recruiting. He's told me that both privately and publicly — most notably when I hosted a charity event with him two years ago. So what better time to get fed up with your contract negotiations and walk away than two days into the July Evaluation Period that requires coaches to be on the road recruiting? No sense in resigning in May or June because you can, if you want, get away with not doing much in May or June and still collect those big paychecks. But in July you have to be out on the recruiting trail for a total of 15 days. So I'm not surprised by the timing at all, because Brown never liked being on the recruiting trail for 15 days.

And demanding a five-year extension from SMU — which is what Brown was reportedly demanding — is pretty brazen for a 75-year-old coach who spent nine games suspended last season, and whose team was banned from the 2016 NCAA Tournament, because of NCAA violations that happened on his watch. SMU would've been foolish to give Brown that five-year extension, and for two reasons: 1) It would've likely led coach-in-waiting Tim Jankovich to seek other opportunities, and 2) Larry Brown IS 75 YEARS OLD! Do you realize the average life expectancy for an American male is 76?

That means Brown was demanding an extension to coach Division I basketball four years past the age at which the average American male dies. He was demanding a contract extension that would take him to the age of 80, and do you know how many men have successfully coached Division I basketball at 80?

Zero!

To be clear, Larry Brown might've and could've been the first. He's great. Nobody denies that.

But it would've been silly for SMU to give him that contract. And isn't it funny that Brown wanted a five-year extension that would've theoretically kept him at SMU for a total of nine straight seasons even though he's never coached anywhere in his life longer than six straight seasons?

So here we are, on a Friday in July, with Larry Brown having again left a job abruptly, with time still left on the contract he signed, less than five months after <u>publicly stating it would be silly for him to walk away now</u>, and with a third NCAA scandal on his resume. Again, it was all so predictable. Being the only man to coach an NCAA champion and <u>NBA</u> champion will be a big part of the Hall of Famers' legacy, to be sure. But this — and the other times he did something very similar to this — will likely be what most remember most. https://www.cbssports.com/college-basketball/news/larry-brown-leaves-smu-in-the-most-larry-brown-way-possible/

After my dad's passing and the subsequent shenanigans, I had zero interest in stepping in to represent Larry. Like Woodson, Larry went "Big" and through some incredible coincidence he had the same agency represent him as well. As of this writing he has never signed another contract with anybody! After the scandal at SMU and the subsequent probation, it looks to me like SMU tried to redo his deal. It didn't go well and when Larry tried to negotiate a 5-year extension with SMU, apparently they refused. Larry resigned as a result. In other words, business-wise Larry's career turned to crap.

I wonder what changed??!! Something was missing.

Or maybe someone!

To those Larry Loyalist's out there and I can hear some of you already who will be angry with me for writing all this, ask this question: Are you mad at me for telling the truth or because I had the balls to tell it?!

Just when I thought I was done with this saga, my youngest, Luke suggested that I wrap it up by telling the "Gramp Exit Story," and relate it to all those who will find an issue with what I've revealed here. At first, I said no I've said enough but thinking it through it was apropos.

For a period of time whenever possible my parents and I used to spend a weekend at Caesars in Atlantic City. We had a ball! My dad and I loved craps while my Mom favored blackjack or the slots. She really thought she had a system for the slots and we never discouraged that theory. On some occasions though, she would join us at the crap table. On one such evening, the 3 of us were playing when a thirty something guy approached the table to join in.

The guy had obviously been "comped" a few too many drinks and was acting inappropriately. Two minutes into his visit he started cursing:

> **DAD**: Hey, there's a lady present, please watch your language!

A few minutes went by before the guy lost some more money and started up again:

DAD: You know I asked ya NICE! Now shut your mouth!!

DRUNK: You want to take it outside?!

DAD: WHICH EXIT?!

My dad was 81 at the time. I never saw him afraid or even fearful of anything in his life!

To all those who have an issue with the truth that appears here I can only say:

WHICH EXIT???!!!

CHAPTER SIX

THE TWO MALONEY'S

OK, that's settled, I had the best father ever!!! Matt Maloney's wasn't too bad either!

In December of 1980, some fairly significant events occurred. John Lennon was murdered outside his home in New York City. Iran requested $24 billion in US guarantees to free the hostages held there. Jim Baker and Jessica Hahn had intercourse of some kind leading to the downfall of Jim & Tammy Faye's "Empire!" On a much more personal note in that December long ago, I found myself in Tokyo, Japan as a part of the of UCLA basketball team!

Asking why we were even in Tokyo in the first place is a reasonable question. We had lost in the National Championship game in March, so there was interest based off that fact but the trip had been planned well before that occurred. The main reason was the overwhelming interest in UCLA basketball period. Due to a previously discussed unparalleled string of success of UCLA in the 1960s and 70s, the people of Japan thought that UCLA was the ONLY University in America. I guess 10 National Championships in 12 years coupled with the attendant TV presence will do that.

We were to play the Japanese National Team in our first game in Tokyo and then Temple University from Philadelphia the next night. Let's just be kind and say we weren't very winded from the "contest". The Japanese team was no match for us. It was a strange atmosphere in the arena as well. Even though the place was packed, there was an eerie feeling to it. I finally realized that stemmed from the fact that the Japanese did not cheer or yell and certainly there was no booing. They respectfully clapped if they approved of something. Coming from New York that took a little adjusting to. On Long Island, we yell just to stay in shape!

Temple was going to be different. Temple was usually a very tough Club. Maybe the Japanese food didn't agree with them but whatever the reason they weren't as tough on the Island of Japan as they typically were in Philly. The final was 73-49! You would think that would have been the low point of their day but no. The popularity of our team was so huge that our bus was held up for over 2 hours as we were leaving the arena so that fans could reach through the windows for autographs! The problem for Temple was that they were stuck behind our bus with no escape route available. Imagine being beaten by 24 points and then having to watch the victors sign autographs for two hours. Not high on the bucket list!

On that Temple bus were two people who I would have significant interactions with, although none of us realized this at the time. One of them was Terence Stansbury who was a terrific player and would be drafted two years later in the 1st round of the NBA draft (#17). I would end up representing Terence and it was a pleasure. I don't think I brought up that bus thing until about three years into our relationship though!

The other gentleman on that bus probably more than a bit annoyed was an assistant coach named Jim Maloney. Jim had already been an assistant at Temple for seven years when he had to suffer the indignity of watching a punk like me sign autographs. At this time in 1980, he was Don Casey's assistant. Maloney would go on to coach under the great John Chaney for 16 more seasons at Temple.

On the playing side, Jim had been a star in the Philadelphia high school scene, which is a big deal. Philly was and is still a hotbed of basketball in this country. He went on to play at Niagara University where he was teammates with Hubie Brown, the great coach who today is still one of the best commentator's on TV. When Jim graduated from Niagara, he ranked 8th on the school's all-time scoring list. He was asked to come back and coach his alma mater and did so for three years (1965-68). He coached the legendary guard Calvin Murphy, who would average 38 points per game while playing for Jim. (That's not a typo.)

Jim Maloney was what they called a "lifer" in the coaching profession. A "lifer" is generally defined as a coach who was truly interested in actively "coaching" players. They are people that were much more concerned with the game of basketball and its effect on kids than on where their next job was going to be. Coaches like Jud Heathcote of Michigan State, Gene Keady of Purdue, John Wooden of UCLA, Joe Lapchick and Lou Carnesecca of St. John's, John Chaney of Temple, John Thompson of Georgetown, Pat Summitt from Tennessee, Geno Auriemma of UConn, Bob McKillop of Davidson and the great Pete Carril of Princeton are just some examples. There are many more.

I know that good coaches still exist today. The problem is nobody knows who they are. They reside in some high schools and smaller less marketed environments. Many of these coaches do a tremendous job and still indeed do have a big influence on the men and women they coach. They do so without the fanfare or the money. They do it like Jim Maloney!

Jim was known as a sort of "guard's guru." Having been one himself didn't hurt. He taught and brought along guys like the previously mentioned Calvin Murphy but there were many others who benefited from his guidance. Mark Macon who would go on to be drafted eighth in the NBA. Eddie Jones and Aaron McKie, both in the first round, Rick Brunson, Nate Blackwell, and my client Terence Stansbury just to mention the more famous ones. Oh, and there was one more but he didn't play for Jim at Temple. He ultimately went all the way across town to play for a Big 5 rival at the University of Pennsylvania. The traitors name coincidentally was also Maloney. First name Matt.

The first time I met Matt Maloney I think he was just entering college. At that same time, a family that we were close with had a four-year child succumb to cancer. Obviously, it was an awful time for them but the medical bills they were facing further complicated it. A group of friends approached me to see what could be done to help them. At that time, I was representing 23 NBA players, which is a lot.

We came up with the idea of having a golf tournament and dinner/auction to help with the medical bills. This was expanded to add a charity basketball game, which pitted the "Jersey Shore All-Stars" against the "Keith Glass All-Stars." (I have shirts to prove this). It was a terrific event. 22 of my 23 players showed up. Many of them played in the game and they all played in the golf tournament the following day. Every NBA team sent me some type of signed memorabilia for the auction, which was to follow the dinner after the golf tournament. You can imagine how important that was to us. We ended up raising more money than was needed so we continued the event for five additional years, which enabled us to help more families in similar situations.

The Jersey Shore team had players like Anthony Mason, Rod Strickland, and many others, while I had to struggle thru with Scott

Skiles, Mark Eaton, Robert Horry, and Mahmoud Abdul Rauf etc. etc. We were 6 and 0 for those games. Since I was coaching these games, I will admit to stacking my team. Think how embarrassing it would have been to lose your own charity game!! Plus, my players left after the weekend, I LIVE at the Shore!

It's hard to explain my level of appreciation to my players of that period. I always knew the character of the guys I was representing but it wasn't until these events occurred that all the people around me got the chance to see their personal qualities up close. They not only played golf with strangers who became friends and admirers by the 8th hole but most of them came all six years. They never asked for a thing. They just showed up.

An example I won't forget was when I called my client Marcus Liberty. He was one of the first guys I contacted to explain what had happened, and what I was trying to do. At first, he was quiet and then simply said:

MARCUS: Keith, what do you need?

KEITH: I need you to come to the Jersey Shore next month to play golf!

MARCUS: You got it! But you don't sound good! You want me to come NOW?!

Those were and are my guys. When Mahmoud Abdul Rauf showed up (he was still Chris Jackson at the time), he told me he had never held a golf club. Twenty minutes later, he emerged from the pro shop totally decked out in full golf attire complete with knickers, ready to tee off. He bought all of it on the spot. He had a wicked "slice" but he was terrific as far as we were concerned. What Mahmoud did later that night at the auction is an act of kindness that no one present could ever forget. I've written about this gesture before and like I've said this is a new book.

A Michigan State contingent of Skiles, Mike Peplowski, Matt Steigenga, and Jamie Feick were all there as well. My mistake was trusting them to be on their own after the basketball game the night before the golf tournament. You need to understand that every foursome included an NBA player. That's how we sold the event. You paid and you got to play with an NBA player. People had paid pretty good money to do that.

We had a luncheon scheduled for 12:00 followed by tee off at 1:00. Most of the people started arriving around 11:00. You know, head to the range, stretch, get ready to play and eat some lunch. At noon, there were no Michigan State Spartans on the horizon. 12:15. 12:30. 12:45! Nope. No mobile phones then either. We were in prehistoric times. So now I have four foursomes with no NBA players as promised. Refunds are crossing my mind.

At ten minutes to 1:00, the Spartans arrive and may I say not very resplendent either. Straggling in would be the appropriate description. Skiles clearly was avoiding me and went directly to his designated foursome. Mike Peplowski was their spokesman and offered the explanation for the group.

After the game, they had all ended up on the beach in Belmar. I didn't ask how they got there but apparently, some of them decided to take a naked swim in the ocean. Scott took that opportunity to bury Peplowski's clothes and refused to inform him for the rest of the evening of their whereabouts. I never checked the veracity of this story but to be honest it sounds like something Scott might have done!

Those six events were special! Even though it turned out to be ultimately a positive experience, you can't call it "fun" because of the circumstances that brought all of them to New Jersey to begin with. Hopefully, we helped some people out.

Somehow, Jim Maloney had gotten news of this event on the Jersey Shore. He called me and said that his son Matt, was a big fan of Scott and asked if they could get tickets to the game. I didn't know Matt but I had always had a ton of respect for Jim. They came a couple of the years we held our event. Matt, as I recall, was a sophomore at Penn and had already been named 2nd team All-Ivy. While that was nice, it was in no way a prelude to an NBA career or even NBA interest. I did however take an extra interest in Matt due to his and Jim's presence at our summer charity games. I always looked at the box scores and followed him as much as I could. He was good but I wasn't exactly thinking of recruiting him. He was more of a suspect than a prospect.

Matt's career at Penn went about as well as a career in the Ivy League could go. Since he had originally committed to Vanderbilt and had transferred to Penn after his freshman year, he spent only three full seasons at Penn (1992-95). His teams really struggled with him in the lineup. During his time there, Penn was 42-0 in the Ivy League! For you beginners, that zero means they never lost a conference game while Matt was there.

Accordingly Penn received three consecutive bids to the NCAA Tournament and in fact, the last time Penn won a game in that tournament was in Matt's junior year. They beat Nebraska 90 to 80. I won't go into all the records he still holds from his stay at Penn. Suffice it to say that in his last year he was the Player of the Year in the Conference.

Not bad but it was still the Ivy League, not the ACC. In spite of that stigma, Matt was invited to one of the two most important tournaments for players attempting to further their career in basketball. This tournament was named the Portsmouth Invitational Tournament (PIT) and was held in Portsmouth, Virginia. I have been going to this tournament almost every year for the past 25 years or so. I have had much success there if I must say so myself. And since I'm the only one writing this I guess I must.

Players that I have signed out of the PIT include Marlon Maxey, Jamie Feick, Matt Steigenga, Randy Woods, Mike Iuzzolino, John Crotty, Alex Blackwell, Alan Bannister, Mike Smrek, and Kenny Atkinson just to mention a few. Considering that this tournament is limited only to seniors that is a pretty good haul for an agent. Normally, the PIT is for players considered to be possible second rounders or guys that will go undrafted and therefore become free agents. Either way, the PIT has produced a good number of players who have gone on to the NBA and overseas success.

I'm not 100% sure but it has been pointed out that in those 25 years, I have never gone to the PIT alone. No, I was not importing various women to the tournament. I went with one or two of my three sons every year. It became a bonding trip for us. So I went to Portsmouth the year Matt Maloney was set to play. I had not made any overtures to Matt or Jim expressing my interest but I did see something in him. However, they knew me pretty well from the past and I figured if they wanted to speak me they knew how to find me.

Jim was in Portsmouth as I thought he would be. Both Jim and Matt were very friendly when we saw each other at the gym and around the town of Portsmouth. I figured they were going to wait until after this tournament to start dealing with agents. This was April and there were still two and a half months until the draft and I didn't think Matt was going to be drafted anyway. I realized my theory was not totally accurate when I saw several agents approaching Jim and Matt. They would have conversations with others but showed no interest in talking with me about representation.

Hmmm! Now, I started wondering what I had done or said to them in the past. It was bothering me but I just figured maybe they had good taste. I wrote it off. Matt played well in Portsmouth and that earned him an invite to the NBA pre-draft camp held in Chicago. Today this is known as the "Combine." This one was held in early June. I was curious about who they had signed with agent-wise but the word on the street was they hadn't decided yet.

Given that I had signed two players who were also invited to the combine, I was in Chicago as well. I ran into Matt and Jim together in the lobby of our hotel. There were big friendly hugs all around but no mention of talking to me about representing Matt.

Now, it was really starting to bother me. Don't get me wrong I understand you don't sign everybody you want but this was a little different. I knew these guys and they obviously liked me to a degree. I let it go again realizing that there are also several women who I think made huge mistakes in not giving me a shot (Jennifer Aniston comes to mind) or, at least that's what my Mom used to say!

So I moved on from the Maloney's as I had from Jennifer. That is until two days before the draft.

The phone rang and it was Jim:

JIM: Hey Keith, you busy tonight?

KEITH: Uh, not really.

JIM: Good, meet Matt and me at Exit 8 on the Jersey Turnpike. There's a truck stop there and it's half way from Philly to the Shore!

While I was happy to hear from them, why couldn't it have been Jennifer?! I went anyway. We sat at a little booth and Jim showed his straightforward nature immediately:

JIM: Keith, what do you think of Matt as a player?

KEITH: I think he's really good but he's not the best player I've ever seen. I don't think he gets drafted but

I think he has some NBA skills. I don't think he makes the league in his first year but if he is willing to work as hard as I would for him, I think he could make it in the right situation!

JIM: You got a f...... contract with you?!

KEITH: I always have a f...... contract with me Jim!!

JIM to MATT: Sign it!! If I hear one more agent tell you how great you are I'm going to hit him right in the head!!

And they say I'm not a great recruiter!! Normally if an agent said what I had said to a parent or a player, you'd basically be out of the running! But Jim Maloney knew the score. He knew what was necessary for Matt to make it to a level that only the two of them had dreamed he could. It wasn't going to be accomplished with bull crap. It was going to take a lot of work by whoever represented Matt and obviously by Matt himself. No nonsense! Jim knew what they were going to do all along agent-wise. They knew me but they wanted to hear others out as well.

So I signed Matt Maloney and unfortunately I was right about the draft. The Maloney's were under no illusions about that either. We arranged for Matt to go to the summer league with the Golden State Warriors. He did all right but they cut him as I expected and we headed to the Continental Basketball Association (CBA), which served as the minor leagues for the NBA. Today this has morphed into the "G League." Matt joined a CBA team, which had one of my favorite team names: The Grand Rapids "Mackers!"

Matt played well for the "Mackers." He was teammates with a player I would later represent, Melvin Booker. In fact, Matt & Mel became two of my favorite players I've ever had (although considering the character of most of my guys it's hard to use the word "favorite"). They both were close to getting called up to the NBA at the tail end of the season. Obviously, every player wants to have that happen. That's the reason you become a "Macker" in the first place!

In this case, the Houston Rockets chose to call up Melvin. Matt didn't get the call. The irony of that "call up" is that by "winning" that roster spot in the NBA Melvin would set into motion the opposite results of what we wanted. By becoming an NBA player, he generated more interest from Europe than ever before. The offers from Europe became too great for us to pass up and Melvin Booker became one of the truly great European point guards to ever play there. He also became rich which didn't bother either one of us.

On the opposite end of that decision was Matt. While he was legitimately happy for Mel, he was understandably disappointed that he didn't get that call. Jim and I would talk weekly about Matt's progress. Talking to a parent who was not only an active coach but also a realistic one was a pleasure. There was none of the usual nonsense about how his kid was getting screwed or was underappreciated or wasn't getting enough shots. Jim knew the score and he knew we were all working in the same direction. Instead of whining about where Matt was, we discussed how Matt could make that one final step and get to the League. It was never pressure from Jim but rather it was more strategy. The discussions were basketball based not business related. I don't ever recall discussing money even once with Jim. The goal was to make the NBA. The NBA was "the cake!" The money and everything else was "the icing."

Our weekly discussions stopped on May 3, 1996. Jim was on his way home from the Temple University basketball offices when he suffered a massive heart attack on the Ben Franklin Bridge. His car crashed but nobody really knows whether he died from the heart attack or the resulting crash. Then and now the cause mattered little. Either way, it was crushing.

When I start writing these chapters it's usually very easy. I'm not really a writer or an author, which takes a lot of pressure off me. I'm a storyteller. I enjoy it too. So when I sit down and start telling stories it goes fairly easily. After I wrote the preceding paragraph, it's taken me two full days to tell this one about Jim's passing. I just don't think I wanted to talk about it even though it's 20 years later. Don't get me wrong, it wasn't like I was so close to Jim but his passing and specifically his funeral still remain a very emotional memory for me.

I'm not in the business of ranking funerals (I would be surprised if there even is a business that does that) but Jim Maloney's funeral was truly a remarkable thing. I was debating making the trip down to Philadelphia for the service. In the end, I decided to go just to show my support for Matt and his family.

What I witnessed was an incredible outpouring from the basketball community of that great city. It was basically like witnessing a cross section of Philadelphia. Every race, religion, and height category was represented although the average height of the people in attendance was way above the national average. You can always tell a basketball crowd by the height. When I was a kid, the crowd at Madison Square Garden was always a wonder to me. However, I have come to realize in 2018 that the crowd is getting progressively shorter as the price of the tickets gets progressively taller!

The outpouring of affection for Jim was off the charts! Just getting a place to park and then a spot in the audience was daunting. I recognized many of the faces there but it's not really important to name-drop them here. John Chaney, however, stood out. Coach Chaney and Jim had worked together for 21 years and there was an obvious deep respect and love between them. Coach Chaney delivered the Eulogy that day and to call it emotional just scratches the surface. Just so you don't accuse me of exaggerating this is an excerpt from the book *Palestra Pandemonium- A History of the Big 5* written by Robert Lyons in 2002, six years after that day:

> *"Jimmy Maloney was something special...the kids*
> *loved him because he paid attention to them. He*
> *always took the part of me that was lacking. He was*
> *the other half of me. Here I am the driven person, a*
> *hard person, and he was the guy that always said,*
> *'Hey, don't worry about it, man, the coach loves*
> *you. We'll work on that tomorrow.' I'm the guy who*
> *would say 'No you can't' while he was saying 'Yes*
> *you can.'".........*
>
> JOHN CHANEY

Robert Lyons continued quoting another friend of Coach Chaney's describing that scene:

At the eulogy, the church is jammed. Maloney's casket is right in the middle aisle and John is looking right down on the casket. He gave this unbelievable eulogy about their life together, what they did, scouting trips, and all that. It was the greatest eulogy I've ever heard from anybody. At the end of it, John's pointing down at the casket and he said:

> *"I've always prayed that I would die before Jimmy*
> *because Jimmy could get along without me but*
> *there's no way I could get along without Jimmy."*

When he stopped speaking, there was total silence in that church. But when he sat down in his seat we all stood for two full minutes. Everybody knew that ovation wasn't for Coach Chaney. It was for Jim!

In the season that followed, the chair next to John Chaney was empty the entire year!

Trying to separate myself from the emotions I was feeling after Jim's passing was not going to be easy but I understood more clearly than ever that we needed to accomplish Matt and Jim's dream of making the NBA. I set out to try and find the best spot for Matt to play in the upcoming NBA summer league.

A lot of players don't realize it but many times it is more important for an agent to understand basketball as a sport and therefore where a player might fit best than it is to be constantly "wined and dined." This was particularly true in Matt's case. The basketball side of my brain told me that since Matt's strength was shooting 3's, he needed to get his opportunity with a team that had a player or players who drew double teams in the post. Matt was not a guy who you could leave alone on the perimeter.

Enter the Houston Rockets! They had a guy in the middle named Hakeem Olajuwon, who presented NBA teams with a distinct choice. Either double him or, in the alternative, have him consistently beat your brains in! This looked like a good spot. It was common knowledge that Houston was looking for shooters to surround Hakeem. Not only was it impossible to miss the presence of Hakeem but the Rockets also had two other fairly impressive players. Charles Barkley and Clyde Drexler! Both Barkley and Drexler are Hall of Famers and I consider Drexler one of the most under-appreciated players in the history of the league. Double teams all around!! That's the spot for Matt!

So now Matt and I know the right team, but how do we get him there? It's a long way from understanding the right spot for your guy and having him make that roster. The first step was to get Matt on to their Summer League roster. We had an ally. A gentleman by the name of Joe Ash was the main scout for the Rockets. He was also a friend of mine. Through many conversations, I knew that Joe was a fan of Matt's game and the Rockets were fans of Joe.

Thanks in part to that bit of information and having knowledge that Joe had put in the word for us, my next call was to Carroll Dawson, who was the General Manager for Houston. I had developed a good relationship with Carroll as well and we were able to take that first step of getting Matt invited to their camp.

The Rockets were participating that year in the Rocky Mountain Revue, which was held in Salt Lake City. The Utah Jazz ran the Revue and it was my favorite summer league to put my players in and to visit. While today the NBA holds its premier Summer League in Las Vegas with all 30 teams participating, the Rocky Mountain Revue had eight teams and it was all business! That is the business of *really playing* basketball and evaluating talent. The Vegas version of summer league not surprisingly has turned into what most of the NBA has become, that is selling! The NBA Summer League has now simply become an extension of the overall NBA product. As usual, they have done a terrific job.

I just got home from the 2017 NBA Summer League in Las Vegas. I've seen a lot of things and a lot of developments in this league but even I was somewhat stunned at this year's event. The first night we arrived at the Thomas & Mack Center on the UNLV campus, I was informed that the games were sold out! WHAT!!?? This is the Summer League! I've been coming to the various incarnations of summer leagues for 35 years. I've placed 150 players in these leagues. You CAN'T sell out the Summer League! The players, coaches, agents, etc. are there to work!

What a fool I've become. If I had only known that purely "by chance" Lonzo Ball was playing against Markelle Fultz that night in their initial summer league matchup, I would have contacted Ticket-master weeks earlier. In the good ole days, the game actually would have been between the Lakers and the 76ers but this was 2017. The rest of the players were just there so we can have a game with 10 guys. You see I'm learning. This was Lonzo vs. Markelle.

In the actual game, Markelle turned his ankle and didn't play the rest of the summer. They still sold t-shirts with his picture on them in the lobby though, so all was not lost. Lonzo remained healthy and was 1 for 15 that night! Very entertaining! The great Don Rickles would have summed up the game this way:

> *"I would have rather watched a fly crawl up a drape!"*

Just so you don't get the wrong idea, I really like Lonzo Ball as a bas-ketball player. He is unselfish and really knows how to play. He might in fact someday be a really good player. The part that bothers me is the hype surrounding him. While I'm intrigued by his potential as player, what exactly has Lonzo Ball accomplished? If you want to dole out money and fame to an individual who hasn't participated in a pro-fessional game that's your decision. I, on the other hand, don't have to BUY it.

Obviously, the attention paid to Lonzo and many of his contem-poraries is based solely on potential, marketing, and hype. I often have these arguments with people that accuse me of being "old school" in my approach to these situations. It's not "old school" to want someone to truly produce in their chosen profession before they receive this over the top adoration and financial compensation. In many ways, this unending hype has had very negative effects on a player's growth. This isn't a positive for that player or the game.

So let's try and examine how this has happened. With Lonzo, it's unfair to put the entire onus on his father, Lavar. He is really an easy target in all this! But the reality is all he did was tap into an understanding that in 2017 our society doesn't reward accomplishment. We reward bravado! Well, at least for a brief period of time that is. When that bravado turns out to be just another form of baloney, we move on the next guy who tries to say things even brasher. Whatever gets the most attention is what gets covered.

A couple of years ago, my son Tyler and I put together a radio show. We did it once a week and it was a blast. We would go into Manhattan every Thursday and record it at the "Sound Lounge" right next to the Flatiron Building on 5th avenue. The "Sound Lounge" is co-owned by Marshall Grupp, who I had met recently. Actually, we had met 55 years earlier in the mountains of Pennsylvania at that same place called Keeyumah. Marshall became our producer and the show was starting to get a little traction. We were in several outlets but nothing big.

A "big-time" company in lower Manhattan wanted to talk with us. They had interest in taking the show to a live format and basically have it "blow-up." We sat in a beautiful conference room with about 10 of their employees. Bagels and coffee, the whole works.

I'll never forget one part of that meeting. One of their executives told me point blank that they would like to help me say some type of outrageous statement in order to increase my social media presence. It didn't matter if it was true. It didn't matter if I even believed what they would put out there. It just needed to be "outrageous."

I didn't see Lavar Ball at that meeting but he obviously saw how it works. Two takeaways from this suggestion were: 1) it was our only meeting and 2) we don't have a radio show anymore! I get the feeling that if Lavar Ball were faced with the same suggestion, he would today be a fixture on the nation's airwaves.

What's next?! You do know that Lavar has sons even younger and less accomplished than Lonzo. Why not a line of shoes for his high school kids?! Oh, wait they just did that! I've got nothing against the Ball family. I just know that Lavar has cleverly tapped into a part of our society that is really not healthy. The glorification of the average is making the country average as well.

Sorry! Clearly, that's what my kid's call one of my rants! They even try to secretly tape these rants and use them against me. Family can be a wonderful thing! Let's get back to Matt Maloney and The Rocky Mountain Revue.

The summer league is a series of games and practices spread out over seven to 10 days. An NBA team, therefore, gets to develop a pretty good feel for the players on their summer roster. I had no concern about Matt personality-wise. I knew they would love having him around but now it was on him to show that he belonged on an NBA roster.

Trying to do my job as best I could, I had secured an offer for Matt from Alba Berlin, a very good team in Germany. The deal was for $150,000. We included what is called an "NBA out," which simply means that Matt would have until a certain date to pull out of the agreement. This "out" would only kick in if we secured a guaranteed job in the NBA. Our date coincided with the end of the Summer League, sometime at the end of July. The goal however was the NBA, as it is with every player I've ever represented.

To put it mildly, Matt was more than holding up his end of the deal!! I was scheduled to fly to Salt Lake City anyway but I had to move the trip up after I started getting reports on how well Matt was performing. He was doing everything we had hoped. Each successive game was better than the one before. I was keeping tabs on him from several sources. Some friends inside the NBA and several of my other players who were in the summer league were raving about him. It was time to strike while I thought the iron was hot!

Even though I had set up Matt's participation with Houston with their GM Carroll Dawson, thanks to a big assist from Joe Ash, I knew that their Head Coach, Rudy Tomjanovich would be the ultimate decision maker. Rudy, who was a great player for the Rocket's in his day, had arrived as their coach in 1992. He was therefore instrumental in drafting my player Robert Horry with the 11th pick in the lottery that year.

Rudy and I got along very well and as you may know Robert Horry was a pivotal part of Houston's back-to-back championships in 1994 and 1995. In looking back on Houston's four-game sweep of Orlando in the 1995 NBA Finals, there is an interesting statistic. Out of a possible 192 minutes, Robert played 187 of them. This meant Rudy subbed him out a total of five minutes during those Finals. That is basically a tad over a minute per game that Robert wasn't on the floor. For anyone who understands basketball and coaching that is a staggering statistic. Rudy liked Robert a little bit.

So off to Salt Lake City I went. I felt like we had a good chance to get something done considering the way Matt was playing coupled with my fairly good relationship with Rudy. Specifically, I was looking for a guaranteed contract for Matt for the coming season. While a guarantee doesn't assure that you make it on an NBA roster, it's a helluva start. When you have to pay a guy you have a tendency to keep him around. (This may not apply to the current administration in Washington, but I'm talking generally.)

The "fun" immediately began before I even checked in to my room at the Marriott downtown. As I approached the front desk to get my key, Rudy saw me and came over to talk. It caught me off-guard but after the usual pleasantries the conversation went like this:

KG: I hear Matt's doing pretty well!

RUDY: Not too bad. What are you looking to do with him?

KG: I'm looking to get him guaranteed. I have a job for him in Germany but obviously he wants to stay here!

RUDY: BON VOYAGE!!

It was at that moment, holding my bag in the lobby of the Marriott that the emotions of Jim's passing coupled with realizing how close we were to fulfilling their dreams must have hit me. For the first, and I hope the only time in my career as an agent, I totally lost my composure. Nobody had asked me but I felt like Jim's surrogate at that moment and I launched into a tirade on Rudy that I won't even repeat here. It's not like I'm proud of it.

An hour later, I decided to cool off by taking a walk. The Marriott has a mall attached to it so I went there to look around before the games were to start that evening. I was heading east when I looked across the mall and Rudy was going west. Rudy held up either a white handkerchief or a napkin and began waving it at me. Rudy was laughing as he did it. He was surrendering. I knew that Matt was about to get his guarantee!!

So Matt Maloney now had at least financially fulfilled part of his dream but we still needed to make it onto Houston's roster and start playing in the NBA. As I said earlier, Jim and I had never discussed the financial implications of Matt making the NBA; it was all about being there and playing. This wasn't going to be easy either.

CHAPTER SEVEN

OLAJUWON, BARKLEY, DREXLER...MALONEY??!!

The Rockets already had two point guards on the roster. They were both experienced and clearly ahead of Matt on the depth chart. Both of them went down with injuries and this is when things got really interesting. Houston was now faced with having no starting point guard. Since they were considered to be a strong contender in the Western Conference with Hall of Famers on the roster this was simply not acceptable. As such, they began the process of scouring the league to locate some help. Trades, waivers wires, anything they could to fill the void.

But the story goes that a certain forward on that team approached Rudy on a flight during the preseason. This was right after the injuries had occurred. For whatever reason, he went to bat for Matt. He basically said that he thought Matt possessed similar qualities to the guys who had been injured and more importantly had the tenacity that would be needed. Matt's family and mine as well thank Charles Barkley for the recommendation!!

The Rockets listened and Matt Maloney became the starting point guard for the Houston Rockets right next to Olajuwon, Drexler, and

Barkley. The only analogy I can think of for this situation is from the television show, "Seinfeld." George Costanza somehow lands a job with the New York Yankees as the assistant to the traveling secretary. Jerry and George are dumbfounded:

> **JERRY**: The New York Yankees??!!; Ruth, Gehrig, Dimaggio, Mantle...

> CONSTANZA?!

> The Houston Rockets??!!; Olajuwon, Drexler, Barkley... MALONEY?!

While George Costanza was a serial slacker always looking for shortcuts, true to his nature Matt went right to work! Having gotten his chance to not only make the roster but also being presented with the opportunity to not only play but also become the starter on a playoff team, Matt was going to do whatever was needed! When the season opened, he was indeed in the starting lineup.

In only his second game, Matt scored 17 points and handed out 4 assists. He got 18 more in a win against Boston. He registered 21 points and 9 assists in his hometown return to Philadelphia. That one felt really good. He went for 19 more against the Spurs in San Antonio, 19 points and 5 assists against Milwaukee, and then 17 points and 6 assists in Seattle.

As the first half of the season was ending, Matt and I received notices that he had been selected to play in the Rookie All-Star game in Cleveland. The league had started an exhibition, which pitted the top rookies from each conference to play in a game as part of what was developing as "NBA All-Star Weekend." One day was no longer enough.

I went to Cleveland for All-Star Weekend. I was there to support Matt but also to spend some time with the father of another player of mine from Greece, Efthimios Rentzias. Efthimios had been drafted in the 1st round that season by Denver but since he was under contract in Europe he would have to wait to come to the NBA until I could get him free. His father, Vassilis Rentzias, was accompanied on this trip to Cleveland by Ted Rodopoulos, who was a very close friend and advisor to the Rentzias family. Rodopoulos was also the person who had recommended me to them as their agent. Both are really good people and they were in Cleveland specifically to experience an NBA All-Star game.

I have been lucky enough to go to a few of these games. In 1992, I happened to be in Orlando during "All-Star Weekend." This was the game in which Earvin "Magic" Johnson came out of forced retirement. He had missed the first half of the regular season because he had announced that he had contracted the HIV virus that can cause AIDS.

I was staying with Scott Skiles, who was the MVP and easily the most popular player on the Orlando Magic at the time. We had no plans to go to the actual game until Scott heard that Magic, a fellow Michigan State alum was making his comeback. Scott casually asked me at breakfast if I wanted to go. I said sure but that was going to be a really hard ticket to get. How do we get in?! Anyone who knows Scott Skiles in any way can visualize that grin of his that says:

SCOTT: Are you kidding, you're with me!!

We walked into the game with an escort! No tickets. Try doing that in 2018. Good luck! That was a terrific experience and "Magic" as he usually did, lived up to the hype. He put on a show especially in the 4th quarter and was named the game's MVP! This game was the impetus for "Magic" to realize he could come back and play for our "Dream Team" in the Barcelona Olympics in 1992, the greatest team ever assembled in any sport!

As great as that Orlando game was, it does not in my mind come close to the 1996 All-Star game and it had nothing to do with Matt Maloney. In fact, I recall him not playing particularly well that night. Rather, it was an under-hyped idea that captured everyone fortunate enough to be in attendance that night.

The NBA having been established in 1946 was celebrating their 50th anniversary. If that was to take place today, they would attempt to cancel schools, have a National Day of Celebration and close the city of Cleveland for at least five days. In other words, hype it to death.

In 1996, the NBA got it right and proved the theory that "less can be more." They decided in a fairly quiet way to simply name the top 50 players in the history of the NBA. Get it, 50 years; 50 players. Not entirely rocket science!! That was a terrific idea. Unknown to me or I believe most people in that arena that night was that they had flown in those players, and without publicly making a big deal of it were going to introduce them to the crowd!

At halftime, they brought out 50 pedestals for the 50 guys and started announcing the names. Some of them were current NBA greats and some of them were like watching the legends of my childhood come to life! There was no smoke released, no blaring music accompanying the procession, no dancing girls… nothing orchestrated. It was just names:

Bob Cousy, Bill Russell, Hal Greer, John Havlicek, Billy Cunningham, Dave Bing, Walt Frazier, Bill Walton, Wes Unseld, Earl Monroe.

They had each been given a leather jacket, which was emblazoned with the logo of their team. As they heard their name called, one by one just walked out there. The intros continued:

> Oscar Robertson, Rick Barry, Julius Erving, Dave
> Cowens, Sam Jones, Kareem Abdul Jabbar, Elvin
> Hayes, Nate Archibald, Paul Arizin, David Robin-
> son, Kevin McHale.

Each one of the players announced drew ovations, the likes of which I don't remember hearing. There were no stats presented in spite of the fact that collectively these 50 guys had scored over 1,000,000 points. The names were enough:

> Wilt Chamberlain, George Mikan, Jerry West, Elgin
> Baylor, Bob Pettit, Nate Thurmond, John Stockton,
> Karl Malone, Bill Sharman.

It just kept going and it was thrilling. They simply walked out, got on their pedestal and waved to the crowd.

> Isiah Thomas, Scottie Pippen, Charles Bark-
> ley, Clyde Drexler, Hakeem Olajuwon, Dave
> DeBusschere, Patrick Ewing, George Gervin, Jerry
> Lucas, James Worthy, Lenny Wilkens.

My friends from Greece were totally overwhelmed with this presentation. They were not prepared for it and it was an awesome display of talent and history. They had only dreamed of seeing these players in the flesh while they were falling in love with the game of basketball from a distance of 6,000 miles.

Larry Bird, Magic Johnson, Michael Jordan, Pete Maravich, Shaquille O'Neal, Dolph Schayes, Willis Reed, Robert Parrish, Moses Malone.

I was hoping it would never stop. I didn't even agree with all the selections but that was for another night's discussion. The only players not physically there were the ones who had unfortunately passed away or been sick. "Pistol" Pete Maravich, who had died at age 40 on a basketball court after a pickup game, was represented in Cleveland by his two sons. Dave DeBusschere had also passed and Jerry West could not be there. It was quite a moving experience and I'll never forget it!

With the All-Star Weekend concluded the 2nd half of the season was now underway. Matt kept up his production. He recorded 11 points & 10 assists vs. Orlando. In back-to-back games with Denver, he had 11 points and 12 assists the first night after the All-Star break and followed that up with 19 points the next night. To finish off the regular season, he scored 24 points and handed out 5 assists against Dallas. Not bad for a guy that was a "Macker" the year before.

Summing up Matt's rookie year, he finished averaging 9.4 points per game with 3.7 assists. He also registered a 2.5 to 1 assists to turnover ratio, which is solid. Most impressive of all was the fact that he started all 82 games for the Rockets. He wasn't the greatest player in the league but he was there and acquitted himself quite well. As such, Matt was also selected to the All-Rookie second team.

As solid as his play was during the regular season, Matt turned it up a notch in the playoffs. Houston drew the Minnesota Timberwolves in their opening round. Matt's matchup would be Stephon Marbury, who was their star point guard. While Matt went undrafted, Marbury had been selected 5th overall with all the hype that surrounds such a lofty spot. In the first game of that series, Matt had 14 points and 6 assists in Houston's victory. In the best of five series, Houston swept the T-Wolves in three straight games. In the clincher, Matt torched Marbury and the T-Wolves for 26 points. He averaged 17.3 for the series.

Round two was against the Seattle Supersonics. Matt's matchup here was against Gary Payton, who was even better at that stage of his career than Marbury. This series was much tougher for Houston but Matt kept on going. In the first game, he had 17 points in a win. In Game three, he added 19 points. Game four was his best effort yet. He scored 26 again and had 6 assists in Houston's 4-point win! The series would go all the way to game 7 where the Rockets prevailed and Matt scored 15.

This win took them to the Western Conference Finals! This time though, the point guard lining up opposite Matt was John Stockton of the Utah Jazz. Let's put it this way, Matt was not the first or the last guy that John Stockton "took to school." Stockton gave Matt a clinic. It happens, but being that it happened in the Western Finals magnified things a bit, but only for a minute. To look back on what he had accomplished, it was a remarkable year for Matt!

Matt's rookie season was now in the books and it couldn't have gone much better, John Stockton aside. The following 1997-98 campaign wasn't too bad either. Matt started 78 games that season, so over his two years with the Rockets he averaged 80 games per year as their starter. Overall, I can honestly say that there wasn't quite the excitement that we had the year before. Like a lot of things in this life, the first time is always a little bit more special and different. That first year for obvious reasons felt like a mission while the next year seemed more like a business.

We had signed two successive minimum contracts for Matt after my standoff with Rudy in the lobby of the Marriott. Now, we needed to get paid. As with many situations my players and I have found ourselves in, there were bound to be some extenuating circumstances. Matt became a free agent in the summer of 1998. July 1st to be precise. The NBA decided that they would honor that occasion by instituting a "lockout" of its players the same day. There was no business to be conducted until the lockout was settled.

I was fairly calm during all this. I knew that eventually there would be a settlement. There was too much money going around to not have that happen. This wasn't the first time the league had taken that "lockout" route to try and force the players into a lopsided collective bargaining agreement. In 1995, they did the same thing and I was asked if I would agree to become a member of the newly formed "Agents Advisory Committee." This committee was composed of 11 handpicked agents that the National Basketball Players Association (NBPA) thought could aide them, not necessarily in the actual negotiations but with "advice." Things don't always go as planned!

CHAPTER EIGHT

"THE 22 MINUTE STRIKE"

The NBPA was first formed in 1954 and it was a pretty loose and not a very effective body. In 1962, Larry Fleisher was hired as the director of this union and things began to slowly change. In 1964, the NBPA was still not exactly what you would call a powerful force in professional sports. That type of power tends to be earned not given. But an event would occur in 1964, which would change everything not only for professional athletes but indirectly for me as well.

I was a 13-year-old kid in 1964. The context in which I knew of Tommy Heinsohn, Jerry West, Elgin Baylor, Bob Pettit, Bill Russell, Wilt Chamberlain, et. al. was simply as that of a fan. They were larger than life figures who came onto my television screen only on Sunday. There was one game per week. Take it or leave it. (Today I get enraged if every NBA game is not in high definition). Normally, the Boston Celtics were involved as they won 11 Championships during that period and were clearly the biggest television draw at that time. Personally, I always hoped to see the Cincinnati Royals pop up on those Sundays. That would give me the rare thrill of watching Oscar Robertson play. To those of you who didn't get that opportunity, I can only say you are forgiven when you put some of the players of today ahead of the "Big O" when listing the greatest players in NBA history!

Bob Cousy had started the NBPA and it began having an influence due to some extraordinary efforts and courage of those players I got to watch on Sundays. In 1964, NBA players had none of the advantages or rights that are taken for granted in 2018. They had been fighting for years with ownership in order to accomplish what today would be considered obvious concessions and working conditions. They were seeking a pension plan which would cover a portion of their retirement years, meal money, scheduling concerns such as no Sunday afternoon games after Saturday night games, and other issues.

Try and imagine that landscape today! The NBA in 2017 had to institute a policy in order to attempt to try and stop its players from "resting" periodically during the regular season. If they tried to schedule a Sunday afternoon game after a Saturday night game, the fans might show up but it would be a very lonely experience player-wise. Like many things in society, things change and evolve, occasionally for the better. Day games in the NBA after night games wasn't a good idea in 1964 either but the owners felt it was necessary as it saved money on travel, etc. The fledgling NBPA had been thwarted or in most cases simply ignored up until 1964.

The All-Star game that year was to be held in Boston. The players had enough of the disrespect:

> *"They'd tell us, they were going to do all these things*
> *and then they'd change their minds."*
> OSCAR ROBERTSON

Today, basketball fans outside of New England only know Tommy Heinsohn as one of the biggest "homers" while broadcasting Celtic games. In retrospect, he was a whole lot more than that! He was the

President of the NBPA at that point in time in '64. The word was he got this post partly because his "offseason" job was in insurance. The NBA and for that matter, all professional athletes of that time had "real" jobs in the off-season in order to "feed their families." Not Latrell Sprewell's family; their own families:

> *"The owner's kept putting us off and putting us off.*
> *Finally, we decided, we're not going to play in the*
> *All-Star game."*
> TOMMY HEINSOHN

There was a major snowstorm the day before the NBA All-Star game in Boston, which delayed the arrival of several players. Heinsohn gathered them in the lobby of their hotel and got them to sign a petition to boycott the game later that day. They also included a list of their issues and the demands that needed to be met in order for them to play that afternoon. Heinsohn would years later say:

> *"That was the Magna Carta of the Player's*
> *Association".*

Adding to the drama and pressure of the day was the fact that the game was to be televised LIVE on ABC. As I mentioned earlier this was not an everyday occurrence in those early NBA days. It was a big deal and an opportunity to get their product seen by a mass audience. The idea that this "live" TV opportunity was being threatened by their players did not go over real big with the owners. The owners were getting pissed. My experience in this business is that when owners get pissed they try and do something about it. They are after all extremely successful people in their other careers, which is how they originally got to own teams in the first place.

The time slot for the game was set in stone! ABC made it clear that they would "pull the plug" if the impasse wasn't settled. The players were sitting in the locker room refusing to go out and warm up. Owners kept barging in to yell and/or threaten them. According to Heinsohn, the owner of the Lakers, Bob Short, attempted to enter the locker room but was stopped at the door by a security guard:

> *"He tells this old Irish police guy, 'I'm Bob Short, the owner of the Lakers. You go tell Elgin Baylor that if he doesn't get his ass out here fast, I'm done with him.' So Elgin gets the word and said back to him, 'Tell Bob Short to go f... himself.'"*

In 2011, Baylor's teammate Jerry West told the LA Times:

> *"The players were controlled by the owners. All of us felt like we were slaves in the sense that we had no rights. No one made anything then. You had to work in the summer. It was the dark ages of basketball."*

The more pressure the owners put on these players the more entrenched they became. I have had the opportunity to deal with several of these men in later years as an agent and sometimes even as a friend. As competitive or emotional as a negotiation got with any of them, I could never dream of trying to pressure them. They simply weren't built for that. Apparently, the owners didn't quite grasp that:

> *"We weren't quite united at first but soon got there. It took a little conversation but we got it done. People came in the locker room making threats telling us we were going to kill basketball. What are you*

doing? It was a televised game and we could un-
derstand that, but it was something we had to do.
If you negotiate in good faith and you agree to do
something, you should be true to your word!"

-OSCAR ROBERTSON

Now there's a concept!

With the pressure mounting, game time approaching and ABC in his ear, then Commissioner Walter Kennedy met with his owners and finally entered the player's locker to inform them that their demands would be met. This was not only important for the issues involved but it more importantly set the stage for the NBPA to have a seat at the negotiating table from that point forward!

Even after Kennedy's promises, the Players held a vote to see if they would go out and play. Reneging on promises made over a decade can make people a bit suspicious. The vote was 18-2 in favor of playing:

"There was a lot of discussion pros and cons....and
there were players who still thought we should not
go out and play. I think it was Wilt Chamberlain
who said, 'we've got the commissioner's guarantee
that he'll do everything in his power. We need to
go out and play.' I guess we went out three or four
minutes before what was supposed to be tip-off, took
one or two layups and started the game."

-BOB PETTIT

Oscar Robertson was named MVP of that All-Star game after scoring 26 points, getting 14 rebounds, and handing out 8 assists or as I would put it, just another day of the office for the Big O! Bill Russell had 13 points and 21 rebounds. Wilt got 19 points and 20 rebounds and Pettit had 19 points and 17 rebounds. But those numbers pale in comparison to what they had accomplished in the bowels of the Boston Garden before they ever took the court:

> *"You talk about money, there wasn't a whole lot*
> *of money in that (locker) room in terms of salary.*
> *Today, I think it would be very, very difficult when*
> *guys are making millions and millions of dollars. I*
> *don't know if it would have happened today or not.*
> *I don't think a lot of players today are even aware*
> *that this happened."*
>
> -OSCAR ROBERTSON

Oscar Robertson wasn't quite done either. Six years later on April 16, 1970, Oscar Robertson in his capacity as the President of the NBPA became the Plaintiff in the first Anti-Trust lawsuit in NBA history. The basic point of the suit was an attempt to abolish the "option" or "reserve" clause in a player's standard contract, which served to bind a player to one team for life. Six years later on April 29, 1976, the NBA agreed to settle with the NBPA, thereby changing the balance of power in professional sports. This gave players their first real point of leverage when it came to dealing with ownership. More importantly, it paved the way for me to earn a living.

There were 20 players in that locker room on that snowy day in Boston. Twelve of them are enshrined in the Hall of Fame in Springfield, Massachusetts. Many of them went on to have careers in management in the league. It was in this capacity that our paths crossed many times.

Wayne Embry became a highly respected team executive who I found was a great pleasure to deal with. I had several dealings with Jerry West during his tenure with the Lakers. On the other side of town, the great Elgin Baylor and I also made some contracts happen together in his capacity as the general manager of the Los Angeles

Clippers. Hopefully, I never showed it but a part of me was always in awe of them. For crying out loud, you think it's easy to negotiate with the NBA "LOGO?!"

We can argue all day if you want about who was better, Oscar or Michael or Elgin or Lebron or whoever you want. It's fun and it doesn't hurt anybody. There is, however, no argument about who stood up to power and thereby made it possible for the players of today to enjoy the staggering benefits and lifestyles that the NBA provides.

I don't know how men like these come to be. I just know them when I see them!

So here I am in 1995 and I've been selected to this "Agents Advisory Committee," which is designed to some degree to help prevent the potential "work stoppage" that lasted those 22 minutes in Boston 31 years earlier. Things had changed dramatically in those 31 years. Most of those changes revolved around one main ingredient: MONEY!!

In the early days of my career, I could literally spend an entire summer fighting for a $5,000 roster bonus for one of my players. The minimum player salary back then was $40,000 and you had to battle to get it. Over the years, those numbers have risen dramatically to the point where in 2017 the rookie minimum salary was $815,000! That's not just inflation, that's growth!

In all of these labor stalemates I have been involved in, the issues can get very complicated but the real "meat" always comes down to two main things:

1. What percentage of revenues will each side get and just as significant,
2. Through which mechanisms will the players be able to navigate the "salary cap" in order to attain their own individu-

al contracts? This is where the terms, "mid-level exception", "minimum rookie and veteran scales", "signing with room", etc. get their start.

In 1995, the central issue, however, really became secrecy. The formation of the "Agents Advisory Committee" in retrospect was merely an attempt to keep us agents "close." Godfather buffs know:

"Keep your friends close and your enemies closer!"
-VITO CORLEONE

This would come to totally backfire against the creators of the committee, namely the NBPA and its director. Oh Boy, I'm feeling more history coming!

In 1967 under agent/attorney Larry Fleisher's guidance, the NBPA, and the NBA negotiated the first Collective Bargaining Agreement (CBA) in the history of organized sports. This was no small accomplishment. As such, it was universally looked at as a tremendous cooperative working relationship between those two entities. That spirit of cooperation ultimately led to the very innovative CBA in 1983. The main innovation was the establishment of the original "Salary Cap" in sports history.

People can have different views on the necessity of "The Cap". The time in which it was implemented is important to consider. The NBA was certainly not the "Goliath" it has become today. In 1983, the rationale used to create the "Cap" was that the NBA was not profitable. In fact, they were floating the idea that four teams were certain to fold if some form of restraint or "cost certainty" was not provided to its teams. While I do believe there is some merit to that argument, another rationale in my view was a bit more cynical. The NBA needed a way to protect the owners from themselves. This led them to concoct a system where they were restrained to a degree from spending beyond their means. If I didn't know better, it looked like one of my ex-wives was involved in these negotiations.

My questioning of the motives of management and the league, in general, has only increased as the years have passed. Certainly, none of the 30 NBA franchises currently participating in the league are in danger of folding. Re-locating maybe, but folding no way. In fact, it was recently reported that an NBA owner was proposing the idea of expansion.

The league is so "depressed" in 2018 that such a move to add even one team would put an extra $1,000,000,000 in the owner's pockets without selling a ticket. Yet the salary cap remains firmly implanted in every CBA since it was originally instituted. To the owners, the "salary cap" has morphed into a right which they cannot exist without! One hundred years from now, I believe that people looking back on our times will only ask two questions:

1. What did men do to their former wives to necessitate paying them large sums in order to obtain a separation from them? And
2. What was up with the "Salary Cap"?!

Enough of my personal venting for now. Let's go back to the history of this dispute. After Larry Fleisher stepped down as director of the NBPA Charles Grantham replaced him. Charlie had a grand plan which included the elimination of three key components:

1. The "Salary Cap"
2. The "right of first refusal". This clause enabled a team to sit back and simply "Match" an offer a "restricted free agent" received, and;
3. The NBA draft just for good measure.

Good luck with all that!

The agent part of me was obviously in complete favor of all three of these "dreams," but the pragmatic side knew this was not about to happen. Grantham's efforts at the negotiating table proved very ineffective and the players actually played the entire 1994-95 season without a replacement agreement with the league. The Union then took the step of filing an antitrust lawsuit in order to eliminate those three provisions. In July of 1994, U.S. District Court Judge Kevin Duffy ruled against the players saying that as long as a CBA existed the NBA was immune from an antitrust action.

With no other choice, the NBPA returned to the bargaining table. In the middle of these attempts at negotiations, Charles Grantham resigned abruptly as there was talk of alleged improper expense related activity. As I have said before if I wasn't involved, it's hard to talk about it.

Out of this sudden vacancy emerged Mr. Simon Gourdine. Oddly, Simon had not only worked in the NBA League offices but had served as its Deputy Commissioner. That made him the #2 man in the NBA. I knew Simon from years before and we became closer after he moved over to the Union side. It became very obvious that Simon wanted to get a deal done and surprisingly a tentative agreement was reached fairly quickly.

The problem was that this agreement was reached very secretly and the contents of it were unknown. Neither I nor the other 10 agents on the "Committee" really cared for the way this was going down. Additionally, some of us started to get information leaked to us about the contents of that tentative agreement. That was when all hell broke loose!

This group of agents included some interesting and certainly outspoken individuals. Besides myself, the group included David Falk, Arn Tellem, both Fleisher brothers, Bill Strickland, Steve Kaufman, and others. I think the estimate was that between the 11 of us, we represented over 70% of the players in the NBA at that time. The secrecy involved in trying to get this deal signed caused us tremendous concern.

I'm writing this in September of 2017 and the way the Republicans in the Senate are attempting to ram through health care legislation and tax reform is reminiscent of the attempt between the league and Simon. Pass it before anybody gets a chance to see what's actually in it! The difference here was that while Senators that oppose the health care bill obviously can't call the estimated 20 million people who are in danger of losing their health care, the 11 of us had all the phone numbers we needed. They were our clients.

All the members of the Committee held a conference call and it was an eye-opener. All these men who had fought and stolen from each other literally as a way of life were suddenly on the same side. It took some adjusting but I pulled through. As surreal as that initial call was between the committee members, the next conference call is one I will never forget.

We all arranged to have every player we could get to phone in and join a mass call the following day. They did! I think I was the 6th person to join the conference. If you've never had that experience, they have you call into a specific number and then patch you into the conference call. They announce you as you join. Imagine the thrill of hearing:

"Mr. Keith Glass is joining the conference."

It's a bit awkward at the beginning of this process but the six of us made some small talk and then it started:

"Mr. Patrick Ewing is joining the conference."
"Mr. Scottie Pippen is joining the conference."

"Mr. Reggie Miller is joining the conference."
"Mr. Alonzo Mourning is joining the conference."

On and on it went:

"Mr. Scott Skiles is joining the conference."
"Mr. Michael Jordan is joining the conference."

Suddenly the thrill of Keith Glass joining the conference was beginning to fade!

"Mr. Dikembe Mutombo is joining....."

I think you get the point. By the time the poor conference phone operator finished, there were over 100 of us on that call which is pretty remarkable. The conversation itself was even more important than announcing the participants. It got pretty heated at times but the overall feeling was clear that we all had to collectively stand together to defeat a "bad deal." The issue of why this was happening so clandestinely between the league and Simon was discussed but I am not going to crawl inside Simon's head to identify his intent. All we knew was that for whatever reason the players were being sold out.

It was decided that the only way to stop this agreement was to "decertify" the Union. To understand this process and the need to decertify, you first have to understand the basis for the Union in the first place. As a certified NBA Agent, I am empowered to "negotiate individual compensation negotiations." This basically gives me the right after signing an individual player to negotiate HIS individual contract with an NBA team.

The NBPA as the Player's Union is empowered to negotiate the CBA with the League. They represent ALL of the Players only in Collective Bargaining. If there is no CBA due to a decertification, the

NBPA ceases to exist and thereby ends any prospective agreement with the NBA.

More damaging than that to the NBA is that, without a Union to negotiate with, the NBA would be at risk of losing their exemption from antitrust legislation, thereby opening themselves up to a successful lawsuit by the players. Whether or not they will ever admit it, this was the only leverage that the League was concerned with.

Our Agent's committee's challenge now was to get at least 30% of the Players in the league to individually sign a "decertification letter" seeking to disband their own Union. After Simon's end run it wasn't too difficult. I alone got 20 or so to sign on. The 30% hurdle was easily accomplished and an election to decertify the Union was scheduled for September of 1995.

The NBA's reaction to these events was to:

a. Lockout the Players on June 30, 1995, thereby freezing all interactions with its players and threatening the delay of the start of the season and;
b. Begin to renegotiate terms on the deal that we had stopped.

Both of these tactics helped to bring about a new deal between the parties. The lockout was lifted and the 1995-96 season began on time. Clearly, my players and others did not want to miss any games in the upcoming season, not to mention the paychecks that accompany those games. The cynic in me was in some ways disappointed that the players didn't take things even further.

Thinking back to the events of the 1964 All-Star game made me wonder what they would have done. It's one thing to threaten a strike when you're not making much money. I guess you could say they didn't have as much to lose as the players of 1995 who were beginning to make millions. Clearly, it's a relative argument. A player in 1964 was to some extent risking his entire career while in 1995 it was more about exactly how many paychecks am I going to miss.

At least we caused some trouble for the League and got significant concessions in the renegotiated version of the CBA. There was, however, one clause that would complicate things down the road. Even though the new CBA was a six-year deal, the owners got themselves the right to "reopen" negotiations after year three. This right to "reopen" would kick in only if the player's collective salaries exceeded 51.8 % of the revenues of the NBA. After the 3rd year, the Player's salaries leveled off at around 57%! They blamed the agents for loosening the system up to allow for some flexibility in the Cap! True and you're welcome!

As a result on March 23, 1998, the owners voted 27-2 to reopen the CBA, claiming poverty and citing the "fact" that 1/2 of its 29 teams were losing money. What was not mentioned by the owners was the "actual fact" that they had just secured a new TV deal with NBC and TNT, which totaled $2.64 billion. This new TV contract raised each teams' annual income from $9 million to $22 million.

What the owners were really after was a "hard cap," which would act to eliminate the flexibility that we had preserved in the previous 1995 negotiations. The owners are not stupid. Salaries were rising rapidly and they wanted to control that. On June 22, 1998, the last of nine negotiating sessions ended after only 30 minutes. The players made it clear that they would not accept any form of a "hard cap," and the League announced its lockout for July 1, 1998. The same day as Matt Maloney's free agency was to begin.

Money not only has a way of attracting large groups of people but it often leads to a hardening of positions. My divorces alone taught me that one. The more that's at stake the more people are willing to fight to keep at what they have, if not to get more. That is what happened after the owners opted out of the CBA in 1998. This time there would be no saving of the season.

This time, the two sides dug in and for the first time in the history of the NBA, the season did not begin as scheduled. In fact, the lockout of 1998 lasted 204 days. The NBA owners lost $1 billion while it was estimated that the players lost approximately $500,000,000 in salaries.

Another ramification was that the questionable motives of Simon Gourdine did not go unnoticed. Simon was out and replaced by Billy Hunter. Billy, who I would become fairly close with came from a football background and was also a former prosecutor. He was a pretty tough guy.

There is no way I'm going to recount all of those 204 days. It's still frustrating just writing about it because I always felt that it could have been settled far earlier than it ultimately was. If the owners and the players thought it was ok for them to lose great sums of revenue that was their prerogative. During all of these labor disputes, I always think about the effect on all the people that earned their living off the NBA. The parking garages, the concessions etc. Those people weren't dealing with millions; they were relying on those revenues to feed their families, literally.

When Latrell Sprewell uttered his infamous line about turning down a guaranteed $36 million on the grounds that he "had to feed my family," I could only imagine what the average sports fan felt upon reading that! Obviously, they didn't feel too bad as the revenues and popularity of the NBA has probably tripled since that statement was made.

Okay, that is enough of my moralizing, for now. There was BIG money at stake and both sides were fighting for it. To understand where both sides were coming from, you need to understand how the finances in the NBA were beginning to escalate. When the original cap was instituted for the 1994-95 season, it was set at $3,600,000 per team. For the approaching 1998-99 season, it had grown to $30,000,000. Individual "star" players' salaries were going up at an alarming rate, at least from the owners' perspective.

Hakeem Olajuwon signed a five-year extension with Houston for $55,000,000. Dikembe Mutombo went to Atlanta for $50,000,000 over five years as well. In 1996, Shaquille O'Neal signed a seven-year contract with the Lakers for $123,000,000 and in 1997, the deal that seemed to epitomize the lack of control by owners and general managers was the signing of 21-year-old Kevin Garnett for seven years at $126,000,000 with the Minnesota Timberwolves.

The Garnett signing prompted general manager Kevin McHale to say:

> *"We have our hand on the neck of the golden goose*
> *and we're squeezing hard!"*

I would like to point out though that the general manager of the Minnesota Timberwolves who negotiated the Garnett deal was KEVIN MCHALE! So they all knew. They couldn't help themselves! At least they thought they couldn't.

One can only imagine the maneuvering and conversations that went on during those 204 days of the lockout. We were not allowed to discuss anything with anyone even loosely affiliated with an NBA franchise. NBA Commissioner David Stern threatened heavy fines to any employee who violated these orders. These orders extended not only to forbidding any discussion with an agent but even to a ban on any NBA employee commenting on any subject.

As an agent, we were left to reassure our clients that things would ultimately work themselves out. It was, however, becoming obvious to me that the players were beginning to have significant divisions in their ranks. It's only natural especially when you realize the disparate salaries involved and therefore the different incentives for each player. Even though a Patrick Ewing stood to lose more per paycheck than a player making the minimum, that minimum might represent a lot more to the 11th guy on the roster in terms of his specific lifestyle.

Patrick was the President of the NBPA during this tumultuous time. He took a lot of crap from fans and the league for his staunch defense of the players' positions. Personal attacks of Patrick were commonplace. Patrick Ewing gained an awful lot of respect from me during that entire period. He was one of the guys who stood the most to lose both financially and reputation-wise. He never flinched at what he thought was the right thing to do. I always admired Patrick as a player but he took it to another level during the "lock-out" as far as I was concerned!

I recall specifically the meeting that was called by the NBPA in the midst of the lockout to discuss where things stood. The meeting was held in Las Vegas. Why Vegas?! There's no NBA team in Las Vegas. It's not geographically convenient. Maybe they felt that there was some other attraction to that particular American city. Probably the museums! We had come a long way from a cramped locker room in Boston to a conference room at Caesars Palace! Or had we?

Whatever the case, it became clear to me during those two days in the desert that even within my own list of clients there was no unanimity. To be clear, none of the "stars" of the league were on my client list but I did have players across the rest of the NBA spectrum and they were all concerned with different things. While in Vegas one of my guys told me point blank:

"Keith, I don't give a crap about the guys that come after me! I want my check!!"

The public and the media weren't buying into the whole dispute either, which was totally understandable. My childhood friend, and actually the author of the foreword to my earlier book, Tony Kornheiser declared the lockout as one:

> *"Between tall millionaires and short millionaires"*

Newsweek termed the lockout:

> *"An incomprehensible and unconscionable dispute*
> *between rival gangs of millionaires"*

The problem I was having, which was similar to my feelings in 1995, was that I was in agreement with those sentiments. Of course, I am all for the players and their efforts to be fairly compensated. It's actually my job to help that happen but I was increasingly uncomfortable and clearly remain so to this day with not only the players' compensation but also with the staggering amount of money being generated by TV, ticket prices, etc. etc. These bloated numbers across the entire spectrum are moving the game further and further away from the average fan. Goodness, what are we going to do as a society when we can no longer afford those big foam fingers at the games! It could happen! It is happening!

After several contentious and heated meetings coupled with the usual threats from the Commissioner, Billy Hunter and David Stern held one final meeting on January 4, 1999. We were then summoned to New York City by the NBPA on January 6th along with player reps and players to discuss agreeing to a deal that had been struck at that January 4th meeting.

It was quite the scene. We all went up to some law offices right above where the Apple Store now sits off 5th Avenue. I realized this was going to be settled but I was concerned about the details. The

NBPA had agreed upon several elements in order to get the lock-out lifted. Salaries were capped. A rookie wage scale was instituted, which would have a median salary set for each drafted player in the 1st round of the NBA draft.

A luxury tax was put in for good measure. This was established as a financial punishment for any team exceeding the hallowed salary cap. Deep down, however, I knew that even though these were concessions the league was never going to curtail the salary growth of its players. My real worry was that what they were accomplishing was going to separate the "stars" from the rank and file of the Union and that is exactly what has been happening.

What really annoyed me about this process was the date it was settled. After 12 years as the head basketball coach at Mater Dei High School in New Jersey, I retired in order to watch Tyler play for his high school, Middletown North. Tyler proceeded to start 77 games in a row for his three seasons. When he was a sophomore, he was playing against my old school, Mater Dei and the game was January 6, 1999. It was the only game I missed during his career and it still pisses me off.

Many of the rules and exceptions coming out of these negotiations were designed to eliminate or at least reduce the influence of agents. The establishing of these "scales" was in part to minimize what we as agents could negotiate. After the "Rookie Scale" was instituted, the NBPA took the additional step of reducing what an agent could charge a player for a minimum. These are just a couple of examples of the overall desire to rid themselves of us. The theory was that if we "scale" salaries then what do you need with an agent?! This, however, assumes erroneously that an agent just sits back fielding offers. This is the case for just a small percentage of players. Most players in any professional sports league need an advocate in order to even get into a position where there will be offers.

As I was coming down the elevator after the deal was ratified and the doors opened, there was a huge crush of media. Apparently, they were so desperate for information from anybody that a reporter from *Sports Illustrated* grabbed me and asked about this perceived attempt to rid themselves of agents. My response was and still is:

"Agents are like city rats. We can survive in any environment."

This has been borne out in almost ridiculous proportions. Today, NBA players and their agents are splitting up tremendous amounts of money. Clearly, the misguided attempts to reel in the influence of agents in their sport have failed. Currently, the average NBA salary hovers around $9,000,000 per year with "Stars" commanding $200,000,000 contracts. This calculation is based primarily on the ten-year television package that the NBA negotiated in recent years.

Not only has the impact of agents not diminished but, recently NBA owners have come to realize that the power and knowledge that some agents possess might be useful. Several NBA teams have decided, that since agents have beat their own front office people on many occasions at the negotiating table, instead of fighting them they've employed them. This has happened in various cities including, Phoenix, Detroit, Utah & also with the reigning NBA Champs in Golden State. If you can't beat 'em, hire 'em.

Three plus years had elapsed. Two subsequent CBA's had been negotiated between the Union and the NBA. We as agents were smack in the middle of that struggle. We won some concessions but probably lost more. Bizarrely, we had come together to fight for a better deal for our players. When leaving that office on 5th Avenue the night of the settlement in 1999, I did, however, find myself longing for a simpler time, where instead of uniting and fighting for the common good, my fellow agents and I could return to stabbing each other in the back!

CHAPTER NINE

SHOW MATT THE MONEY!!!

That certainly was a roundabout route to Matt Maloney's contract. Regardless of any roadblocks, he does now need to get paid. Sometimes, I do this for the money!! There's no need to go into elaborate detail on these negotiations. The one thing that was clear after the lockout ended was that everything was going to be done in a hurry.

Even the schedule itself was rushed and truncated. The NBA had decided to play a 50 game schedule in spite of the advanced date. The season was condensed to fit between the months of February and April for the regular season. To get 50 games into that time frame was a challenge. There were many back to backs and I seem to recall even some three in a rows.

Because of this accelerated pace, the actual contract negotiations for free agents were not the typical "dance," where the team would downgrade your guy and you would then have to battle back. In normal seasons, this could sometimes take an entire summer to finish. In January of 1999 after having no contact with the Rockets at all, both sides knew that we didn't have the time or the inclination to screw around.

Matt was their starting point guard for two years and we both knew that there was a value to that. Add in the fact that he started 160 games out of a possible 162 and further adding in his performance during the playoffs for those 2 years, it didn't take a genius to figure out a salary.

The going rate was going to be between $2,300,000 and $2,900,000. This was pretty clear. I therefore had two issues. The first was naturally to get towards the top end of that range but the more important one was for how many years!? That's where I faced resistance from Houston. They obviously wanted to keep it short while I realized that Matt and I had landed in the perfect situation for him and the odds on Matt continuing to do this with the Rockets in my estimation was remote. I had seen too many fickle things happen in the NBA.

Teams fall in and out of love with players more than I did with women!! They always look for something else around the corner (teams, not me). They make trades. They waive players and sign new free agents and so on. I was very concerned about that for Matt. Also adding to that concern was the fact that a big part of Matt's success with the Rockets was clearly due to the fact that he had been surrounded by three future Hall of Fame players during the time he was there. There is this thing called age which happens to all of us and that was approaching with Hakeem, Clyde, and Charles! Without those guys Matt's value would, to be kind, seriously plummet!

I first established the number at $2,800,000,000 per year and then I dug in on the length. Even though it was a relatively smooth contract to navigate, there was some push and pull. There always is, even in this unusual situation. I ended up getting Matt seven years guaranteed by "giving up" some of the per year salary. In the end, we signed for approximately $17,000,000 for those 7 years. Not bad for a kid from Penn who wasn't drafted and who no one outside of his own family ever dreamed would ever even play in the NBA.

Nine months later, the Houston Rockets CUT Matt Maloney!

I guess this calls for some explanation.

In June 1998 a few days before the League locked out its players, the NBA held its annual draft. The 2nd pick overall in that draft was a young man named Steve Francis. Steve had played one season at the University of Maryland and had then decided to leave school early and enter the draft. There is nothing unusual about that and he was indeed rewarded in his decision by being drafted #2 by the Vancouver Grizzlies. What a thrill! At least, it was for Vancouver.

It seems that Steve and his representatives had, primarily for marketing reasons, spent the better part of the months leading up to the draft informing the Vancouver Grizzlies not to draft him. This occasionally happens in professional sports. John Elway and Eli Manning successfully pulled this off on their draft nights. Both of them were the #1 picks in their respective drafts and I think just as importantly they were quarterbacks. They took their share of flak for their seeming ungrateful response to the cities of Baltimore in Elway's case and San Diego in Manning's. Steve Francis took things up a notch.

Steve according to accounts "went into a full-court pout." On National TV immediately after being selected, an obviously upset Steve Francis said:

"Hopefully tomorrow when I wake up I'll be happy."

Tomorrow?? To most people watching tonight seemed pretty good. Michael Wilbon the current co-host of PTI writing for the Washington Post at the time remarked:

"Francis is a one year wonder who looked very selfish and completely ungrateful."

The lockout hamstrung Francis and his reps to a degree. In spite of Commissioner Sterns edit on communications I'm sure they were working behind the scenes to get Steve out of the apparent hell that is Vancouver. Francis, his reps, and Francis' brother visited Vancouver for a press conference prior to the lockout. They had dinner with Stu Jackson, the GM of the Grizzlies.

The press portrayed him as a greedy young millionaire. At an airport ticket counter, his agent was asked if they were a rap group. This question was apparently shared with Steve. When they returned home, his agent called Stu Jackson:

> "*Stu, we have to work this out." That meant get him out!*

Although Francis was trying at first to say the right things even if it didn't come with any form of sincerity, his tenor and words became a bit more strident as the summer dragged on. Initially, he claimed that Vancouver was too far from his hometown in Maryland. Geographically, that is plausible but then he switched to complaining about the taxes in Vancouver. Interesting! Then came the claim that it wasn't the right fit for him from an endorsement or marketing point of view. Getting closer! Finally, he invoked the idea that it was "God's Will" that he doesn't go to Vancouver. Call me crazy, but I don't think he wanted to play there!

On August 27, 1999, seven months after Matt and I signed our seven-year $17,000,000 guaranteed deal with Houston, Steve Francis was traded to Houston in an eleven-player blockbuster deal. Even if Matt didn't know it at the time, he was on his way out. Two months after the trade, Houston released him, along with our $17,000,000. (And you wonder why you're paying $11.50 for a hot dog!)

The Rockets would go 34-48 that season but certainly not solely because of the trade. As expected, they were getting older. Hakeem was injured. Barkley popped a knee and retired. It happens. Matt and I continued to find other NBA teams for him. We went to Chicago with the Bulls for a brief period and then found a home in Atlanta with the Hawks for a minute but it was never the same as it was in Houston. After he was released again by Atlanta, the San Antonio Spurs came after me twice for Matt. Both times he turned them down. I finally asked him why did he keep turning down such a terrific franchise like the Spurs:

"Keith, I don't think you realize it but I really don't like playing that much!"

OK!? That can be a problem!!

It would be really easy for me to get maudlin, sentimental, or even make a futile run at being profound in some way at the conclusion of this chapter on Matt and his dad, Jim. The truth is that I don't have any particular insights on what these events really mean in the universe. Since all this went down with Matt and Jim, I too have lost two of the people closest to me. I would love to believe that they are "looking down on me," watching, guiding, and most times proud of what I'm up to. The bottom line is that none of us really know. It's all just hope and faith. If Jim Maloney is "looking down," all I'm sure of is that he would be really proud of his son! Sometimes when I get to the point where I'm having trouble expressing exactly what I'm thinking someone else does it for me:

Sports Illustrated VAULT ARTICLE:

*"A POINT PROVED GROOMED BY A FATHER
WHO DIED TOO SOON TO SEE HIM PLAY IN
THE NBA, ROCKETS ROOKIE POINT GUARD
MATT MALONEY DID HIS DAD PROUD
AGAINST THE SONICS"*

BY: DAVID LEMING

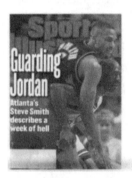

*THIS IS AN ARTICLE FROM
THE* **MAY 19, 1997** *ISSUE*

ORIGINAL LAYOUT

Sometimes it's the little things you remember about a person once he's gone. For the Houston Rockets' rookie point guard, Matt Maloney, it's the videocassette tapes that his father, Jim, a longtime assistant coach at Temple, filled up with basketball games. Jim didn't care if it was a Final Four game or a high school scrimmage airing on a cable access channel. If the game had something he could use to teach his son, Jim wanted it on tape. Soon, tapes were everywhere inside the living room of the Maloneys' house in Haddonfield, N.J., a Philadelphia suburb. They were stacked a dozen high in some places, occupied every inch of space atop the coffee table and were strewn about.

They're all put away now. Jim died of a heart attack on May 3, 1996, at age 62, and the family placed the tapes neatly in boxes and stored them in the basement. But often during this improbable rookie season of his, Maloney has thought about the tapes and his father's many lessons. "The game was his life, and he knew it inside and out," says Maloney. "Now I'm just an extension of what he lived for. This is all a tribute to him. I'm just applying his knowledge when I play."

"Every ounce of Matt is Jimmy," says Temple coach John Chaney, who left a seat on the Owls' bench empty this season in honor of Coach Maloney. "It's almost enough to make you believe in reincarnation."

The connection was never so clear, or as profound, as it was on Sunday. With 36.8 seconds left in overtime, Maloney collected the ball behind the three-point arc, then calmly (as his dad always preached) dribbled to his left to avoid a lunging Hersey Hawkins and sank the game-breaking basket that lifted the Rockets to a 110-106 win and a 3-1 advantage over the Seattle Supersonics in the NBA Western Conference semifinals, which were scheduled to resume on Tuesday in Houston.

Maloney, 25, the youngest Houston starter this season by eight years, matched his career-high of 26 points on 8-of-13 shooting from three-point range. After averaging just 9.4 points during the regular season, Maloney has made the Sonics pay dearly for their double-teaming of Hakeem Olajuwon. Maloney scored 17 points in the Rockets' 112-102 win in the series opener and 19in a 97-93 win at Seattle's Key Arena last Friday. And after Sunday's performance he was shooting .526 (30 of 57) from beyond the arc in the postseason.

So on a team packed with aging stars like Charles Barkley, Clyde Drexler and Olajuwon, the child with the legendary father may be leading the Rockets to the NBA Finals. "In terms of being a warrior on the court," says Houston coach Rudy Tomjanovich, "he's exactly like the rest of 'me."

Maloney's father toughened him as a teenager by including him in Temple practices and scrimmages. Matt attended Vanderbilt on a basketball scholarship in 1990-91, but he grew homesick and transferred to Camden County (N.J.) Community College in the fall. The following year he enrolled at Penn, where he broke all the school's three-point records and earned 1994-95 Ivy League Player of the Year honors. When he wasn't selected in the NBA draft, Maloney spent a year with the Grand Rapids [Mich.] Mackers of the CBA, working on his foot speed and on the art of breaking down defenses by—you guessed it—studying more videotape.

The last time his father watched him play, during the CBA play-offs in March '96, Jim returned home as happy as anyone had ever seen him. "He told us all, 'Matt's ready. He's ready to make it to the league.'" says Matt's brother Paul, a medical researcher in Palo Alto, Calif., who attended Sunday's game. "Dad knew before he died that Matt would make it."

Maloney might never have made it off the Rockets' bench, though, if Brent Price hadn't broken his left elbow in the preseason—and if Barkley and Drexler had not approached Tomjanovich on the team plane shortly afterward, asking that Maloney be given a chance to run the team. He responded by becoming the only rookie to start every game in the NBA this season and by leading all first-year players with a .404 shooting percentage from three-point range (minimum 82 made). "Every time I tell that story I get goose bumps," says Tom-janovich. "I love that kind of interaction and that kind of trust and leadership because it's extremely rare, yet you have to have that to be a winning team. The guys just said Matt was ready and, ever since, it's been like watching a little brother coming out and finally being able to keep up with his older brothers."

If Maloney had yet to pay back Sir Charles before the weekend, he settled his accounts on Sunday. Barkley, busy all game long bullying the Sonics' mascot and yelling at fans—"You're a good goddamn rea-son not to have cloning," he told one heckler—nearly blew the game when he missed two free throws that could have put Houston up by five points with 11 seconds to play in regulation. Thereupon, Hawkins drained a three from deep left to tie the game 98-98. Seattle rode that momentum to a 106-105 lead in the extra period before Maloney's eighth three-pointer nearly snapped the net inside out.

After a pair of free throws by Rockets forward Mario Elie with 3.2 seconds left put the game safely out of reach, Maloney sat on the Houston bench pumping his fist in a moment of solitary triumph. But one got the feeling, even then, that he wasn't entirely alone.

I have said it many times and strongly believe that I have been as fortunate as anybody I have ever met! I've worked my ass off but I was also exposed to opportunities that others did not get the chance to capitalize on. It's worth repeating that, of the more than 170 players I've represented over 33 years in a really cutthroat business, there have been only 2 that I didn't personally like. You know guys that I didn't look forward to seeing or going to dinner with or have at my home! That's pretty extraordinary! Obviously you can't have 168 "favorites" but Matt was and is at the upper level of that group. It wasn't just his story. He was simply a pleasure to represent, like 99% of "my guys."

I try to stay in touch and I'm always happy to hear from my former clients. I don't do as good a job of communicating as I should but neither do they. We have all moved on with family and career obligations but the bond is always there. There isn't a week that goes by that I don't hear from at least one of them and now through social media I actually get to see them and their families grow!

You can categorize people in many different ways. Most times my players were "good guys" and sometimes they were different. Different isn't necessarily bad either. Different can be interesting, fun, and sometimes quite the ride!

Lloyd Daniels was DIFFERENT!!

CHAPTER TEN

PRODIGY

Recruiting isn't all-bad!!

Coming from me, that might seem a little strange. I'm not talking about the seedy stuff. I'm referring to the actual process involved. You get to meet new people. People you wouldn't ordinarily get to interact with. In my business, it's the players and many times their families and coaches that become a major part of the recruiting process.

Having represented over 200 professional athletes, I would estimate that this would have enabled me to meet 1,000 people that I otherwise would not have had the chance to. 800 or so were a pleasure to meet and talk with. I like people and normally when you recruit a player you sit down with him and his family at a restaurant or in their home and just talk. I like that. A story here another one there and maybe I have a shot!

That scenario was accurate even in a cutthroat business like mine up until about ten years ago. Today, I can tell three minutes into a meeting whether or not the people I am sitting across from have ever signed with an agent before I walked through the door. It has always puzzled me as to why they even agree to these meetings. Sometimes,

I think it's merely to appease a coach they played for. Many coaches who don't know me tell me I can meet with a player I've shown interest in once the season is over. This is done because it keeps agents away from distracting his player during the time the coach is generally concerned with, the basketball season.

The problem is that I am probably one of three agents, who will honor this request. There are another 50 or so that won't and another 100 that will bypass the coach completely. It's that damn "coach" part of my background that screws me every time. So before I walk in, I'm OUT!

I'll never forget my initial introduction to the then coach at Michigan State, Jud Heathcote. I was interested in talking with his center, Kevin Willis but I didn't know Jud at the time. My best friend, George Irvine, knew Jud and called him to give me an introduction:

KG: Coach, this is Keith Glass.

JUD: Who???!!!

KG: Keith Glass, I think George Irvine called about me.

JUD: Oh yeah, George is a great guy. You want to talk to Kevin Willis right?!

KG: Yes I do.

JUD: Well, Kevin and I have been invited to participate in the Aloha Classic in Hawaii in early April. Come out and you can talk with Kevin there.

KG: Coach I appreciate that but this is November and by April Kevin will probably be signed already.

JUD: Well he'll be signed then!! CLICK! (That's the sound of Jud hanging up)

I did it Jud's way and met with Jud and Kevin Willis in Hawaii that April. I didn't sign Kevin Willis. He was long gone but that abrupt phone call led to a 30-plus year friendship with Jud that I wouldn't trade for representing Kevin Willis or anyone else.

If you weren't already aware, I am writing this in 2017-18. The recent College Basketball/FBI scandal really tells you all you need to know about how recruiting truly is conducted. Although recruiting athletes has never been easy and never been 100% clean, sometimes you just get lucky.

I don't specifically remember why Lloyd Daniels came in to my life but I do remember his recruitment. It consisted of an incoming phone call from Lloyd during the 1994-95 season:

LLOYD: Keith Glass?! I hear you're the man!!!

Obviously, he had spoken with a person who had known me or was delusional and needed help. Either way, I agreed to meet Lloyd and he showed up in my office the following day. You see recruiting is really hard!

This began a relationship that has lasted until the present day. Not always smooth sailing but always interesting. We've had numerous adventures together both in the NBA and in Europe. When Lloyd first arrived at my office, he had just been released from two NBA teams in a short period of time. He was in a down moment in his playing career. Compared to what he had already been through in real life, being released by an NBA team was nothing but an inconvenience. The mere fact that he played at all in the NBA was borderline miraculous.

When I sit down to write these stories, I am very mindful of the fact that while I give background information on the characters depicted in these pages, I try and stick to my personal involvement with them. Lloyd's stories of what happened to him before he met me are HIS stories not mine. As such, all I will do here is repeat what is common knowledge and then deal with my personal relationship with him and discuss those instances in which I was actually involved.

Lloyd's history is fairly well known, at least in basketball circles. There have been several books devoted to his upbringing and events in his life. There is even a recent documentary produced by Carmelo Anthony, which depicts some of those moments in Lloyd's life. It's not like I'm unveiling some deep dark secrets here. I appear several times in that documentary and I believe I was voted "Best Looking Basketball Agent in a documentary for 2016." Who even knew they had that category!

If it's possible to be a "basketball prodigy," then Lloyd Daniels was it! It was obvious to anyone who watched him at an early age that they were witnessing something very special. After seeing the 6'8" high school sophomore play every position on the floor, NCAA championship coach and future Hall of Famer Jerry Tarkanian remarked:

> *"When they write the history of great guards to ever play basketball they will talk about Oscar Robertson, Jerry West, Magic Johnson and Lloyd Daniels"*

That is pretty heady stuff for a fifteen-year-old. It should have been a great place to start. Unfortunately, that is not where Lloyd Daniels "started." He started fifteen years earlier in Brooklyn, New York, and THAT would define who he was more than his athletic gifts. When I looked at Lloyd, I saw and see a guy born in almost the same exact place that I was, some years before, near Foster Park in Brooklyn. But our paths became very different.

My parents moved eleven miles away to Lynbrook on Long Island. Lloyd's didn't. Think of it Brook-lyn to Lyn-brook. It wasn't just the order of those letters that changed things for me. Those 11 miles may as well have been 11,000, when you consider the environment and therefore the opportunities that I had that Lloyd didn't.

Tarkanian's comments should have been an incentive for Lloyd to better his situation. Instead, it unintentionally contributed to the subsequent over-the-top adulation and recruitment that placed Lloyd in the precarious spots he ended up in.

Lloyds' upbringing was to be kind less than ideal. He grew up without much or any parental supervision. His mother had passed when Lloyd was three. When someone asked Lloyd in 1991 who the major influences where in his life, he simply said: "Myself." His grandmother was influential throughout his childhood but Lloyd was left to his own devices at a very early age. As I've indicated earlier, the details of that part of his life are Lloyd's story to tell, not mine.

What is common knowledge is that Lloyd attended four high schools in three different states and never graduated from any of them. In Lloyd's own words in a Sports Illustrated article from 1991, you can get a brief glimpse into those times:

> *"Any kid like me who doesn't go to school can't read.*
> *How are you going to learn if you aren't there? I*
> *wasn't there. I was one of those kids who just got*
> *passed through. It's bad. People keep telling you*
> *you're a helluva ballplayer and kiss your butt. Then*
> *they don't teach you nothing. But I'm no dummy."*

Now THAT I can vouch for! I'm almost an expert on that! Lloyd happens to be really bright. Not from a "book smart" vantage point but take it from me, he has a high intellect and is as "street smart" as anyone I've ever dealt with. He also can charm the skin off a snake and he knows it. This combination is not always beneficial, especially when you use them as aides in an addiction rather than qualities to employ on your road to success.

By 1986, Lloyd Daniels and Marcus Liberty of Chicago were the two best high school players in the country. How I ended up representing both of them I will never quite understand. Marcus did not have the troubled background that Lloyd did and signed a scholarship to attend the University of Illinois. Lloyd having taken a totally different approach to school and life had to take a totally different approach to his future. That's the way it works.

Even the way Lloyd ultimately ended up at Mount San Antonio Junior College, which for some reason is located in Walnut, California, is unusual. A college assistant coach, Mark Warkentien, became Lloyd's legal guardian after high school. In what I'm certain was a total coincidence, Mark Warkentien was an assistant at UNLV, where just as coincidentally the Head Coach was Jerry Tarkanian. That is the same Jerry Tarkanian, who had initiated a lot of the hype that helped turn Lloyd into a "legend."

Tarkanian's nickname was "Tark the Shark" and to my knowledge this was not due to any particular seafaring ability! So in 1987 Jerry Tarkanian, we can assume with the aid of Lloyd's new legal guardian, arranged for Lloyd to be enrolled at the University of Nevada Las Vegas (UNLV). It would be difficult to think of a worse place for Lloyd Daniels to go to alter the trajectory of his life but Tark never forgot that fifteen-year-old he watched years earlier. It turned out that neither Tark nor Lloyd would ever forget each other.

In the interest of full disclosure, my Dad and I had many interactions with Tark and were very fond of him. He was a character all the way through and he wasn't afraid of a good fight. You can ask the NCAA about that one. My father, in particular, really enjoyed his company. Tark reminded him of many of the people he had grown up with back in New York.

We entered Tark's world in an unusual way. I was in Italy in a town called Perugia. This was at the very beginning of my own journey in to sports representation. This was sometime in the early 1980's. I was there watching a game that one of my players was playing in. My guy was playing against the team from Rome. After the game, as is the norm in Europe, both teams had dinner together in a local ristorante. I was invited and really enjoyed myself. These dinners are a total departure from life in the NBA where the player's normally go their separate ways after games.

The meal ended but not until around two in the morning. It was then that I realized I had no hotel, no car, and about $30 in my pocket. This was pre-mobile phones and the streets were empty. Just as I was about to panic I realized I was from New York and therefore would figure something out. Seemingly out of nowhere a bus emerged around the corner of the winding streets of Perugia. It was the Rome team's bus and they were leaving at that moment. I had just met the coach from Rome at dinner and he asked me where I was headed. I asked him the same question and when he said Rome I said "ME TOO" even though I was trying to get to Milan.

I went to the back of the bus, sat down, and across the aisle from me was one of Rome's American players, Jackie Robinson. No not that Jackie Robinson! This Jackie Robinson was from UNLV and was part of the famous "Hard Way Eight." Tark played eight guys exclusively and being that there were quite a few pairs of dice in Las Vegas, the nickname fit and stuck. They were his first real stars during his time at UNLV. To this day, the "Hard Way Eight" are beloved in Las Vegas.

The trip to Rome was two hours long. When I got off the bus, I had a signed contract to represent Jackie Robinson! Jackie became one of our favorite clients ever and his signing led me to sign other

UNLV players including Robert Smith, Moses Scurry, and the late Glen Gondrezick, among others. This series of events led to our relationship with Tark. My Dad's favorite story about Tark was when we were in Vegas and Tark invited us to dinner:

> **TARK**: Hey Joe, I'm taking you and Keith to dinner. I'm comped!
>
> **DAD**: Which casino are you comped at?!
>
> **TARK**: ALL of 'em!!

Tark owned Las Vegas in those days! It was said, and it was no exaggeration, that during Tark's heyday in Vegas, tickets to a UNLV basketball game were harder to get than a ticket to see Frank Sinatra. For you youngsters, Sinatra was pretty big.

Lloyd enrolled at UNLV but never played for Tark. Before the season even began, Lloyd was busted at a Las Vegas crack house. The arrest was videotaped by the police, at least the part that showed them putting Lloyd in a police car and his subsequent appearance in court. I had not met Lloyd at that time but I do recall feeling awfully bad for him. I had heard all the accolades as well the details of his issues but you could feel his shame and desperation right through the TV. But these issues had been there for all to see, unless for whatever reason you didn't want to see. This was no shock to anyone.

Alcohol and drug abuse ultimately led him to a street corner in Queens, New York on May 12, 1989. I was about to label this incident a "drug deal gone wrong" but don't all drug deals start and end wrong?!

Lloyd was staying with his Grandma. According to newspaper accounts Lloyd made a "clerical error" while purchasing crack cocaine.

Seems he gave the drug dealer two 5's instead of two 10's. Apparently, drug dealers don't like that. Being in the public eye as well as being 6'8," everybody knew Lloyd Daniels and where he was staying. They confronted him and shot him three times. He basically was left for dead in the street. He lost seven pints of blood. I hear we only get ten. He was almost gone and he told me as much. He told me that he saw a white light and thought he was dead but he could still hear the doctors talking as they were working on him, trying to bring him back.

DANIELS CRITICAL AFTER SHOOTING
By The Associated Press
Published: May 12, 1989

Lloyd Daniels, a star high school basketball player whose playing career stalled because of drug and alcohol problems, was in critical but stable condition in a Queens hospital after being shot three times yesterday, the police said.

At about 2:10 a.m., Daniels was shot by two men outside his home in South Jamaica "during a possible drug-related dispute," said Detective Vincent Jones, a police spokesman. He underwent surgery at Mary Immaculate Hospital.

Daniels, 22 years old, attended four high schools without graduating. He later attended the University of Nevada-Las Vegas, but was dismissed after being arrested in February 1987 on charges he tried to buy cocaine from an undercover police officer. Daniels pleaded guilty to a misdemeanor and entered a drug program.

He turned pro, but was suspended from the Continental Basketball Association for unspecified reasons. He was later dismissed from the

New Zealand Basketball Federation for missing practice and excessive drinking, his coach said.

(http://www.nytimes.com/1989/05/12/sports/daniels-critical-after-shooting.html)

He managed to survive the shooting and somehow began an unproductive journey of attempting to come back from what had almost killed him. There were various stops including several stints in minor league basketball. 12 in all. The names of these teams and cities tell you a lot about not only Lloyd's travel schedule but his desperation to realize all that potential.

There was the Topeka Sizzler's, the Miami Tropics, the Quad City Thunder, the Greensboro City Gators, the Fort Wayne Fury, the Idaho Stampede, the Sioux Falls Skyforce, the Bayrunners, the Trenton Shooting Stars, the Strong Island Sound (I love that one), the Tampa Bay T-Dawgs, and the Long Island Surf, who had great T-shirts! These stops were not back-to-back but rather over the course of his entire playing days but you get the point.

By 1990 or so, at the ripe "old" age of 23 Lloyd Daniels, the "basketball prodigy" was washed up! All the hype, all the talk of him being a "legend" in New York City was now another of many similar cautionary tales. Lloyd would join the list of all the other "playground legends," who never made it to the NBA. Player's like: Richard "Pee Wee" Kirkland, who is famous or maybe infamous for turning down an NBA contract because it would have been a pay-cut from his regular job of dealing drugs. Joe Hammond, "Jumpin" Jackie Jackson, "Fly" Williams, and Earl "The Goat" Manigault who rumor had it not only grabbed silver dollars off the top of backboards but left change with the other hand!

Lloyd never totally gave up on basketball even though the basketball world had clearly given up on him. In 1992, three years after he was left for dead on that street in Queens, Lloyds' hometown New York Knicks offered to bring him in for a look. They quickly sent him packing and a scout for the Knicks actually told the new head coach of the San Antonio Spurs:

"Lloyd can't play!"

Normally that is not considered a ringing endorsement for an NBA prospect. But the new head coach of the San Antonio Spurs was Jerry Tarkanian!

I truly believe that sometimes the difference between an NBA player and a guy who pays for his own ticket to watch an NBA game is two things:

1. The opportunity to show what you can do and;
2. Someone in a power position has to truly believe in you in order for you to get that opportunity.

Lloyd got both of those from Tark. Let's really understand how remarkable that relationship was. Remember that when Lloyd got busted in Las Vegas it caused Tark tremendous problems. Problems with the NCAA that started when there were allegations that Lloyd had received cash and a car. Marty Blake, the NBA's head scout at the time:

"Lloyd Daniels was the biggest mistake Tarkanian
ever made."

Tark himself, when asked about Lloyd said:

"He's been nothing but a problem for me, but he's not malicious. He has great talent, he's very sweet, and he's a good person."

The San Antonio Spurs signed Lloyd Daniels just before the 1992-93 season. In his FIRST Preseason game, Lloyd scored 30 points. In his 2nd game of the regular season, his stat line was:

26 points…. 8 rebounds…. 6 assists…. 3 steals & 3 blocked shots.

I hope we all can agree on how incredible that is. It's hard enough to play in the NBA, which despite what may seem like criticisms of the league in these pages, clearly has the best athletes in the World! To perform like that after what Lloyd had put himself through was almost unbelievable. I don't think I could put up those numbers if they locked me in the gym by myself.

Like many points in Lloyd's life, achieving success wasn't the problem. Sustaining it was a whole different story. It was totally analogous to his issues off the court. He always understood how he wanted to conduct himself but as we see with so many others once you get into that lifestyle "wanting to" and "being able to" are completely different mindsets.

Lloyd had a really solid rookie season as he averaged 9.1 points per game. The Spurs brought him back for a second season but when Tark was fired during that second year they may as well have released Lloyd with him. Lloyd was waived after the 1994 season. He was signed by the Philadelphia 76ers but lasted only five games before being waived there as well. For those five games, he scored a total of 23 points. After not getting another opportunity, Lloyd Daniels ended up sitting across from me in my office in Red Bank, New Jersey.

I admit to agreeing to the meeting in large part out of curiosity. Being from New York, I had heard all the stories. I wanted to see for myself what this guy was all about. I didn't really know if I could even help him. I did know that he was there at least in part because of my reputation for "reclamation projects" or under-appreciated players.

We talked for over two hours! By the time he left, my attitude went from curiosity to hoping he would sign with me. That Lloyd Daniels charm had worked and I'm not that easy. There was no BS from him. He told me openly about his issues and we ultimately decided that we were the right fit for each other going forward.

With Tark no longer employed in the league, we had lost Lloyd's "guardian angel." At least Lloyd had done some things while he was with the Spurs that could help us now. I knew that if we both put in the work we could get some interest. That interest finally came in February of that same season. We agreed to sign with the Los Angeles Lakers.

Lloyd played his first game for the Lakers on February 22, 1995 and he spent the rest of the season with them. In one game, Lloyd took over a tight game and scored 20 points in the 2nd HALF to lead the Lakers to a win. He started the next 14 games. On March 13th, he had 22 points in 32 minutes. In 25 games with the Lakers, he averaged 7.4 points per game. If I had him doing that in 2018 those numbers would equate to around $11 million per year.

What I also understood was that Lloyd's play in both San Antonio and more recently in LA had made him an attractive candidate for Europe. They love former NBA players and they love a good story to go with it. Lloyd had both! The main issue that we discussed in detail was that newspaper articles and being characterized as a "legend" doesn't pay too well. You need an actual job to go with it. To put it more bluntly, Lloyd was not independently wealthy. One of the top teams in Europe at the time, Scavolini Pesaro was interested in providing that job. I began negotiating a contract with Pesaro. When the Pesaro offer climbed to 600,000 euros, Lloyd and I found ourselves in the business class compartment of Alitalia Airlines on our way to discuss the final details of an agreement.

Pesaro is a beautiful smaller town on the east coast of Italy. It sits on the Adriatic Sea just across from Croatia. They also historically were one of the biggest teams in Italy and in the Euroleague. An offer from Pesaro was something to consider strongly especially in light of the fact that we did not have interest from an NBA team. At least not one who would guarantee him a salary. The 600,000 euros that was on the table was guaranteed. When you add in the additional tax benefits and other perks that come with a European offer, a 600,000 euros contract is worth north of $1,000,000 to an American player.

Lloyd and I had a wonderful trip across the Atlantic (business class will do that to you). We got a chance to really talk about a multitude of things. The one thing that struck me and I remember distinctly was my asking him:

> **KG**: Lloyd, how good are you now compared to before you got shot?!

He didn't answer quickly. He thought it through very seriously:

> **LLOYD**: About 60%.

It hit me that I was talking to a guy who had played the season before in the NBA, the highest level of basketball there is and he was only at 60% of what he formerly was.

> **KG**: Why only 60?

LLOYD: Glass, back then I could HOP! (Translation: JUMP)

We landed in Bologna, which was about 90 minutes from Pesaro. A representative from the team picked us up and off we went for Pesaro. While it is a beautiful city, Pesaro is not a large place. The drive was uneventful and unless you've driven in Europe you have no idea how fast you can get where you're going if there's no traffic issues. Everything was fine until we got within range of our hotel.

As we approached the hotel, we got stuck in the middle of huge traffic jam, which was totally out of place for a town of Pesaro's size. We were literally stopped dead in traffic and there were thousands of people milling about. I commented to our driver that there must be a festival of some kind and was wondering if there was another way to get us maybe to the back of our hotel. He laughed at us:

DRIVER: They are here for you!

Let's just say that I had been to Pesaro several times before and never had any trouble with crowds waiting to see me. Obviously they were there to get a glimpse of my travel companion. In my many subsequent trips overseas, I still haven't seen anything close to that scene. Lloyd's reaction was to smile and typically say:

LLOYD: Glass, I'm larger than life!

We were checked in by another member of the Club and were shown to our rooms. Both rooms overlooked the Adriatic Sea and it was quite the sight for two transplanted guys born in Brooklyn. We were also each given a bag full of Pesaro basketball gear—t-shirts, shorts sweats, etc. Here we were about to sign for a good sum of money, but we were clearly most excited about the treasures we discovered in those bags. I immediately thought of what I could have done trading this swag back in Camp Keeyumah 25 years earlier. These thoughts were drowned out from a voice down the hall:

> **LLOYD**: Glass, come on down here! Let's see if we can work a trade!

> **KG**: You want to negotiate with ME?!

> **LLOYD**: I'll take my chances!

After one of my most difficult negotiations, we settled on two of my t-shirts for one of his sweatshirts. But before we could seal the deal, Lloyd wanted to try on my shirts to make sure they fit him. He took off his shirt to try on his prospective acquisitions. There was no way not to notice what was clearly the result of the shooting. There was a half-inch thick scar that began in the middle of his chest, continued all the way around to his midsection and then wrapped around to his back. I was startled and Lloyd naturally took notice:

> **LLOYD**: Glass, you never saw this before?! This really freaks white people out!!!

> **KG**: Just white people?!

> **LLOYD**: Black people have seen this shit before!

He then almost with a strange sense of pride proceeded to show me the bullet that was still lodged in his neck, pointing to a dark bulge under his skin. The doctors were afraid to remove that one since it might kill him being dangerously close to a major vessel. After witnessing the chest scene, the bullet in the neck was not a problem for me. I guess you can get used to seeing just about anything!

Shirts and shorts aside, the purpose of the trip was to finalize our contract. We accomplished that the next day. I took my sweatshirt from the Lloyd negotiations and went home. There clearly were some bumps in the road during Lloyd's stay in Pesaro but Lloyd managed to finish the season and was beloved in that City by the time he left. In fact, all these years later, Pesaro was the setting for one of the premieres of the documentary on Lloyd. This would unfortunately not always be the case with other stops we made, specifically the one in Greece a few years later. That one ended up with a car accident and Lloyd leaving the car and Greece the same night!

As usual not only with Lloyd but with most players that I have represented over the years, there is an assessment of what that particular guy's market is after each season. Overall, we had a very positive experience in Italy. That helped. We also had put up some good moments in the NBA. Given those two factors I had more juice than I usually did.

Lloyd and I had several talks concerning his future and since he had moved 15 minutes away from my family and I on the Jersey Shore, we got to spend a lot of time together. One of those days found me hosting Lloyd, his family and another client Marty Conlon at my house for a bar-b-que. It was during these types of settings that we really got to see Lloyd's true nature and personality.

People have, from afar, naturally been critical of him due to his failings but I view Lloyd as someone who did the best he could. I often think back on a conversation I had with Lloyd when he was stuck in the old CBA, the minor league system. I have probably had 40 players play in the minors and not one of them didn't understandably bitch about some aspect of it. In those leagues, players had ten-hour van rides before games, cheap hotels or motels, etc. It's really not the glamorous lifestyle that we associate with professional athletes. But when I spoke with Lloyd:

> **KG**: It's tough down there isn't it?!

> **LLOYD**: Glass it's not bad man. They give us money to eat and I've got a roof!

To me that meant that he didn't always have those "amenities."

Although I didn't respect many of the choices he made in his life I always got the sense that he was trying to do better for himself and his family. He would fail but he would always try. Coming from where he started, he didn't do too badly.

There were times when he flat-out lied to me but he was never a phony. That differs from many of the con artists I have to deal with in this business. Guys who look you in the eye and try to assume the pose of integrity. These are guys who think they're slick but you can tell they're full of it even as they're talking to you. Lloyd would BS me but at least he did it in a way that I wouldn't realize it until a little later. All you could do in those moments when you realized you'd been "had" was shake your head. He got me. I respect that. I think back to a conversation I had with Bob Ferry, the ex-player and General Manager of Washington. We were at the pool in Hawaii during a tournament and I asked him for his opinion of a rookie I had just signed. Apparently Bob didn't think much of him:

> **BOB**: Keith, can I call you when we get back to the mainland?! I consider you a friend and I don't like to lie to my friend's faces!

That's respectful!

Although it was not done in a malicious way, Lloyd always loved to start some trouble or at least make an existing issue just a little worse. If a situation was diffusing itself, that was no fun for Lloyd. He seemed to thrive when there was tension, like when a game was on the line.

Right around the time of that bar-b-que I had back surgery. One of my several ex-wives celebrated that festive occasion by purchasing a yellow Labrador puppy while I was hospitalized. I guess that's a normal reaction. Let's help my husband through the surgery and recovery or buy a dog while he's under anesthesia! Tough one!

Naturally just having had back surgery I was of no use in training Casey, who was actually already named by the time I came home. As such Casey began acting…well like a dog! He was completely out of control and I actually found three of my kids sitting on the kitchen island with Casey trying to bite their feet. Terrorizing OUR children was fine but when Casey starting hunting our next-door neighbor's kids it was time for him to go. While all of my children were upset with this especially Tyler and Maggie, Tyler held a particular grudge and it was centered squarely on me.

He was ten or so at the time and we really didn't speak much for about a week. At the time of the bar-b-que things were finally thawing out. Even though Ty was only ten, Lloyd and Ty had developed a special bond. Tyler didn't look up to Lloyd like some big time NBA player. Tyler just loved Lloyd.

They would talk, just the two of them for an hour at a clip. They talked about everything. Even though, I was painfully aware of Lloyd's errors in judgment and life choices, as a father I never worried about this friendship. I always trusted Lloyd when it came to interacting with my kids and still do but that didn't mean Lloyd wouldn't try and do a little instigating along the way. Lloyd and Tyler had been in my library at the house and when Lloyd heard me passing by:

LLOYD: Dad gave your DOG away Ty??!! That ain't right!!

That added another week to the "freeze."

Being that our relationship had somehow survived the bar-b-que, Lloyd and I now had to decide on the next step of his journey for the 1996-97 season. In spite of some interesting offers from overseas, we decided that this was his last real opportunity to get back to the NBA. We first went to Sacramento. That didn't go well. He was there for five undistinguished games.

While we were anticipating a fairly long wait to get another chance at the NBA, we caught a break. Only three weeks after the Sacramento release, John Calipari, whom I had been acquainted with for some time, called me to talk about Lloyd. John had just signed a very lucrative contract with the New Jersey Nets to become their head coach. In fact, upon that signing when I called to congratulate him he answered the phone by saying:

"Keith, is this a great country or what!?"

Lloyd signed with the Nets and was playing for them by Christmas. This stop was actually terrific for my kids and me since we could go to his games just up the New Jersey Turnpike, Exit #16 to be exact. Lloyd had his moments, probably more moments than John did that season but overall he didn't set the world on fire in New Jersey. He played in 17 games for the Nets and was released again.

This is a nice spot for some basketball analysis from a guy who knows a bit about it. In fact, it has often amused me when I speak to a few NBA and overseas coaches, general managers and scouts. They give me their "view from the mount" regarding their expert opinions of the game in general and my player's place in it! While most of these people in decision-making positions work really hard and do a good job, I also understand that most of them look at me as an agent. What does an agent know about THEIR game? I've had to accept this attitude as part of my job and hold my tongue quite often. I've spent 16 years as the head coach in high schools, in addition to my two years at UCLA. I know a bit about the game. It's frustrating that I can't really give my true opinions for fear that something I might disagree with could adversely affect one of my clients. It's been an interesting "dance" and I've pulled it off in spite of the fact that I'm not a very good dancer.

All that being said when I stepped back and looked at Lloyd objectively and solely from a basketball perspective, I understood why he kept getting released. While he was gifted and could have controlled games almost by himself that was not what he was called on to do. At this point in his career he was looked upon as a "role player." A guy who could score the ball and pass it. He was never a good defender although he was so smart that he always covered his ass defensively. He was asked to come off the bench for 15 minutes or so and give the team a little juice.

Outside of that first season with Tark and San Antonio, that was not his thing. If you look at his numbers in Philadelphia and LA and Sacramento and New Jersey, he never shot a great percentage either. If you couple this with his defensive flaws it equates with being released. This was always the case except for our next chance, which came via the Toronto Raptors. Toronto was our last NBA stop and it is a story, which details and illuminates just how nutty the NBA can be.

After Lloyd was waived by New Jersey, we did indeed get our expected long wait to return to action. The 1997-98 season had begun without Lloyd Daniels. Therefore, we decided that since Lloyd needed to play rather than sit home, we returned to the minor leagues. He needed to stay in shape and also remind people that he was still around and kicking. So off Lloyd went to the Fort Wayne Fury to play and wait out a possible return to the NBA.

This time, the wait took us in to early January. I got a call from Isiah Thomas, who was running the Toronto Raptors. Over the years, Isiah and I had some unusual dealings together (read *Taking Shots*) and this would become another one.

Isiah and I agreed to sign Lloyd to a "10-day contract." A "10-day" is just what it sounds like. It is an NBA contract that is only guaranteed for 10 days. That puts an enormous amount of pressure on the player signing it because any misstep or bad game or even a bad practice could be the end. The player is guaranteed 10 days of a prorated salary and that's all. Normally a player on a "10-day" may get a few minutes if the game is a blowout in either direction. They usually have been brought up to the league due to an injury. It's a fairly temporary gig.

Lloyd had played for Fort Wayne the night before we signed with Toronto. Isiah wanted Lloyd to suit up that same night against the Cavs in Cleveland. When you're signing a "10-day" out of Fort Wayne you don't argue. I knew Lloyd wouldn't play much anyway. Typically, an NBA coach will at least want a new player to have a practice or two before putting him in to an NBA game.

Lloyd played 23 minutes that night for Toronto. He scored 21 points and Toronto won. A remarkable debut to say the least. I have probably signed players to fifty "10-day" contracts in my 30 plus years but never had anyone do what Lloyd did that night. The next game he didn't have the same success but he did play 30 minutes, which is a lot. So Lloyd had played 53 minutes in two games on a "10-day" contract and we were feeling pretty good about our chances at signing for the remainder of the season. Things abruptly changed. Specifically, his minutes started changing. For the next four games, he played a total of 29 minutes. I confess that I began to worry that Lloyd had done something off the court to screw this situation up. It wouldn't' have been the first time. I confronted him and he said that everything was fine. No run-ins, no attitude, no lateness, no nothing!

Isiah and I had spoken after Lloyd's first game and everything was terrific. Eventually our "10-day" was up and in spite of the reduction in minutes, I assumed that Isiah would call to extend Lloyd for the rest of the year. They had seen what he was capable of in pressure circumstances. Isiah did indeed call:

ISIAH: Keith, Lloyd's been great! He's done everything we asked and more. He's also been a model citizen. But we're not keeping him!

KG: Huh?! (I've always had a way with words) You've got to be kidding!

ISIAH: I'm not kidding.

KG: Well you've got to explain this one to me. Lloyd's played well.

ISIAH: No doubt. He's been terrific but the problem is that we drafted a kid who is 19 years old and right now Lloyd is better than him! Lloyd's really good, but this kid is gonna be GREAT!! As long as Lloyd is here our coaches won't play the kid and I can't have that. If we get rid of Lloyd my coaches won't have a choice.

This was how Tracy McGrady and all his potential essentially ended Lloyd's NBA career. It's not like Isiah was wrong either. McGrady would go on to earn over $100,000,000 for his career and was inducted into the basketball Hall of Fame in 2017.

Lloyd and I ended up in Istanbul. Not just Istanbul either. His stops after Toronto were with such teams as Polluelos de Aibonito in Puerto Rico, Galatasaray in Turkey, AEK in Greece, Panteras de Miranda in Venezuela, Rida Scafati back in Italy, Ovarense Aerosoles in Portugal, and finally with the Shanghai Sharks in China.

All because he was better than Tracy McGrady!

I was involved with most of those stops. While I'm happy that my relationship with Lloyd has continued to the present time, our agent/player combo stopped in 2000. In my swan song as Lloyd's agent, I organized a special workout for him with NBA teams. I arranged to have the New Jersey Nets host this workout at their practice facility just outside New York City. In order to get the maximum amount of NBA teams and therefore the max exposure for Lloyd, I knew I needed to get someone in there to go against him. Teams don't like one on none!

I arranged for another client of mine, Ibrahim Kutluay from Turkey to be at the workout with Lloyd. "Ibo" was a European star and while he was a terrific shooter he was not in Lloyd's class as an overall player. Thirteen teams agreed to come to watch this workout. "Ibo" shot the hell out it and we actually parlayed that workout into a 2-year guaranteed contact with the then Seattle Supersonics, today's Oklahoma City Thunder!

Lloyd didn't show up!

Jerry Tarkanian died in February 2015. The day after Tark passed, Lloyd was asked for his reaction:

> **LLOYD**: "Tark was a great man…a great man. When everyone else was looking down on me, he was there for me. Not only in basketball, in life. He only wanted to see me do well, off the court, in school. And being a father now with three kids, I appreciate that even more now. He was a great man and he was great to me. It's a sad day."

Lloyd had visited with an ailing Tark about six months before he passed. They had never lost touch. Obviously, there were heartaches and betrayals involved in their complex relationship but without being overly dramatic, from my vantage point, there was a lot of love there also.

The no-show for his workout in New Jersey was the end for me professionally. It's not great for your rep in this business to arrange a special workout and then not have you client show up. I know why he didn't show but like I said at the beginning of this chapter, it is HIS story to tell or not to tell.

Lloyd may not have been the easiest client I've had but he was clearly among the most interesting. Even though you couldn't trust him to always "show up", for some inexplicable reason I always did and still do trust him.

Except at Bar-B-Ques!!

CHAPTER ELEVEN

THE SUN (YUE) ALSO RISES

"Keith, just to let you know, there are so many people who are watching [the results of the NBA draft] tomorrow, including the Chinese government. The biggest TV network, CCTV, will broadcast the news throughout the country. So, please take this seriously. China is watching."

JUNE 27, 2007 EMAIL FROM BEIJING

I'll admit it, some bizarre things have happened to me in my career as a sports lawyer/agent. Phone calls, and emails such as the one above may seem unusual but to me it didn't and doesn't seem bizarre at all. You never really know what an agreement to represent a player will encompass. It is one of the reasons that this business has kept my interest for so long. If you think signing a prospect means that he is the only individual that you will deal with, then you are badly mistaken. There are mothers, fathers, aunts, uncles, high school coaches, AAU coaches, friends, etc., etc. that you sometimes have to deal with as well. In this case specifically, I had to deal with an entire country and its customs!

The email above came the night before the 2007 NBA Draft. Taking into consideration the twelve-hour time difference between New Jersey and Beijing, I actually read it right before I went to sleep. As long as there's no pressure!!

Like most of my stories, the beginnings of this saga originate in an unusual way. Jack Mai, who at the time was an executive with the Sacramento Kings, had been silently watching our efforts on behalf of Quincy Douby during the run-up to the 2006 NBA Draft the year before. (See APPENDIX)

As is my usual practice, I made a tremendous assault on the league on behalf of Quincy. Without exaggeration, there had been 300 to 400 phone calls, which were made to every conceivable employee of NBA teams. Anyone who could possibly have input in the selection process was targeted. Douby was projected as a middle 2nd round draft prospect at the time he signed with us. People had mistakenly assumed that we had pushed Quincy into making a poor decision on entering the NBA Draft at all. I would have to say that we at least had some role in Quincy going 19th in the first round of that draft.

Apparently, our efforts and results were duly noted. Four years later Jack Mai called asking me directly if we had any interest in representing a player named Sun Yue. Jack was involved in the Douby drafting but we had never really had much interaction prior to that. Jack did, however, leave an impression on both Tyler and myself as someone that you could trust! That is not as normal as it should be. He was also very knowledgeable about the league, its players and its future prospects. Most importantly, we had always viewed him as a guy with unusual integrity. If he was approaching us about a prospect I was going to pay attention.

Sun Yue was and still is a 6'9" POINT GUARD from China. He was playing for a team named the Beijing Aoshen Olympians (Aoshen). I assumed, looking at the name of the team that they were playing out of Beijing, China. Aoshen, actually was playing in Los Angeles, California, my old stomping grounds. Sun was playing in the ABA, which was a loosely run minor league. The reason for this geographical anomaly involved a struggle between Aoshen and the Chinese Basketball Association.

The Chinese Basketball Association (CBA) was urging Aoshen to sell the rights to Sun Yue to a more powerful and prestigious team in the CBA. To put it mildly this idea did not go over very well with the ownership of Aoshen. Additionally the owners of the Aoshen Basketball Club were extremely powerful, influential and intelligent men in their own right. Don't take my word for it. Wikipedia describes the owner of Aoshen this way:

> *"....the controversial & mysterious owner, a Chinese real estate tycoon and billionaire named Li Su, often referred to in the Western media as Winston Li...."*

Although I never actually spoke with him throughout this entire episode, the owner was known to me as "Mr. Li." He declined both requests of the Chinese Basketball Association. Instead, he removed his team from the CBA completely and moved them lock, stock, and 6'9" point guard to L.A. Aoshen and Mr. Li eventually went so far as to televise their games back to Beijing. The cost of each telecast was rumored to be around $35,000 per game. Clearly, Mr. Li was not a guy to trifle with.

This entire story sounded a bit bizarre on its face. In other words, it was a perfect situation for me. After checking into Sun Yue's reputation as a player and watching what limited video there was to see of him, I called Jack:

"We're in!"

My cursory research of Sun Yue revealed another interesting fact. We here in the U.S. are very aware of the 7'6" former center for the Houston Rockets, Yao Ming. However, there were two other Chinese players of some renown who were drafted and had played in the NBA prior to Yao. The first NBA player from China was Wang Zhizhi. He was a 7'1" forward who made his original appearance in the league for the Dallas Mavericks in April of 2001. He played a total of 137 games and an additional 16 playoff games. Recently, there were two commemorative stamps issued in his honor back in China. I think the Chinese are into basketball! The second player was Mengke Bateer, who played for the Denver Nuggets, the San Antonio Spurs, and finally with the Toronto Raptors between 2001 and 2004. Bateer was a 6'11" center. He played a grand total of 46 games between those three teams.

On the opposite end of the basketball spectrum, Yao Ming was the first pick in the 2002 NBA draft. At the time of my introduction to Sun Yue, Yao was an NBA All-Star and a national hero in China. His wedding there had 70 guests and 130 security guards. Yao is big in more ways than one.

That made three Chinese born players in the history of the NBA. Another interesting part of my sudden involvement with Sun Yue was that there was a player in this draft class named Yi Jianlian. Yi was also from China and was a seven-footer to boot. He was supposed to be a tremendous prospect, which the entire NBA was already acutely aware of. Friends in the NBA told me he could go as high as third in the June draft. Yi was supposed to be very athletic and a tremendous shooter and was being projected as a small forward or power forward. He was billed as a Dirk Nowitzki type prospect. The relevance of this to me was that after only three total players of Chinese descent had been drafted in the history of the NBA, what were the odds of having two drafted in the same year?

Between these two prospects from China, Sun Yue was more interesting to me despite their disparate reputations. My background has always been to represent the underdog. The guy who most people have overlooked. Certainly the guy without the hype. The guy without the backing. The other aspect of this preference was that I could very rarely successfully sign a top prospect due to the nature of recruiting. If you want details of what I'm referring too, read the accounts of the current FBI basketball probe.

Another facet of this situation which intrigued me dealt with the actual type of player that Sun Yue was. A lot of non-basketball people will try to promote a player by exaggerating his talents. Someone is always trying to sell a big guard as a point guard. That is a very rare commodity. The notion that a 6'9" guy is truly a point guard is difficult to accept. I admit to my own skepticism about Sun Yue being a real point guard. Everyone is the next "Magic" Johnson. There has never been a next Magic Johnson. After getting to watch more of Sun Yue on film I understood that he truly was a 6'9" point guard. "Magic" comparisons aside that is not the norm.

In Sun Yue's case, point guard was actually the only position he had ever played on a basketball court. He had great vision and could really push the ball. He played a much more open American type of game. None of this half-court crap for him. Sun Yue wanted to run.

Because of this style, I was informed that Sun was actually the more popular player of the two Chinese prospects. This was not in terms of marketing but from the fans' perspective. They could relate to and enjoy the way Sun Yue approached the game. This was not another seven-footer who was merely bigger than the others. This guy had the ball in his hands and was flying across the floor.

The logistics of how the two players were going about their respective careers created a difference in the exposure they would receive as well as. This would extend to the backing and promotion they would get from the Chinese Basketball Association. Yi was their "golden boy" who would be promoted constantly. Sun Yue and Aoshen were rebels who had struck out on their own. Sun Yue and the entire Aoshen Basketball Club did not end up in Los Angeles through some massive travel agency screw-up. They went there to make a point and it clearly was an act of defiance.

From my own vantage point, this was a fascinating situation. My initial calls and conversations with NBA people indicated that while they all seemed to have some knowledge of Sun Yue, many of them did not even realize that he was currently residing in the U.S. and competing in the ABA.

Even the process of how I became his agent was a bit strange. I never once spoke with Sun Yue. I became his agent through Aoshen/Mr. Li and thus began an education process for both sides. I became aware of the fact that there were going to be some cultural differences in the way the Chinese approached this business of being someone's agent!

The first departure occurred immediately after I signed the Standard Player Agent Contract (SPAC) with Sun Yue and Aoshen. They asked for my banking information. When I asked them why they needed it, they informed me that they were going to send money immediately into that account. I told them that this is not the way it's done. I am paid a percentage of what I negotiate for a player. Since nothing in that regard had been done, there was no fee owing.

Their response to that statement was a revelation, especially to an NBA agent. Their view was that they would not have me working for them for nothing. In other words, Aoshen realized immediately what the NBA players association (NBPA) and many players in America don't. That is, that an agent who is properly doing his job for his client is working hard long before a contract is actually negotiated.

When people ask me how long did it take me to negotiate one of my larger professional contracts, my stock answer is:

"About 30 minutes"!

Obviously, this is not the case. The actual negotiations may be brief but the process of being an agent is not what you think. If you sit around, smoking cigars and waiting for offers to flood in, you're going to starve. This is true at least for the type of players that I have primarily represented. There have been numerous times when we have gone years without making a dime through a particular client. Many times, in my case, the job has not been negotiating contracts to rather, getting a team to want to negotiate!

The rules that exist between a player and his agent are drafted by the NBPA and are terribly slanted in an inequitable and sometimes damaging way towards the players. Aoshen, from many thousands of miles away, would have none of that inequity. Two days later, $10,000 was deposited in my account after we agreed that Aoshen would hire me as their consultant. (Note to my ex-wives' and their attorneys: I declared the income.)

All of this occurred in November 2006. We, therefore, had six or seven months before the draft in June. This gave us ample time to do what we do; try to get the league interested in drafting one of my relatively under-publicized or in some circles unknown prospects. Fortunately or unfortunately, I've traveled this path many times.

Our first goal was to try and make sure that Sun Yue was invited to two particular camps in order to maximize his exposure. The first was the camp for international players, held every June in Treviso, Italy. Treviso was home to one of the real classy professional teams of Europe: Benetton. I had been representing their point guard from Greece, Nikos Zisis.

We secured the invite to the Treviso camp but it was then that I got my first real glimpse into the previous warnings I received concerning dealing with Aoshen and Mr. Li. They objected to several items mentioned in the camps standard release and participation forms. These forms were very straightforward and were automatically (and gladly) signed by camp invitees for years. I patiently tried to explain to Aoshen that there was no issue here. Mr. Li to say the least was suspicious of signing any papers when it came to Sun Yue.

After two months of wrangling, I still couldn't get them to agree to sign the forms. I even enlisted the help of the woman who ran the camp administratively to try and help with Aoshen. Her name was Jelena Soce and she was as professional a person as I had met. She spoke several languages and worked at that time for both and Benetton and Reebok. She was incredibly patient and very articulate.

Our last attempt to get this seemingly easy issue resolved came when I was physically in Treviso, visiting Nikos Zisis. This was a month before the camp and Jelena and I got on a conference call with the management of Aoshen. Forty-five minutes later and in spite of herculean efforts on Jelena's part, it was determined by Aoshen that Sun Yue would not be allowed to attend the camp. The sole reason being to those innocuous non-issues in registration forms. I knew that this was the wrong move. I also knew that in this business you have to pick your battles and I could sense that there were more battles on the horizon.

Although we were extremely disappointed in that lost opportunity in Treviso our main objective was still ahead of us. Get Sun Yue invited to the NBA pre-draft camp. This was held at the very end of May and today is referred to as the "Combine" and is held in Chicago. In 2007 it was held in Orlando. We got this invitation as well and this one we just accepted on its face. No discussions.

Sun Yue, his coach from China, and an interpreter arrived in Orlando a few days before the camp began in order to get acclimated. Sun had come directly from Beijing and there was naturally some jet lag involved. The trouble began almost immediately after the camp began.

As previously discussed, Sun Yue was the point guard on the Chinese National team and had played that position exclusively his entire life. He had never played anywhere else on a basketball court. The NBA people at the pre-draft combine, in their infinite wisdom, decided to ignore that little bit of history and miraculously converted him into a small forward. This happened either upon his arrival or somewhere over the Pacific.

To put it quite mildly, this did not go over very well with Sun Yue, his coach, Aoshen, Mr. Li, the interpreter, or the country of China as a whole. I spent the bulk of the next four days of the pre-draft camp on the phone with everyone involved convincing them to not leave the camp and return to China.

This battle I won! He stayed and played very well especially for a newly minted small forward. Several NBA teams called me from the gym to say they thought Sun was the best player in the camp. This is always a nice thing to hear about a client. I also started to get a bunch of calls inviting Sun to come to various NBA cities for private pre-draft workouts.

Aoshen had originally told me that Sun Yue and the coach were only allowed to stay in the U.S. until June 8th. He needed to return so he could begin training with the Chinese National Team. As the interest in Sun kept growing, this arbitrary deadline was becoming a problem. Even though Sun Yue was still never mentioned as a draftable player, I was starting to get the sense that this assessment might not be totally accurate. I had been in similar positions before with other players and the ultimate draft results were remarkably different than early predictions.

It was during the first day of this Orlando camp that I actually got the chance to speak with my client. I had been very cautious and borderline paranoid about even asking to speak with Sun Yue. I didn't want to overstep. When I realized we were in a crisis situation that first day in Orlando I knew that I needed to have some direct contact. I called Sun at his hotel and the conversation went something like this:

SUN YUE: Oh, I finally get to speak with my agent! I told another player today that I never spoke to or met my agent! I don't even know what he looks like.

KG: Just tell everyone that your agent is the best-looking one. They'll understand.

SUN YUE: Oh, just like me!

My initial reaction was that I think I'm going to like this kid. My next thought was: Why the hell is he traveling with an interpreter?

After the Orlando camp, we went to work not only scheduling the NBA pre-draft workouts but more importantly building the case for drafting Sun Yue. I was met by resistance anytime I advanced the notion that Sun was legitimately a point guard. The teams thought I was crazy. He was a small forward. After all, they had all just seen him play in Orlando.

I met resistance from the other side of the water as well. This edict from Aoshen, (which I was catching on was really Mr. Li) that Sun Yue could stay only until June 8th was going to seriously complicate my life. I realized however that we could use it to our advantage. I would tell interested teams that we only had a finite number of days for these workouts. Therefore, I could only schedule him in those cities where I was convinced there was a legitimate interest.

Let's understand what these workouts are really all about. The rationale or purpose for these workouts and the way they are approached can vary in importance for each individual prospect and from team to team. They are actually a fairly recent development. They didn't even exist when I began in this business. They are an offshoot of the influx of money available to NBA franchises which affect the number of employees on each team.

Where there used to be maybe five people employed on the basketball side of these franchises that number has since exploded. There has to be something for these folks to do, so let's do some workouts! To be fair, the fact that players' salaries have exploded as well makes evaluating talent a lot more important. A workout for a prospect can give a team an additional opportunity not only to see a player again in the flesh but also to spend some extra time assessing character.

In the case of Sun Yue however, these workouts could prove to be a valuable tool on both sides. Many of the NBA teams had only recently become acquainted with his skills or even his existence. I thought it could only help to expose him to as many teams as possible. Another positive for us was that by meeting Sun it would eliminate any question about his English speaking abilities. Just one less thing.

The very first team expressing an interest in having Sun Yue come in for a workout was the Portland Trail Blazers. (This will have major significance later in this chapter.) They seemed genuinely interested. I informed them of our time constraints. I was honest with them regarding what I considered their geographical problem. A visit to Portland would take Sun out of the mix for several days due to the distance. However, they were adamant and I believed them regarding their interest.

Aoshen/Mr. Li had other ideas. They were borderline obsessed with the notion that Sun Yue should not only be drafted (which in early June was a stretch) but he should be drafted ONLY in the first round! In other words, the top 30 picks. While anything is possible, it was still very unlikely. We would need to have everything fall perfectly into place for that to happen.

To better understand this situation, certain factors need to be pointed out. Portland had the first pick in the entire draft and with that pick, they were going to select Greg Oden, the 7-foot center from Ohio State! They were obliged to do this in spite of the fact that Oden posed a known injury risk. Everyone knew that. It was not a mystery. We all know how that turned out. Kevin Durant was sitting there as well but there were very few people who, before the draft, would have taken Durant over Oden. There are a lot now!! Oden would be habitually injured and never got his career off the ground. Durant is mentioned as a possible top-25 player of All-Time.

That was Portland's only first-round selection. This is normal since initially, every team gets one first rounder. Remember that Aoshen/Mr. Li only wanted Sun Yue drafted in the first round. After the initial shock that Sun was not going to be selected first OVERALL, it dawned on them that Portland couldn't select him in the first round at all. The formula for Aoshen was:

1. Sun Yue has to be a first-round draft choice;
2. Portland doesn't have another first;
3. Portland is no good for Sun Yue!

I saw something different. Even though Aoshen/Mr. Li didn't want to discuss it, Portland had FOUR second-round draft choices. These had been acquired through various trades through the years. If used correctly, this is a valuable asset for any franchise to have. However, teams also don't want to draft four players in the second round because there is usually no room for them on their roster. In Portland's case, it was obvious that coupling these potential picks with Greg Oden would give them five rookies. No team wants to do that. These draft choices are usually packaged together to "move up" in the draft or to acquire draft picks in future drafts. They also on occasion can be sold, and for good money!

A good example of this selling occurred in the 2016 draft. I represent Matt Costello from Michigan State. It turned out that Matt's best chance to be drafted was by the Atlanta Hawks. Matt had worked out for them in the pre-draft period and the Hawks kept in almost constant touch with my youngest son Luke. On Draft night, the Hawks called us several times. They had the 52nd pick in the second round and informed us that they were seriously considering drafting Matt at that pick. In fact, when the draft got to the 51st pick, Atlanta called us again. This time to actually tell us they WERE drafting him.

I couldn't help but notice that when it came time for the 52nd pick, the Atlanta Hawks selected Kay Felder. There had to be a mistake. Maybe they had the wrong picture up on ESPN. Matt looks nothing like Kay Felder. Atlanta called soon after that and explained that Cleveland bought the pick from them for over $2,000,000. I would have done the same thing.

The lesson is that the way the draft looks even on the day of is not necessarily the way it's going to end up. I tried on a multitude of occasions to break this down to Aoshen and Mr. Li. The message I thought was clear. We should not look at Portland the way they were currently constructed draft-wise but rather for the interest they displayed, and for the potential of them making a draft day deal. Portland clearly had the "chips" to be a major player! Unfortunately, as was the case with the Treviso camp a few weeks earlier, the answer came down from Aoshen: Sun Yue would not be allowed to work out for Portland.

The news from China was not all negative. Due to the increased interest that we were experiencing, Aoshen/Mr. Li did agree to not only extend Sun Yue's stay but they would allow him to remain in the U.S. all the way up to the draft on June 28. Overall, Sun would work out for eleven NBA teams—some of them twice. There was another unusual aspect to Sun Yue's travels around the United States. His coach and the interpreter was still present. This entourage traveled with him on every stop for the entire month! NBA teams only pay for the player. Aoshen and Mr. Li were paying the freight for the interpreter and the coach. This team from China was paying quite a sum to ensure that their player got the opportunity to be seen and possibly drafted in the NBA. This was in spite of the fact that very few people thought this was "in the cards." If they accomplished this, they would then lose their best player to the NBA. It's extraordinarily unselfish when you look at it in that way.

Just when it seemed that we had too many obstacles in our journey to the draft, we got another one. This one was friendly fire. The head coach of the Chinese National team was annoyed with the fact that Sun Yue was pursuing his dream of being drafted by the NBA instead of training with the National Team back in China. As a result, he came out with an unsolicited statement, which was carried throughout the media in China and ultimately made its way to the States. In his statement, he basically said that Sun had no business staying in the U.S. for these workouts. Sun was not ready for the NBA and had little or no chance to be drafted anyway.

I dealt with this assault in my usual diplomatic manner. I released a statement, which was translated on Sina.com, the Chinese version of Yahoo. In it, I blasted the National coach and I meant every word of it. I didn't appreciate anyone trying to throw cold water on this kid's dream of being drafted in the NBA, not to mention screwing with my potential commissions. Sun Yue was working his behind off. I truly felt that the Chinese people should have been very proud of the way he was competing as a player and conducting himself as a person. He at least deserved the support of the coach from his own National Team.

This certainly hurt us in our quest. It wasn't fatal but I did have to explain to a few teams in the NBA why Sun's coach would have the opinion that he wasn't really worthy of being drafted and in essence wasn't good enough to play in the NBA. Coaches and management types have a tendency to listen to opinions especially when they come from someone who has personally coached a prospect.

It was interesting that this same coach said nothing about Yi's absence from those same National Team's workouts. Yi was holed up in L.A. working out for specified NBA teams. Yi and his representatives had made a master plan. They would manipulate the draft or at least try to. They would allow Yi to workout only for designated teams. Teams that his representatives deemed worthy of his talents in cities with large Asian populations. L.A., New York, and San Francisco were at the top of the preferred list. These were the places they all felt they could "max out" on his marketing opportunities. Basketball itself had ceased being an actual sport a few years earlier. The notion of "Branding" was now in vogue.

Yi ended up in Milwaukee!! Brand and all! A poet immediately came to mind…

"The best laid schemes o' mice an' men, Gang aft
a-gley"
ROBERT BURNS

On the flip side, Sun Yue and I went basically wherever we were asked, provided I was convinced of a team's interest. After all, we had an uphill climb simply to try to be drafted. We weren't exactly in a position to exclude entire population' centers even if we wanted to.

I got my opportunity to actually meet Sun Yue in Washington D.C. The Washington Wizards and I had arranged for him to have a workout against other prospects for the June draft. I drove down to meet Sun and watch the workout. They wouldn't let me in. I did, however, get to spend some quality time with Sun, his coach from Aoshen, Paul Coughter, and the interpreter.

It was during these days that I was able to confirm my initial phone impression of Sun Yue. He was bright, communicative, had a keen sense of humor, and was indeed extremely tall for a point guard.

I now understood the general reluctance of NBA types to consider him a pure point guard. He didn't look the part. It was easier to dismiss that notion than to actually watch him to figure it out.

In almost every stop, the feedback was very positive including our stops in Washington D.C., Boston, Philadelphia, Dallas, San Antonio, Golden State, and finally in Los Angeles after his workout for the Lakers. The only stumble was in Phoenix, which was, in my opinion, the best place for him due to their "open" style of play. In Phoenix, Sun Yue hit a bit of a wall and cramped up during the workout. It was understandable if you looked at his travel schedule, which had taken him from Beijing, up to Washington D.C. and then across the country to Arizona. But the NBA is an unforgiving place and excuses don't cut it.

In spite of the difference of opinion regarding the Portland situation, Mr. Li through Aoshen showed their support in many ways. The fact that they kept telling me that we could continue the workout process was extremely helpful. This was their first experience with the NBA Draft and I did have to spend a good deal of time explaining what can be a very confusing situation.

At the end of the day, they usually supported me in my suggestions and most importantly they always supported Sun. It became very obvious as the month of June was concluding that Aoshen's and thereby Mr. Li's main priority was that Sun Yue would be taken care of properly.

The concept of money was never even discussed with Aoshen or Mr. Li. On the contrary, I informed Aoshen that they could, if drafted in the right situation get a buyout payable to Aoshen of up to $500,000. The NBA contract has a clause, which allows an overseas player who is under contract to an overseas team to have his NBA team pay a buy-out to the players existing Club. This was compensation for that player leaving his team. It's negotiable but it happens. This payment does not affect the player's salary. This is on top of that salary and therefore costs the player zero. Overseas teams have made some very lucrative deals for themselves using this approach.

Mr. Li and Aoshen indicated that they didn't want any part of it. It wasn't totally altruistic either. It was business. They reasoned correctly that it could be construed later, after Sun Yue finished a possible career in the NBA, that this buyout terminated their contract with Sun. They never wanted to be in a position where Sun could play in China for any team other than Aoshen.

Mr. Li was a very shrewd man!

CHAPTER TWELVE

A LITTLE BIT OF KNOWLEDGE IS A DANGEROUS THING!

Draft day was finally upon us. Emails from China aside, I was feeling pretty good at least about Sun's chances to be selected. I realized I was in a minority position on that view. Sun was in San Francisco the night of the draft. He had worked out for the second time for the Golden State Warriors the day before the draft. He was scheduled to leave the next morning for a flight to Dallas to meet up with the Chinese National Team. The team was going to play some exhibition games in Texas and then compete in the Las Vegas Summer League in early July.

According to Aoshen, the Philadelphia 76ers were on the exact opposite end of the spectrum from Portland. The Sixers had three first-round draft picks. Based on that alone, the Sixers was their team. That was the team they thought I should concentrate on. In spite of my warnings regarding the volatile nature of the draft, Mr. Li/Aoshen believed that the draft order was cemented in place! It never is and it wasn't that night either.

I had actually traveled to Philadelphia to visit with Sun and the 76ers during his workout with them. At the time of that meeting, the 76ers held picks #12, #21, and #30, the final pick in the magical order of things for Aoshen and Mr. Li. While I was doing everything I could to help accomplish this desired goal, I was really hoping just to be drafted. I knew that would be enough of an accomplishment.

I had long ago come to realize that the NBA draft, like the NFL draft, had become a "Show". It is pure style over substance. The suits, the hugging, the shoes. The "branding" is out of control. But without going too far afield, these drafts in 2018 are pretty reflective of our times. The Kardashian's have a long-running "reality" show and are worth millions and Donald Trump is the President of the United States. That's no style and no substance!

The crazy part of this "Draft Show" is that in many cases players drafted in the second round or not drafted at all, have had careers far superior than the "Stars" taken in the first round. It is this "snub" that fuels them throughout their careers. I refer you to Tom Brady who was drafted #199. Recently, I saw a statistic, which indicated that there are currently more undrafted players in the NFL (434) than there are total players in the NBA (432). The drafts have become theater but Mr. Li and Aoshen clearly wanted to be part of that performance.

As with any player entering the draft, there were some hot spots for us going in. Places where there was some serious interest. I felt that the earliest we could look to get picked was at #30, to the 76ers. They had expressed a good deal of interest in Sun. I was more than a bit disappointed and confused when they selected Peter Koponen from Finland. Kopenen played for a team named the Honka Playboys which is fine but he also was a foreign point guard like Sun Yue.

My confusion ended about 15 minutes later. I received a call from the 76ers draft room. They wanted to let me know that they were still very much interested in drafting Sun Yue. This was interesting to me since my understanding was they didn't have another draft pick. That would seem to preclude them drafting anyone else. They then told me that they now owned the 42nd pick in the second round. Portland had bought the 30th pick from the 76ers for $2,000,000 and in addition, had conveyed the 42nd pick to Philadelphia as part of the deal.

Portland had been sincere all along!! They had told us that there was a good possibility that they would be active with their picks. Mr. Li and Aoshen had been kept in the loop on this the whole way. I just don't think they understood how this all might work itself out. Portland never had the opportunity to have Sun work out for them. More importantly Portland didn't get to spend time with him thereby getting to know him as a person. This was clearly was a major factor in their drafting of Kopennen.

Koponen had taken Portland up on the work-out invitation. They went for a point guard but he was clearly ranked below Sun Yue on Portland's rankings. No disrespect intended as Koponen was not the player that Sun Yue was. Peter Koponen never played or signed in the NBA. He has had a very nice career in various spots in Europe and that is where he is playing today. The final irony was that the dream of Mr. Li and Aoshen in having Sun Yue drafted only in the first round was derailed, not by any lack of ability on Sun's part but rather because they didn't understand the inner workings of the draft. They also didn't trust me enough to listen.

The 76ers were straight with me as well. They planned on pocketing the cash and hopefully would get the chance to select Sun with the 42nd pick anyway. Pretty shrewd! I'm sure they realized there was a risk to this but it was worth it to them and I really didn't blame them. It was the right move.

The Los Angeles Lakers spoiled that master plan shortly thereafter. They selected Sun with the 40th pick. This marked the first time in the history of the NBA that two Chinese born players were selected in the same NBA Draft! I was tempted to call the Chinese National Team coach to gloat a little but I clearly am not that type of guy. I had also misplaced his number.

This was a cause for celebration in China! Not only was Sun Yue drafted and drafted fairly high, but it was also the Los Angeles Lakers that drafted him. The Lakers were a very high profile team in the league and therefore extremely prestigious for China. Mr. Li and Aoshen recovered quickly from not being drafted in the first round and they were very excited to have their player in a major market in the NBA. The additional fact of there being a large Asian population in Los Angeles didn't dampen anyone's spirits either.

Mitch Kupchak, the General Manager of the Lakers, called me. We had a very good talk and he indicated that we would work together on this to see what the best course would be for Sun Yue. No contract numbers were discussed. My interpretation of this discussion was that the Lakers had drafted what they thought to be the best player on the board at #40. This is not an earth-shaking statement.

They also had the idea that since Sun Yue was an international player maybe they could have him remain in China for a while and then bring him over at some later time. This is called "stashing." This type of plan enables NBA teams to expand their rosters by having a drafted player not even show up at their training camp. Stay overseas, we keep your rights and we'll talk to you next June. It's a good plan! Unfortunately, they had never let Sun Yue, Mr. Li, Aoshen, or me in on the plan's formation.

That plan was all well and good for the Lakers but what were our rights in this situation? The rules governing a second-round draft choice in the NBA are ridiculous! In a world of over-regulation which many times put the creators of these rules into their own straitjackets, the rules regarding second-round NBA draft choices are just priceless. I have, in fact, been in an almost constant running battle with the Players Association over this for over twenty years.

The NBA is a league of stars. It is the stars that are marketed. It is the stars that get the lion's share of the salary cap. Now that we are in 2018 the "stars" have in many ways taken over the league by putting their own franchises together. There is no indication that this practice will change anytime soon.

As in all industries, the ultimate power lies in the money. While I understand that the bulk of the money still rests with the owners, through the escalating value of their franchises, the league has also empowered a select group of "stars" in ways that players from previous eras never dreamed of.

There are no projected "stars" in the second round of an NBA draft. Therefore, there are no rules to protect them. In short, an NBA team selecting a player anywhere from #31 to #60 has the obligation only to "tender" that drafted player a contract by a specific date and for the minimum salary allowable. This "tender offer" is usually sent sometime in August. The critical element of this contract is that it does not have to be guaranteed in any way. Not $1 has to pass to a second-round draft choice.

If you are a first-round pick (potential "star"), you are currently guaranteed at least two years of salary. This used to be three years but apparently, some of these "stars" didn't quite pan out. If you are drafted #30 you get two years automatically guaranteed, for around $2,000,000 or so. However, if you go one spot lower at #31, you are guaranteed $0. Through your agent you can try and negotiate your way around this but most of the time you have no leverage. You yourself can experience the exact sensation of slipping that one draft slot simply by getting in your car and driving off a cliff!

My suggestion has been to have these second rounders get some kind of guarantee. This is apparently too much to consider. A year or even a half of a year of guaranteed money would do much to level the playing field in a negotiation between a second-round draft choice and an NBA team armed with every conceivable piece of leverage imaginable.

You would think this lack of any financial commitment would be enough of an edge for the teams but there's more. If the player and his agent refuse this magnanimous offer of nothing, the team gets to keep the rights to that player until he does accept. In Sun Yue's case it became apparent to me early on in my discussions that the Lakers drafted him so they could have him remain with Aoshen in China. This would give them their "expanded" roster at no cost to them. My concern was not with the 2007-08 season, but what would occur beyond.

We received the required "tender offer" on August 22, 2007. It contained the bare minimum that the Lakers, by rule, had to include. Specifically, it contained the minimum salary with no guarantees. If we rejected this, Sun remained the property of the Lakers. Because they sent the required "tender offer," the Lakers maintained the rights to Sun. Next year they would only be required to send the identical offer again. This can go on forever. There are players drafted in the second round of NBA drafts in the 1990s who are still the property of the original team that drafted them. Those players rejected the offers made and went to Europe and stayed there.

Another of my players that I represented was Joseph Blair out of the University of Arizona. The Seattle Supersonics drafted Joe in the high second round, #35. This was in 1996. He never played for them but remained their property until I got him released from Seattle in 2007. That's 11 years later. Joe became an actual "star" in the highest levels of Europe. Joe didn't want to do that NBA dance where they dictated to him what he was worth. He went out and established his value through his talent and efforts. Not every 21-year-old has the intelligence and the "nuts" to do that! In fact, it's pretty rare.

Sun Yue was obviously a different case from Joe. His decisions were really not his own to make. There was the added component of the fact that I knew that Mr. Li and Aoshen would love to keep Sun with them, at least for a year. Aoshen's motivations were purer than the Lakers. They truly believed in Sun Yue and loved him as a player and as a person. Take also into account that they had signed Sun Yue and moved him and his family to Shanghai when Sun was 14 years old. Mr. Li and Aoshen had invested time and money in Sun Yue. The Lakers were merely exercising their power under an unfair section of the collective bargaining agreement. The age-old question and attendant answer is apropos: Why does a dog lick his balls? Answer: Because he can!

So here I am in what amounts to an international game of chicken. The ironic element of this is that the Lakers used the 40th pick in the draft to select Sun Yue and have now "tendered" him an offer that they clearly don't want him to sign. If Sun Yue signs that offer, the Lakers to my mind, lose all of the previously mentioned inequitable leverage. They now would be forced to bring him to camp and make a decision on him much earlier than they had planned. If they released him in October, they would have wasted a fairly high draft choice. A draft choice they could, in a worst-case scenario, have sold for $1,000,000 or more.

Sun Yue, on the other hand, would now be a very talented 6'9" point guard, who would be the starting point guard on the Chinese National Team. That team would compete in the 2008 Olympic Games. Oh, by the way, the Olympic Games were to be held in Beijing. That's in China! Branding anyone?! In addition, he would become an unrestricted free agent. He would be able to sign with any

NBA team with no rules attached. Believe me, the Lakers didn't want any part of that scenario.

I fought the Lakers very hard all summer about this. I had several fairly heated discussions with Mitch, who I have known and respected for 30 years. I even played the Long Island card with him as both of us grew up there. No dice. He understood my position but that understanding ear didn't change any terms of their "offer."

Looking back at it, I think Mitch knew that at the end of the day although I was right I also had some problems. Namely Mr. Li. As in the situation with the Draft and Portland, I knew that my strategy regarding signing the Lakers "tender offer" was likely to suffer the same fate. Specifically, that they would listen to me respectfully over and over again but it would be their decision, not mine and certainly not Sun Yue's. Mr. Li was calling the shots here. That was becoming very clear. It didn't matter how convincing I was on the phone with other management people from Aoshen. They were just relaying what we discussed to Mr. Li. His was the only vote that mattered.

Many of the freedoms that we in the United States take very much for granted are not even thought of by the citizens of China. Sun Yue was signed at the age of 14 and informed me that he would be free to make his own career choice when he was 45. That was the length of his contract with Aoshen. What I found odd was that as he told me this there was absolutely no anger about it. No resentment. To the contrary, Sun was extremely grateful to Mr. Li and Aoshen for what they had done for him and his family. He saw no problem with basically having his team and owner decide his future.

As I mentioned earlier, Sun Yue was headed to the Las Vegas Summer League shortly after the draft. Tyler and I met him there. It was during this seven-day period that we finally got to spend quality time with Sun. We got to hang together. Surprisingly, there seemed to be very little pressure on him. He was in his element. He was playing with friends for his country's National Team. Most importantly, he was where he belonged on the court, at the point!

He totally ran that team. He really was a joy to watch. Trust me, I have seen many pure point guards and I've represented my share of them as well. One of them, Scott Skiles, set the NBA assist record 25 years ago. It still stands. I know point guards. Sun Yue was terrific! The difference between Sun Yue and Matthew Dellavedova or C. J. Watson or Ramon Sessions or Jose Calderon or Tyler Johnson and yes Jeremy Lin and probably 20 more NBA point guards, was simply the opportunity to play! Due to circumstances explained in these pages, he never was afforded that chance.

During that week I got to enjoy watching him flying around the floor but always under control. He totally understood the game and was very intelligent. I also spent some time meeting with the Lakers, who were in Vegas with their own team of Laker rookies and free agents. Normally, Sun would have played for them but with the Chinese National Team being there that was not to be. Although my discussions with the Lakers continued, my main objective was to get Mr. Li and Aoshen to understand what was best for Sun. That never happened.

When it came time for Tyler and me to leave Las Vegas and therefore say goodbye to Sun Yue, who by this time we had grown extremely fond of, Sun grabbed me around my neck:

"Keith, I'm going to miss you!"

We never saw each other or spoke again.

Mr. Li and Aoshen refused to follow my advice concerning the course we needed to take with the Lakers. I wasn't going to keep silent again. This time it led to an argument. I knew the NBA and they didn't. This had unfortunately been borne out on Draft night. If they weren't going to listen to their representative why was I even in the picture? The way I looked at it, if I wasn't willing to make a stand at this point I was, in essence, screwing my client and I had no interest in doing that.

Looking back at things now, I think that is why my goodbye with Sun ended with his indicating that he would miss me. I think he knew that I wasn't going to take too much more of this. He also knew that in a battle with Mr. Li over Sun Yue's future I was going to be the loser.

On October 1, 2007, four days before the start of training camp and with Mr. Li and I still at odds over Sun signing the Lakers "tender offer" I received a termination letter from Aoshen. They still didn't get the concept that I don't sign a team! In essence, they terminated me from nothing, but I got the point and was oddly relieved to get out of what had become a frustrating situation for me.

I heard that Aoshen had attempted to rejoin the CBA. When that body refused to allow Aoshen to relocate to Macau, Mr. Li's desired location, Aoshen refused to rejoin. They ended up playing in Singapore that season with a very talented 6'9" point guard, who was also the 40th pick in the NBA Draft four months earlier.

In August of 2008, Sun signed a minimum non-guaranteed contract with the Lakers. Mitch Kupchak had won that battle. He spent most of the 2008-09 season in the D-League, the NBA's minor league, with the LA Defenders. For the year, Sun Yue played in 10 games for the Lakers. He took 11 shots, making three of them. He had two assists and three turnovers.

The Lakers won the NBA title that season and while Sun didn't play in the playoffs, he was on their roster. He became only the second Chinese player to win an NBA Championship.

The Lakers waived him on July 31, 2009.

Three years passed. According to Mr. Li and Aoshen, I am now back as Sun Yue's agent. The team signed the contract. Once again none of this had any validity since Sun Yue has never signed an agency contract with me, but what the hell. Intermediaries told me that Mr. Li had realized my sincerity and belief in Sun. This was gratifying and since I really did like this kid I was happy to have him "back" with us.

While Mr. Li and Aoshen had apparently understood my past motives, my advice continued to be treated as mere suggestions. I never got to speak directly with Sun Yue and these "suggestions" as before were not exactly followed through on.

We needed to figure out a way to get the NBA interested in him again. His initial go around with the Lakers was not the stuff of legends. My thought was to try the Euroleague. The Euroleague quite simply is the next best league in the world next to the NBA. It is a very high quality of basketball and extremely competitive. My thoughts were that if Sun Yue could ever spend a season with a Maccabi Tel Aviv in Israel or Milano in Italy or Barcelona in Spain or CSKA in Russia, etc. we would have an excellent chance to be seen by the people in the NBA who needed to see him. Those games are constantly scouted because of the number of future draft choices and European free agents that perform there. Today, there are well over 100 European players in the NBA. A productive season could lead Sun Yue back to the NBA where I still thought he could thrive.

OK, I can almost hear you through the pages. Get off it, man! Just because this kid was your player don't be such a "homer!" The guy was waived, cut, and released. Obviously, he can't play. The problem with that argument is that I've heard that my whole career. Let me give you some information. I've made the point before that the difference between Sun Yue and other point guards was the chance to play. I truly believe that. That chance doesn't always come.

In that 2007 draft when Sun was drafted #40, the Lakers had another pick at #48. Obviously, they thought Sun Yue was the better player and took him before they took Marc Gasol at #48. Marc Gasol was involved in the trade that actually sent his brother Pau from Memphis to the Lakers, which solidified the Lakers front line for years. It didn't hurt Memphis either because the trade gave Marc Gasol the "opportunity" to actually play! I was told by a friend with Memphis that one of the reasons that Marc was included in that deal was because, although Memphis requested Sun Yue as part of the deal, the Lakers wouldn't give him up. Marc Gasol is an NBA All-Star and has signed contracts worth over $150,000,000, all guaranteed. According to the Lakers, Sun Yue was the better player.

My guy could play people!

This all brings me to an early morning in August of 2012. I set my alarm for 5:45 am. I wasn't happy about that! The Olympics were being played and the Chinese National Team was playing their Australian counterparts in the London Olympic Games. Both teams were winless after two games and this game would determine who remained in London and who would politely be asked to leave England.

Obviously, my interest was in watching the progress of Sun Yue. Since I had been back on the case I had been talking him up all year to everyone I could think of. I had their attention too, especially since I could point to the idea that Sun would be competing at these Olympics and against NBA competition. I was out there on a limb and Sun Yue was on the same branch!

The player I watched that morning bore no resemblance to the player I knew. He simply had regressed due to the lack of adequate and consistent competition. Even his own National Team didn't play him purely as a point guard anymore. He really seemed to just occupy space. Sun Yue scored three points and the Chinese National Team lost by 20. This would be their last game in London and they went home without winning a game there. For Sun Yue, this meant Beijing, Singapore or wherever Aoshen and Mr. Li decided to move would be his next destination. It also meant that I wouldn't be hearing anytime soon from the various NBA teams that were in London partially to see Sun Yue and this alleged vast potential his agent had been extolling for over a year!

In September of 2013, Mr. Li died suddenly due to acute myocardial infarction. He was 55 years old. Just so no one thinks I'm inflating his significance to the Aoshen Basketball Club, the team DISBANDED on December 4, 2013. Mr. Li was the key! As a result of Mr. Li's death and the folding of Aoshen, Sun Yue moved to the Beijing Ducks, where he is their point guard today. I hear he makes a bunch of money there and I'm truly happy for him. The fact that we are not involved in the Fee Side of that is just part of this business. I've been on both sides of it.

The Wikipedia description of Mr. Li remains. He was "mysterious" to the end. But he was a lot more than that. Besides being tremendously successful in his business life, he showed that he truly cared about Sun Yue. Mr. Li and Aoshen went the extra mile in financially supporting Sun Yue and there can be no doubt of their feelings and commitment towards him. All of us wanted the same thing. We all wanted Sun Yue to be in the NBA and fulfill his potential. We just couldn't agree on how to get him there. Aoshen or to be specific, Mr. Li never fully entrusted me to take the steps necessary to make that happen.

Unfortunately, Mr. Li is gone now and so is Sun Yue's dream!

CHAPTER THIRTEEN

WHAT SO PROUDLY WE.....

Since I apparently won't be writing again for 10 years I thought I should conclude this volume with some profound and truly meaningful thoughts. Unfortunately, I don't have any of those so we will have to be content with a summary of my feelings and hopes.

I don't have many of those either. Observations however I have plenty of.

We are living in one of the strangest times in history, not only in the sporting world but also politically; at least that I can remember. It's hard for me and many of my friends to even understand how old we actually are. I don't feel old. My back and my right knee do but other than that I feel great! But "maturity" has enabled me to see things across a broader and more experienced landscape. When I rail against the direction of professional sports it is not done out of anger or bitterness or jealousy. Rather the source of my observations comes from a place of concern with a splash of frustration.

Sports in general and basketball specifically have not only given me and my family almost every financial benefit that we have but they have provided me with more joy than anyone could ask for. How could that make me anything but grateful? My frustrations stem from a desire for coming generations to at least have the chance to enjoy that same experience. To allow people who want to see a professional or collegiate sporting event to be able to afford it. To stop taking for granted that fans will pay any price just to get into an arena and then still have something left over to buy a hot dog.

I know that there are still many people who attend these events but there is also no disputing that you need to be of a certain strata of financial means in order to do that. That is not good. That does not bode well for the future. That precludes certain economically strapped families from having that experience. It's a potential problem for both sides. Franchises will start to see some erosion of their base if they haven't already. I also know that I'm writing this at a time of extreme if not historic levels of popularity specifically in the NBA. This doesn't mean that there aren't problems bubbling just below the surface.

The issues confronting sports in this country are not only financial. "Grassroots" issues abound as well. Let's not be naive. Not a day goes by that we are not alerted to another example of parental interference which has tainted youth sport in this country for the past several years. Money issues I have discussed throughout this book. Probably for some too much so. Then again you have always had the option to stop reading. I made that offer on the first page.

As I have indicated throughout this book, I only want to talk about issues with which I am familiar with have actually been a part of in some way. Having some nexus to a subject is important. The over the top involvement of many parents today is one of those issues. I hear you! What makes this guy an expert of that issue? Well to begin with I had two parents of my own. While they did not attend every practice I ever had, as today's parents attempt to do, they did try to be at as many games as they could. They sat in the top row and watched me play.

The thought of voicing their displeasure at anyone besides me was not even a consideration. If they had thoughts or questions about how I played or more importantly how I conducted myself in public, they did that at home. They didn't always like what the coach was doing but they never discussed that. The coach was to them another teacher of mine. If one of my teachers had an issue with me it was my fault not the teacher's. Believe me I tried many times to shift that blame but they wouldn't hear it. They subscribed quietly to the motto that:

> *"He's not the coach because he's always right, but*
> *he's always right because he's the coach!"*

Our coaches weren't always right. Many times they weren't even very good. You would never know that talking to my parents or for that matter to the parents of most of my teammates.

I began coaching when I was maybe 16 or so. This was way back in those mountains in Pennsylvania. As I moved along in playing and coaching I got the close up view of how things had devolved in terms of parenting. Obviously, this is not all parents. Even in 2018 the majority of parents truly understand the real benefits of having their sons and daughters participating in organized sports. More importantly they get the concept and benefits of being part of a team. Most of my best friends are the guys I played next to in grammar school, middle school, high school, college and camp! The parents of all of those players supported us but were otherwise almost invisible.

As my coaching career expanded things changed. Not all at once but change they did. When I was at UCLA we had a standard answer when we encountered a parent with an exaggerated sense of his child's abilities:

*"You should play one level below where you think
you should play; and two levels below where your
father thinks you should play!"*

This little quip was meant mostly as a joke in the 1980s. Today unfortunately it's an admonition that not enough people take seriously. The only change I would add would be to now include the mothers along with the dads. I'm not even sure what the motivations are for these parents. I guess it could be the dream of a scholarship years down the road. If that's the case they'd be far better off putting their energies into band practice or an actual academic endeavor. Maybe there's some reflected glory for a career in sports that they didn't have. Whatever it is, it's unseemly at its best and destructive at its worst.

Anyone even peripherally involved in youth sports has witnessed these parents. They inhabit every gym in the country. Their focus is exclusively on their child. The team doesn't matter. Learning doesn't matter. According to them they've taken care of all that at home already. The other players and certainly the coach are merely props designed to showcase their son or daughter. It's embarrassing and it is harmful mostly to their own child. Sometimes it gets totally out of hand!

In 2002 I was the head coach at Rumson-Fair High School in New Jersey. It was and is a terrific place and was located a mile from our house in Rumson. I loved to coach and I envisioned myself coaching at Rumson until my youngest son Luke graduated from there. All was well until the middle of my 2nd season. I found myself in Freehold, New Jersey for a game against Freehold Boro High School. During the first half my point guard chose the wrong occasion to act like a fool.

I realize that my reaction to this behavior doesn't play too well in print. Suffice it say that I clearly indicated that if he ever spoke to me like that again that I would take my right foot and.... This wasn't the first time he had acted out but I was clear that it was his last. That six second encounter ushered in a series of events orchestrated by his "mommy" which included the Freehold Police Department, 2 Freehold detectives, the Rumson-Fair Haven School District, the County Prosecutor's office, a Municipal Court Judge and actually placed me in front of a Grand Jury.

While this is clearly a case of parental interference on steroids, the sad part is that it actually was allowed to happen and go forward. There was no question that all of this was conjured up by a woman for the simple fact that she understood that her son was no longer going to start on his high school basketball team. It sounds bizarre but it's not the only case of this. Mine was unusual in its scope and in its disposition as well. The following article sums the case up pretty well:

One coach who refused to surrender to the new order

In olden times, growing up usually meant learning right from wrong, among other things. In today's moral marketplace you have three options to choose from: right, wrong and politically correct.

This is what's known as progress.

Political correctness is an ever-expanding term, and an equal-opportunity deterrent to plain speaking. Under today's rules, the great thinkers of the past could not have shared their wisdom quite as openly as they once did. Many of them would have been afraid to do so without first checking the latest edition of

BILL HANDLEMAN

● ● ●

See **Handleman**, Page **C9**

So they screwed with the wrong guy. It happens. Now I'm stuck with a check for $10,000 minus my lawyer's fee, and I really don't know what to do with it. I do know that I don't want the money. It felt dirty to me. This family had tried to pervert the purpose of a sport which had given me so much. The fact that they did not understand any of the principles of what athletics was all about doesn't mean I should profit from it. There was no way that I even wanted this money in my account.

I set out to try and reverse their attempt at "perversion" into something positive. The problem was even though I was consciously looking for a place to donate this tainted money I just couldn't find the right place for it. A year after I received this check there was a reunion at…yep Keeyumah! It seems to always come back to Keeyumah!

When you are at Camp, if you're lucky, there are a few people who inspire you. Usually the tremendous age gap of two years or so provides you with enough of an age difference for that admiration

Handleman

FROM PAGE C1

the lexicon of acceptably neutral and inoffensive thought.

Mark Twain could not exist today, Harry Truman never would have made it past dog catcher, and they would've had to put a muzzle on Vince Lombardi in the name of political correctness.

Still, there are those who continue to resist. Take Keith Glass. He used to be a basketball coach. Then one day he crossed the line, which seems to shift from minute to minute depending on which way the wind is blowing.

He doesn't believe he did anything wrong, but someone certainly does. Meanwhile others keep quiet, choosing safe over right or wrong.

Glass was an assistant under Larry Brown at UCLA for two years. After that he was the head coach at Venice High School in southern California for two years. After that he was the head coach at Mater Dei High School for 12 years.

At Mater Dei he won more games than he was supposed to win, no matter how you look at it. One year he won 23 games with a 5-foot-10 power forward. The next year he won 22 games with a 5-foot-1 point guard and a 5-foot-3 shooting guard. A couple of years later he went 27-2 and beat St. Anthony, which had its usual complement of five or six Division I players.

The guy can coach. It's not how he makes his living — he's an agent who represents basketball players — but he likes coaching and he's good at it.

So 15 months ago he's in his second year at Rumson-Fair Haven High School, and there is an incident during a game at Freehold. One of his players does something to provoke him, and he pulls the kid out of the game and tells him to make himself comfortable on the bench. Then he starts to walk away and the kid says something, and Glass turns around and lets him have it.

"You know what?" he says. "If you ever speak to me like that again, I'm gonna stick my foot up your rear end." Or something to that effect.

The kid never got back in the game. Afterward, in the locker room, Glass was in the middle of his post-game talk when he noticed the kid wasn't paying attention. He was taking his sneakers off instead. Glass told him to listen up, but the kid continued to ignore him. At which point Glass saw red again and told one of his assistants to get the kid out of the room.

That was the end of the relationship between the coach and the player. The kid never played for Glass again. But this was hardly the end of the story.

After a 2-6 start to the season, Rumson-Fair Haven finished strongly and wound up with a 15-9 record, winning a game in the state playoffs for the first time in many years. Since Rumson is not a traditional basketball power, this was generally considered a successful season.

But the incident in January would not go away. The kid's mother was convinced that her son had been wronged, and she wanted the school to fire Glass.

"I think they wanted me to resign because it would've been easier for them that way," says Glass, who makes it clear that he was "disappointed" that the school didn't back him all the way.

"They basically treated me like I had leprosy," he adds.

Dr. Peter Righi, the principal at Rumson-Fair Haven, declined comment.

"Technically, I resigned," says Glass. "But I don't think they were terribly disappointed that I left."

This wasn't enough. In July, Glass got a letter in the mail notifying him that he was to be the central figure in a grand jury hearing. After several delays, the grand jury was convened in February, heard the evidence against Glass, and declined to indict on the more serious allegations of verbal abuse.

The lesser allegations — disorderly persons offenses — were returned to the municipal court in Freehold. According to Peter Boser, one of the assistant prosecutors who worked on the case, these are the equivalent of misdemeanor allegations in other states.

Aside from that, Boser could not comment on the case.

Fred Klatsky could, though. He is representing Glass in the case, which he feels strongly about. Not just because he's his lawyer, but because he has been a coach himself, and because he's appalled by this litigious state of affairs, even if he is a lawyer himself.

"Nothing happened here," Klatsky insists. "Yet here's a coach who's been dragged through the criminal process and the civil process basically because the kid didn't do as well as the mother expected."

He went on to note that Denzel Washington's character in "Remember the Titans" became a lasting motion picture hero the moment he told one of his out-of-line players that he would "stick my size 12 John Brown so far up your rear end that it'll come out your mouth." Or something to that effect.

Let's see him try that today, with more and more parents complaining that coach doesn't like little Johnny, with administrators cowering, with coaches forced to become politicians, whether they like it or not.

Either that, or you stand up for yourself.

"It's easier to see in sports, because sports is so public," says Glass. "But across the board in our society today we've basically become paralyzed.

"We can no longer act, either due to a sense of political correctness, or for fear of rocking the boat. We've surrendered, all of us. Administrators, teachers, coaches, we've all surrendered to a large degree.

"I didn't surrender. So I guess the lesson here is, if you don't play along, you can end up in front of a grand jury."

There's another lesson here as well: Let little Johnny do whatever he damn well pleases. That way you keep the parents off your back and you keep your job and nobody has to make any tough calls.

The kids? Well, they're on their own.

Bill Handleman is an award-winning Asbury Park Press columnist. E-mail: handle@app.com to develop. Two years gives you the feeling that whoever it is you are emulating is sufficiently old enough to admire but not too old to not be able to relate to.

Jody Forstot fit my criteria to a tee. Jody was 2 or 3 groups ahead of mine and always seemed to have things under control. It wasn't just that he was the best athlete of his group either. He was a leader. He was my guy! When I reached the ripe old age of 17 and Jody was an aging counselor of 20, we became the starting back court of the counselor team at Keeyumah. In those days not a small feat. It was a thrill for me and probably meant very little to Jody.

30 or so years later, the first person I see at the Keeyumah reunion was Jody:

> **Keith**: What's up?! Besides being a heart surgeon, what else is going on?

> **Jody**: Keith, I started a basketball league for handicapped adults down in Florida. It's the greatest experience I've had! It shows you how much good the game can do.

> **Keith**: Does the program need any money?!

The check went out the next day. That was easily the happiest I've ever been while writing out a check. I knew that when I saw the right place for that settlement money it would be obvious. The circle had been completed. The game was supposed to bring people together as teammates, not to function as a selfish enterprise to benefit one mother and her little boy. Their attempt to alter the meaning of the game had failed miserably. It took a lot of time and money but we managed to turn their attempt into something positive.

It's a funny thing but when I was coaching in the mountains or in the San Fernando Valley or at UCLA or Venice High School or at Mater Dei High School and finally at Rumson-Fair Haven, I should have known that in spite of our success as a team, there were people talking negatively about me. The great Al McGuire once said that the key to coaching was:

> *"Keeping the five guys that hated you away from the five who were undecided!"*

Coaching elicits many emotions in both players and some parents. That has always been the case. There are after all only five starters on a basketball team and only one ball. It's the guys who play the most and score the most that generally have the best feelings towards the coach. A great coach is the one who can get those feelings from the entire team and that's not easy. When this new crop of over-involved parents gets in their kid's head the problem grows exponentially.

Even though I knew that somewhere up in the bleachers someone was talking trash about me, I honestly never heard it or even thought twice about it. This actually served me well during one of my many marriages. While I was married to my wife from Turkey, I naturally had in-laws. Her parents were terrific people and I loved them. They were in reflection the perfect in-laws. Her father was an interpreter for the Turkish government in Ankara so he therefore spoke English. We could communicate and got along very well. I miss him. "Baba" never complained about anything. As long as I got him a large Mountain Dew at 7-11 he was good to go.

My mother-in-law on the other hand while extremely sweet would let her displeasure be known. This displeasure was never serious and usually revolved around where or what we were having for dinner. The beautiful part of our relationship came from the subtle fact that she didn't speak or understand one word of English. So while she was clearly agitated, I could easily pretend that the source of her irritation had nothing to do with me.

My Grand Jury saga as they would say in a courtroom "qualified" me as an expert in the parental interference field. Out of control parents however are not our sole problem. Not in 2018. For whatever reason social and political issues have become interwoven into professional sports as well. In fact professional sports have become the launching pad for some of the country's issues. I even hesitate to call them "issues" because issues by definition have two sides. This debate over the national anthem does not. It has a correct side and an erroneous side. Ipso facto it's not even an "issue."

Ok, but how do I now come to a discussion of Colin Kaepernick and his kneeling during the national anthem?! I wormed my way into qualifying to discuss parental insanity through my own personal experience but what do I have to do with the anthem discourse?

On March 12, 1996 after leaving my office and minding my own business, I turned on ESPN radio. 15 seconds later they announced some "breaking news"! Mahmoud Abdul Rauf of the Denver Nuggets had been suspended by the NBA for failing to stand for the national anthem. This was obviously newsworthy in itself but a bit more relevant to me as I was Mahmoud's agent and lawyer.

This began an extremely turbulent time for Mahmoud and for me. I had no idea about any of this in advance. Although Mahmoud and I obviously talked all the time, he had never mentioned his intention to "protest" the anthem. He had never even discussed any issue he had with the anthem in general. One can therefore only imagine my surprise at hearing this for the first time on the radio.

After speaking with Mahmoud that night he informed me that he been doing a "silent protest" for weeks. No one had noticed because he was simply not coming out for the anthem. He would stay in the tunnel and come out for the introductions and then play the game. On this particular night for whatever reason he decided to come out and "stretch" during the anthem. When the NBA league office saw this they suspended him without pay. That "without pay" part would prove significant later on.

Naturally Mahmoud and I had a discussion based on why was he doing this?!

> **Mahmoud**: Keith, the flag stands for tyranny and oppression. I will NOT stand!

While I clearly did not agree with his assessment regarding the flag, I instinctively understood that he had the right to his opinion and the founding fathers gave him the right to express it. I not only didn't agree with his opinion but it was even clearer to me that the way he went about expressing it on the night in question was disrespectful. To stay in the tunnel was his choice and no one even noticed or could be offended by his belief. To stretch during the anthem was an expression of disdain and was beyond unacceptable to the NBA and quite frankly to me as well.

For someone like me would stood for every anthem (even some on TV) this was an interesting spot to be in. I did more media in that period than I ever want to do again. The whole country had thoughts on what a diabolical person Mahmoud was. I knew first hand that this was not even close to being accurate. I received my share of nasty comments from the "patriots" in our midst. There was however no issue here. It wasn't MY beliefs about Mahmoud's rights that mattered. I didn't draft the 1st amendment to our Constitution. Jefferson and

Adams and Franklin etc. did. They were our first real patriot's, willing to give up everything including their wealth and their lives if necessary in order to advance the cause of democracy.

The foundation of that philosophy is enumerated in our Constitution generally and in the Bill of Rights specifically. As most of us know the Bill of Rights is the first 10 amendments to our Constitution. It was ratified in 1791 and as far as I've heard it had not been abolished yet. Mahmoud was exercising those rights when he refused to stand for the anthem. I didn't like it, didn't agree with it and certainly objected to how he went about his "protest". There was however no question that as ill-conceived and clumsy as it was, he had the absolute right to express it.

In actuality what Mahmoud did in 1996 and what Colin Kaepernick and other NFL players did in 2017 is not technically even an exercise in "free speech". It is an exercise of what courts in this country have described as "symbolic speech". Unfortunately for our newly minted "patriots", "symbolic speech" is specifically covered by the 1st Amendment as well. But let's not let little things like the Constitution or our judicial system get in the way of some people's gut reactions. That wouldn't be right.

In August of 2016 during the San Francisco 49ers third preseason game, Colin Kaepernick was seen sitting during the playing of the national anthem. He had done this for the two prior games as well. It was a peaceful silent protest. When he was ultimately confronted by the media after this third preseason game he responded:

"I am not going to stand up to show pride in a flag for a country that oppresses black people and people of color. To me, these issues are bigger than football and it would be selfish to look the other way. There are bodies in the street and people getting paid leave and getting away with murder."

He didn't actually start kneeling during the Anthem until September 1st. He explained that he decided to change to kneeling rather than sitting after he had a lengthy conversation with Nate Boyer. Boyer was a former NFL player and a US military veteran. Kaepernick explained that after his meeting with Boyer he switched to kneeling in order to show more respect to current and former members of our military while still protesting.

It couldn't be any clearer what Kaepernick's protest was about. It had nothing to do with disrespecting the military. The military component merely became part of the growing popularity of "alternative facts" which in reality don't even exist. There are facts and there are lies. But the people wrapping themselves in the flag across the country didn't need any facts. They distorted the message. They attacked the messenger.

Kaepernick later went on to wear a ridiculous pair of socks depicting police officers as pigs! He wore a tee shirt with Fidel Castro's picture on it. This further distorted his message. Critic's labeled Kaepernick and all the other NFL players who supported him as a bunch of ungrateful spoiled athletes. They should just be happy that they had money and shut up, as if financial success automatically forfeited your rights as a citizen. Later in 2018 this "shut up and dribble" refrain was used against LeBron James and other NBA players. It doesn't take a genius to see a pattern here.

The message was easily lost. After all distractions have become the new National Pastime. In today's society we can't agree with a person or a party or a principle unless we blindly agree with every other position that person or party has ever uttered. It's why the President of the United States can correctly say during his campaign that he could shoot somebody on 5th Avenue and not lose a vote. In hindsight it is one of the more accurate and honest things he has said. This is a dangerous way for a free society to operate. This "lock step" mentality is stifling the greatness we used to have.

I thought that Colin Kaepernick's choice of socks and tee shirts were horrible. I don't think police are pigs. I never admired Fidel Castro. That doesn't mean everything he has said can now be dismissed. I also have eyes. I've seen the videos of unarmed black teenagers lying dead in the streets. If you don't think those images are way beyond merely troubling then I question YOUR patriotism! Not his and not mine!

I hate to "let facts get in the way of a good story" but let's further examine just how far the hypocrisy of the NFL representing our military extends in the 1st place. The evolution of how the national anthem, the NFL and "patriotism" came to be linked is quite interesting.

It wasn't until recently, 2009 to be precise, that the NFL changed its policy on the issue of players' involvement during the national anthem. NFL players were merely "encouraged" to participate in these staged pre-game activities, which included the playing of the anthem. Before 2009 there really wasn't any specific instructions on any of these activities. Some player's stayed in the locker room as Mahmoud had done before his "public stretching" brought the anthem issue to public attention back in 1996.

During our recent past and I'm talking about 2014-2016, the US Department of Defense had spent millions of taxpayer dollars in payments to the NFL for flag unfurling, military flyovers, emotional color guard ceremonies, enlistment campaigns and yes…national anthem performances. Interestingly, these payments have come after this shift in policy that the NFL made for its players in 2009. So the reality seems to be that Colin Kaepernick and others who didn't follow this policy change towards the anthem weren't actually guilty of being "unpatriotic." They were guilty of not playing along with a marketing strategy cooked up between the NFL and our Defense Department.

More facts demonstrating the blurred line between patriotism and marketing emerged in 2015. Two Republican senators from Arizona, John McCain and Jeff Flake revealed in a joint oversight report that 14 NFL teams had received over five million dollars to stage these elaborate "patriotic salutes" to the military. The years covered were 2011 to 2014. I guess it was pure coincidence that in May of 2016, after the oversight report came out, the NFL refunded $724,000 of these payouts back to the Defense Department. As of September 2015 the Defense Department started prohibiting payments for "patriotic ceremonies".

They must have been embarrassed. That's the emotion that all the people who booed NFL players for exercising their rights in a peaceful manner should feel as well. Where is it written that if an athlete makes above a certain amount of money, he or she forfeits the right to protest?! Who made up the rules regarding what the flag really stands for?

Colin Kaepernick and the others never mentioned disrespecting the military. They are against cases of possible police brutality. If you vilified them, are you saying you are in favor of police brutality?! If you are, then stand up and say that! Stop hiding behind the flag. THAT'S disrespectful!

I've discussed the idea that in today's society "short cuts" are the way to go. This was discussed in the context of athletics. Apparently they spill into this discussion of "patriotism" as well. Even in this age of the superficial and simplistic, stopping men and women in airports and shopping malls to "thank you for your service" is very nice but it doesn't excuse the basic lack of understanding of why they are serving.

It's as if we, who haven't fought in a physical battle for our country, can ease some sort of misplaced guilt by uttering phrases or using our flag in inappropriate ways. More short-cuts! OK, maybe I haven't served my country in any meaningful capacity but if I thank someone who has, I'm good. The only way we can possibly honor the sacrifices of the men and women who literally risked their lives for us is to adhere to the principles upon which the nation was founded.

Is it truly "patriotic" to CHARGE the government for these displays of "patriotism"?! On the bright side it did give the sitting President of the United States another opportunity to totally wrap himself in the flag. He called the NFL players who didn't agree with unarmed citizens being killed in the streets:

> *"Sons of bitches."*

He called on NFL owners who coincidentally had excluded him from owning an NFL team years earlier to "fire" these infidels. The pandering on this issue knows no bounds:

> *"Courageous Patriots have fought and died for our great American Flag-we MUST honor and respect it".*
>
> DONALD TRUMP TWEET

Forgetting the fact that he never served in any military branch and actually sought and received five deferments for bone spurs during the Vietnam War, this was "low-hanging fruit" for him and his hopefully shrinking band of supporters.

> *"What the President failed to acknowledge in his rant was that many of the military displays present at NFL games were financed by the government. Rather than the organic, wholesome expressions of patriotism - the kind Trump has claimed NFL*

*players are disrespectfully protesting - the tradition
of players standing for the national anthem is a recent tradition that coincided with a marketing ploy
meant to sell cheap, manufactured nationalism."*

MELANIE SCHMITZ- 2017

"Cheap manufactured nationalism" is what won the Electoral College for him. Why quit on a winning formula? In 1989, well after Donald Trump's deferments, a federal law was established prohibiting flag desecration. Vietnam Veterans (you know guys that actually served in Vietnam) burned the American flag in protest of the law which curbed the rights granted under the 1st Amendment. Their argument was that they fought for the freedoms enumerated in the Constitution, not for a piece of cloth and to curtail these freedoms was an insult to their sacrifice.

Personally I marched against the Vietnam War while in college. I would do again. That doesn't mean I didn't respect the men and women who didn't agree with us and did indeed go to fight in Vietnam. My "service" was in my protest. I'm not comparing my protesting in any way to what those who actually fought in that war went through. Many in my generation felt strongly that the war was unjust. History I would say has validated those beliefs.

I guess I also was just lucky. When I became eligible for the Draft we were subject to a lottery system. We sat in our dorm rooms waiting for our birth date to be drawn from a drum of some sort. Guys whose birth dates were in the top 120 dates randomly selected were going to Vietnam. My friend across the hall got #7. He left for Canada in the morning.

My number was #323. Technically this meant that I would be called into active duty if there were Viet Cong soldiers on the George Washington Bridge. I still wonder what I would have done if the lottery had come up differently. If you were staunchly against the war your choices were varied and none of them were good. Would I have had the courage to serve in the military? Would I have had the courage not to and risk everything. Would I have had the conviction to go to Canada like so many chose to do?

What's lost in this silly debate on the anthem is that during this Vietnam era there were true patriots on both sides. John McCain's service and actions after his capture are obvious signs of a true patriot. Muhammed Ali's protest while derided viciously at the time has turned out to be patriotic in its own right. Both were certainly courageous. No one can physically compare what John McCain went through at the hands of the Viet Cong to any form of protest. But Ali's conviction and courage can also not be dismissed.

I wonder what the more courageous stance is today. You can take a knee in protest of acts of brutality, or you can stand by and criticize those who have that courage. The fact that you do that out of the almost total ignorance of their protest is not exactly a profile in courage.

I don't know what number Dale Hansen of Dallas got in that long ago draft lottery. I do know that he is a Veteran of the Vietnam War. While thinking of Trump and others who stand in judgment and pontificate about the meaning of "patriotism" without ever having served themselves, I was randomly treated to a commentary of Mr. Hansen.

On September 26, 2017, Dale who is a broadcaster on WFAA in Dallas, had enough of the distortions and hypocrisy:

> *"...any protest you don't agree with is a protest that should be stopped. Martin Luther King should have marched across a different bridge. Young black Americans should have gone to a different college and found a different lunch counter and college kids in the 60s had no right to protest an immoral war.*

I served in the military during the Vietnam War and my foot hurt too. My best friend from high school was killed in Vietnam.....and he did not die so that you could decide who is a patriot and who loves America more.

The young black athletes are not disrespecting America or the military by taking a knee during the anthem. They are respecting the best thing about America. We have white men in America who wave the Nazi flag and he (Trump et.al.) is concerned about taking a knee because it disrespects the American flag.

We use that flag to sell mattresses and beer. We wear it as a swimsuit and we wrap our bald heads in a flag bandana and stick it in our pants. Because we disrespect that flag every day!

Maybe we all need to the read the Constitution again. There has never been a better use of pen to paper. Our forefathers made freedom of speech the 1st amendment. They listed 10 and not one of them says you have to stand during the national anthem and I think those men respected the country they fought for and founded a great deal more than the self-proclaimed patriots who are simply hypocrites because they want to deny the basic freedoms of this great country. A country they supposedly value and cherish."

DALE HANSEN

Obviously, Mr. Hansen doesn't need any help from me expressing himself. The flag represents a lot more than simply our military, both to veterans and others like me. "Service" does as well. Police and fireman "serve". Doctors and nurses "serve" every day! Charitable organizations "serve!" Ordinary citizens "serve" their neighbors on a daily basis! Teachers "serve!" (Have you been in some of our schools lately)?!

My father and grandfather fought in World Wars for this country. They did it out of a sense of duty and country. They didn't expect those sacrifices to be trivialized or converted in to a catchphrase for those of us who didn't make the same sacrifices. Stopping them in airports and shopping malls to utter "thank you for your service" doesn't cover you for not adhering to the principles that the founding of this country were based on. It's not that easy. Continuing a democracy takes real effort and sacrifice.

My grandfather was World War I veteran. He died when I was 2. Obviously, we never talked about his "service" or anything else I guess. One of us had a very limited vocabulary at that time. My father was a navigator in World War II, which is really remarkable in that we were constantly lost on family outings. He very rarely talked about the war. His "go to" story was about his shower situation while he was in basic training. My Dad was a very "clean" guy. Showers were important to him:

> **Dad:** In basic training we had a 5 mile run every morning before breakfast. I never finished worse than 3rd!

> **Keith:** Why?

> **Dad:** We only had 3 showers and I wanted the hot water!

To illustrate how little he and his generation of true heroes understated their heroism, I point to another story. I was 55 years old when my Dad first told me that he had parachuted out of his plane over the then nation of Yugoslavia. Even then he didn't exactly volunteer this information. I found out because he was annoyed that my brother had set up an interview with him for the next morning with the "Yugoslavians". He was still in the hospital from his heart surgery but was being released the next day:

> **Keith**: You must be excited. You're going home tomorrow!

> **Dad**: Yeah but your brother has me being interviewed by the Yugoslavians at the house on Friday.

> **Keith**: There are no more Yugoslavians Dad. The country broke up. More importantly why are the former Yugoslavians coming to talk to you?

> **Dad (annoyed)**: It's from when I parachuted out of that plane. The Yugoslavian Liberation Front rescued me from the woods after 3 days.

> **Keith**: What the hell are you talking about?!!!

> **Dad (annoyed)**: I've told you about it Keith. Our plane was shot down and we parachuted out. It's no big deal!

> **Keith**: Dad I would have remembered this. I remember the shower story, I think I would've recalled this one.

> **Dad**: Maybe I told your brother.

Can you imagine this type of modesty today? Of course not. Maybe among actual military members themselves this is still the case, but not for us new "patriots" who need to wear our loyalty on our sleeves or lapels for all to see. You better wear it as well or we will make sure that you do while you're standing for the anthem! Where in the world are we?!

Certainly, the military is part of what the flag and the anthem represents but it's not all of it. The ironic part of this is that I believe most current and former military personnel would agree. I see freedom when I look at the flag. I see the founding fathers, who through their genius established a system of government that was revolutionary then and if followed properly, still is today. I stand for the anthem in part because of our right to protest and think independently. I stand because others have the right not to. And if I ever choose not to stand, I won't! Not even if a guy in a red hat who doesn't quite understand the purpose and origins of the American Revolution or of actual "service" tells me to!

The Constitution and the Bill of Rights guarantees all of us the right to express ourselves how we see fit. It seems that my friends who would disagree with me on this need to stop confusing the Constitution with a Chinese restaurant. You can't take one from column A and one from column B. You don't get to pick and choose which amendments you like and which you don't. You love the 2nd but not the 1st. Give me the 6th with no MSG and get rid of the 8th. That's not how this works!

That was fun!! This was not how I planned on ending this book but it is what it is. My kids would describe much of this chapter as one of my rants and a "rant" is never really planned I guess. No apologies.

I may however need to rethink that 10-year next book plan. There's just too much going on! Additionally, I'm running out of decades.

I may be back in 5!!

APPENDIX

In the Matter of the Arbitration
Between
Keith Glass and KGG & Co. L.L.C.
- and -
ASM Sports, Inc., Andrew Miller,
& Jack Ringel

OPINION AND AWARD
In the Matter of the Arbitration
Between
Andrew Miller
- and -
Keith Glass

APPEARANCES

For Glass & KGG:
Polloway & Polloway, L.L.P.
By: Merric J. Polloway, Esq.

For Miller & Ringel:

By: Barry I. Siegel, Esq.

Keith Glass and Andrew Miller are sports agents who primarily represent professional basketball players and are certified to do so pursuant to the Regulations Governing Player Agents issued by the National Basketball Players Association (the "NBPA" or "Union").

On October 31, 2007, Glass sued Miller, ASM Sports and Ringel in the Superior Court of New Jersey (Docket No. L-5339-07), asserting, inter alia, that defendants had tortuously interfered with his contractual relationship with Player Quincy Douby. Defendants denied the claim and Ringel also filed a counterclaim against Glass asserting that he was due a percentage of the commissions Glass was receiving following the latter's negotiation of an NBA Contract on Douby's behalf. Then, in 2009, Miller sued Glass in the same court alleging that Glass had tortuously interfered with his contractual relationship with player Taquan Dean.

After the taking of depositions and the filing of motions, the Parties decided, in place of an in-court resolution, to submit their disputes to me as an arbitrator with final and binding authority. Their Agreement, signed by counsel on January 25, 2010, reads:

> Our signatures to this letter will confirm our Agreement, on behalf of our respective clients, regarding the arbitration before you, which is currently scheduled for January 28-29, 2010. We hereby agree that any award or decision by you as arbitrator of the claims and counterclaims made in the disputes known as *Keith Glass & KGG & Co., LLC v. ASM Sports, Inc., Andrew Miller, Jack Ringel .et al.* and *Andrew Miller v. Keith Glass* will be final and binding upon all parties, and will be appealable only to the extent that an American Arbitration Association award or decision is appealable. Subject to

the foregoing appeal right, said award or decision may be entered and enforced by the parties in any court of competent jurisdiction.

Pursuant to that Agreement and an Agreement the Parties themselves had previously signed in November, 2009, I held a hearing on the aforesaid dates, at which all Parties were afforded full opportunity to offer evidence and argument and to present, examine and cross-examine witnesses. Testifying in the Glass/Miller proceeding were Plaintiff Glass, his son and business associate Tyler Glass, Defendant Miller and Defendant and Counter-Claimant Ringel. Testifying in the Miller/Glass proceeding were Plaintiff Miller and Defendant Glass. In addition, various depositions, as discussed below, were received into evidence. Following the testimony, counsel, who, at my request, had submitted pre-hearing statements, submitted post-hearing briefs and reply memoranda, with the Record closed on May 29, 2010, the day of their receipt.

Glass v. Miller

Glass had Douby under contract in April, 2007, having signed him to a Standard Player Agent Contract ("SPAC") on May 9, 2006 and having subsequently negotiated a maximum rookie contract on his behalf with the Sacramento Kings. On April 26, 2007, Douby served Glass with a written notice advising that he was terminating his services, which under the SPAC he had a right to do. Though Glass concedes that Douby had a right to terminate the SPAC and considered that Douby, by his action, had also terminated the endorsement and money management agreements, he contends that it was Miller and Ringel who wrongfully induced Douby to do so and thereby tortiously interfered with the relationship causing monetary damage. Miller and Ringel contend that they did not so interfere and that what occurred was solely Douby's decision, which he had the right to make. As will be seen, a determination with respect to these contentions depends to a great extent on credibility.

The Background

Player Douby grew up in Brooklyn, New York. From the time he was in the eighth grade, even before he played basketball, he was mentored and advised by Defendant Ringel, who was then the Dean and a basketball coach at Grady High School (Gx7, p.15). From those days on, Douby considered him "like my other father" (Gx7, p 9). Initially enrolling at Hofstra at Ringel's suggestion, Douby subsequently decided he wanted to play at Rutgers, a short distance from Marlboro, New Jersey, the town to which Ringel had moved. On hearing this, Ringel introduced him to the Rutgers coach and otherwise aided his entrance into the university and his placement on the team (Tr.II, 137-140, Ringel). In his junior year, Douby began considering leaving Rutgers and entering the NBA draft. One of his teammates at Rutgers was Glass's son, Tyler. As it was, Douby met with Glass, who thought he might be picked in the 1st round. He also met with Miller, who was not so sure (Gx7, 20-21, 34-35). During this period, Ringel was also in touch with both agents, as well as an agent named Ken Glassman, from whom he had accepted money when Douby was a freshman.

As it turned out, in a decision to which Ringel raised no objection (Tr.II, 155), Douby, who was anxious to leave Rutgers, went with Glass. The SPAC was signed at Glass's house in the presence of Ringel and members of Glass's family on May 9, 2006. It was at this time that Glass and Douby orally agreed that Glass would also handle endorsement contracts.

Glass testified that the group decided to celebrate and that as he, his son, Tyler, and Ringel were returning to the house after buying some pizza, Ringel said they had not talked about what was in it for him. When Glass asked him to explain, Ringel said that others, such as Miller, were still calling, implying that he could take Douby somewhere else. Then, when Glass asked Ringel what he was going to do for him, Ringel's reply was that he could make sure Douby stayed. At this, Glass testified that he told Ringel he would give him 25% as "long as he is with me." (Tr.I, 55-57). Tyler Glass corroborated his father's testimony (Tr. I, 169-170).

In contrast, Ringel testified that the conversation about 1% [i.e., 1/4 of the 4% commission] came up before the SPAC was signed and that it was Glass who raised it, saying "whatever anyone else was going to do for me, he would do the same." (Tr. II, 157-159).

On May 24, 2006, Glass and Douby signed a Money Management Agreement. Glass testified that the issue was raised by Ringel who thought that Douby, if signed, would be ill-equipped to handle his day-to-day finances (Tr.I, 61-62). Ringel's testimony is that Douby wanted him to handle his money, but he was reluctant to do so and that when he and Glass discussed the matter, Glass said he could handle it (Tr.II, 162-163).

The Agreement (Gx2) reads:

MONEY MANAGEMENT AGREEMENT

Keith Glass agrees to be engaged by the Player for the purpose of budgeting, managing and advising the Player on the day-to-day financial matters pertaining to the player. This management service shall include payment of bills, budget supervision, income tax planning (but not preparation) and planning and advising on auto and home purchasing. Should the Player decide to engage Keith Glass' services as set forth in this Agreement, the fee to Keith Glass shall be 4% of income. The Player will be furnished with a monthly statement of his accounts, and the services set forth in this Agreement shall commence on the date this Agreement is executed by all parties.

Following a good deal of work on Glass's part in which he talked to a number of teams, Douby was selected 19th in the 1st round, after which Glass negotiated a maximum rookie contract with Geoff Petrie of the Sacramento Kings. (Tr.I, 60, 67-69). Following the signing, Glass followed Douby in the summer league, while Tyler set him up in Sacramento, getting an apartment, furniture and a phone, arranging for insurance, including that of Douby's sister, and preparing and supervising budgets (Tr.I, 171).

Though Douby, by all accounts, did not have a particularly good playing year, Glass testified that he thought that his relationship with him was "very good" and that he had received no complaints from either Douby or Ringel regarding his representation and the management of his day-to-day finances or the fact that Tyler, rather than himself, had visited him in Sacramento (Tr.I, 70-76, 100). Tyler similarly testified, saying he would speak to Douby two or three times a day; that there were never any complaints about their services or the fact that he, rather than his dad, was doing the budgeting and visiting him in California, and that he never got any requests prior to April 24, 2007, from Douby or anyone else to see his financial records (Tr.I, 173-175, 203-204).

According to both, the first indication of any problem was April 24, 2007. Tyler testified that he got a call from Douby asking for his bank statements. He then called his father who said he would call Ringel and get back to him (Tr.I 174-176). Glass said he called Ringel who said that Douby's father was concerned about CD rates, which was a surprise since they weren't in CDs, all agreeing instead to let the money accumulate until May or June, then sit down with a financial advisor to decide what investments should be made (Tr.I, 77-78, Glass). After Glass told his son that Douby could have the bank statements, Douby came over and picked them up, talking about basketball awhile and inviting Tyler out that evening, which Tyler could not accept because of another commitment (Tr.I, 176-178).

Neither Glass nor his son ever saw Douby again. Instead, Glass received a call from him on April 26, during which Douby, who seemed to be hesitant, said he might have to make a change in direction. Glass, who said that Douby then stopped as if someone was talking to him, then asked if he could call back. However, he never did. Shortly thereafter, Glass received a fax terminating his services (Tr.I, 79-81). The letter (Gx3), signed by Douby and dated April 22, 2007, was faxed from a UPS store in Tenafly, New Jersey at 2:33 PM on April 26. It read:

> This letter shall serve as written notice that I am terminating our NBA Standard Player Agent Contract agreement per the bylaws of the NBA and any and all other contracts we may have entered in to. In so doing, please cease any and all conversations with regard to my professional basketball career both on and off the court.
>
> I wish you the best of luck in your future endeavors.

As previously stated, it is Glass's contention that his termination, which was to take effective 15 days after the letter's May 26th receipt, was not Douby's idea, but that of Ringel and Miller and that they orchestrated the termination for their advantage. Miller and Ringel deny the allegation and contend that what occurred was the commonplace termination by a player as was his right. They assert that their first contact was over the phone on April 23rd following the preparation of the April 22hd termination letter; that they and Douby then met on

April 24th to discuss the possibility of Miller representing Douby, and that the Miller/Douby SPAC (MxG) was not executed until May 14, 2007, after the effective date of the termination and the 15 day cooling-off period of the SPAC's Section 6. Glass maintains that this was not the case; that contact was made well before April 23rd and that the greater likelihood is that the Miller/Douby SPAC was executed on April 24th, before Glass had been terminated.

The Events as Seen by Glass

What first raised Glass's suspicions was the fax's origination point; a UPS store in Tenafly, about 1/3 of a mile from Miller's office and his sense, upon reading the letter, that it had been written by someone other than Douby (Tr. I, 87-89). Glass says that what actually occurred, including the circumstances of Miller's signing of Douby, was revealed by his research, the aforesaid depositions and the telephone records of Douby, Miller, Ringel (Gx 9, 10 and 29).

Though Ringel and Douby contend they did not talk to each other until April 23rd, after Douby had assertedly reached a decision to terminate Glass, Ringel's telephone records (Gx29) show an 11-minute call from Miller's office as early as March 20, 2007. They also show calls from Miller's office to Ringel on March 20, April 2, April 9, and April 11. All of this preceded the conceded 36 minute call from Miller to Ringel on April 23rd. The next day, the 24th, Douby came to Glass's office to pick up his bank statements. Later that afternoon, he, Miller and Ringel met at Ringel's house in Marlboro. At this point, Glass had not been terminated.

According to Glass, the actual termination notice of April 26th also reveals Miller's direct involvement. As shown by Miller's phone records, he called both Douby and Ringel on April 25th. This was followed on April 26th by a call from Chris Brantley, one of Miller's employee's, to Douby just nine minutes before Douby called Glass saying he might be going in a different direction. In his August, 2008, certi-fication (Gx24) Douby, who did not testify at the hearing, described a litany of "requests, complaints and warnings" regarding his "disap-pointment in [Glass's] services." And in his deposition, Douby stated there was "no way" he was going to stay with Glass (Gx7, pp.25-26). Glass, as previously stated, denies that Douby ever complained about his services. He then asks, in relation to Douby's assertions, that if Douby was as angry as he now claims and wanted to get rid of him, why is it that he waited from the time the letter was assertedly typed on Monday, April 22nd until four days later, Thursday, April 26th when the call was made and the letter faxed? Glass's answer is that Douby was pushed. Why else would Ringel have called Douby twice earlier in the day and Brantley have called him just before the call was made to Glass? And why else was Douby so near Miller's office when the ter-mination letter was sent? Douby's explanation is that the termination letter was sitting in his car for four days because he had "a lot of stuff" to do; that he was in his car in Manhattan when he received the call on the 26th; that he was shopping but preparing to go to Ringel's house (a direction opposite from Tenafly); that the UPS store in Tenafly "came up" on his GPS as he searched for the location of fax machines and he felt comfortable driving to Tenafly because he knew "from papers" that Miller's office was there (Gx7,pp.61-67). This, Glass says, is as believ-able as Douby's repeated assertions, contrary to the testimony of both Miller and Ringel, that he had not seen Miller or had even talked to him until after the 26th (Gx7, pp.86-87, 99).

The Events as Seen by Miller and Ringel

Miller and Ringel contend that Glass has it all wrong. Douby had de-cided to replace Glass all on his own. Moreover, Miller's representa-tion did not occur until after Glass had been terminated.

First, they say the calls from Miller's office to Ringel prior to April 23rd were all between Brantley and Ringel and had nothing to do with Douby. Though Brantley stated, in his May 27, 2010 certification, that he had "no idea" what the calls were about, he was sure that none related to Douby, for, if they had, he would have remembered (GxV). Ringel, in a certification of the same date, maintains the calls were about three other players in which he had an interest and the hope that Miller's office might be able to help their careers and also aid in getting donations of wearing apparel for the Maccabean Games (GxU).

Second, they contend, there is no question from Douby's deposition that he alone made the decision to terminate Glass. Though no reason is needed for a termination under the SPAC, it is also clear from Douby's deposition and his certification that he had ample reason for doing so, including Glass's failure to visit him during his rookie season and the mishandling of his finances, in which his debit card was constantly getting blocked and he had, by the end of the season, $400,000 in a non-interest bearing account rather than in interest bearing investments.

There is also no question from Ringel's testimony that the termination letter had been prepared on April 22nd, before the first contact between Miller and Ringel.

As to that first contact, the Record shows that on April 23rd, Ringel called Miller's office and left a message that it was about Douby. When Miller called him back, Ringel told Miller that Douby had or was going to terminate Glass and wanted to talk to him about representation. The response of Miller, who was "hoping" that Ringel was "calling about Quincy firing Keith Glass," was that he wouldn't agree to be Douby's agent unless they sat down together and that Douby would have to terminate Glass in the proper fashion by sending Glass a letter to that effect. According to Miller, Ringel's response was that a letter had been drafted. Miller, however, do not inquire as to its content (Tr.II, 52-54, 59, 129-130). According to Miller, the meeting on the 24th was exploratory to ascertain whether he wanted to be Douby's representative. His testimony is that from what Ringel had told him, "they were done with their current representation and they were moving along," but if he and Douby weren't on the same page, he didn't want to be involved (Tr.II, 54-56, 107-108).

Thus, Miller and Ringel claim, there was nothing improper in the meeting of the 24th. Miller thought it was all over between Douby and Glass. But even if that was not accurate, talking to a player represented by someone else is not impermissible and the fact is that Miller did not become Douby's agent until May 14, after the termination took effect.

On this latter point, Glass asserts that the Miller/Douby SPAC was not signed on May 14th, but executed on April 24th and back-dated. According to Miller's testimony, he was in Ringel's house twice; the meeting of April 24th and the SPAC signing of May 14th (Tr.II, 122-124). However, Miller's phone records, which show he was in Marlboro on April 24th (Gx10) do not show him in Marlboro on May 14th (Gx30). If, as Miller says, the SPAC was signed in Ringel's house, this must mean that it was signed on April 24th, the only day the records show him at Ringel's residence. Thus, it was improperly entered into two days before Glass was sent notice of termination.

Discussion

All agree that Douby had the right to terminate the agreements at issue. That is not the question. Rather, the question is whether Miller and Ringel tortuously interfered with the Glass/Douby at-will relationship. All also agree that Glass has the burden of proving his claim. Additionally, there is no real quarrel, considering the similarity of the New Jersey and federal cases cited by the Parties, as to the lens through which the testimony and contentions must be viewed.

Pursuant to those cases, the elements of tortious interference are that there was a reasonable expectation of economic advantage, the asserted interference was done maliciously, i.e., intentionally and without justification or excuse, the interference caused the loss of prospective gain, and the injury caused damage.

Given the fact that Glass had Douby under contract and that Douby's playing contract had at least another year to run, the key question is whether there was interference with that relationship and, if so, whether that inference was malicious in the sense stated above. Only if those questions are answered in the affirmative would one need turn to the loss of prospective gain and the question of damage.

Miller and Ringel contend that there was no interference; that the decision was Douby's alone and they had nothing to do with it. This position rests primarily on the contentions set forth in Douby's deposition and certification.

In Douby's certification (Gx24), filed in August 2008 in support of a Motion for Summary Judgment, he repeatedly and emphatically states in Paragraph 12 that he first contacted Miller after he faxed Glass the termination notice and had no contact with Miller before then. This, we now know, is simply untrue. These statements alone, which were given under a permissible form of oath but are contrary to all direct evidence in this proceeding, are sufficient to cast considerable doubt on Douby's credibility and any other statements he might have made.

With respect to other statements in the certification, Douby asserts in Paragraph 10 that Glass had been instructed to send monthly bank statements to his father and Ringel. As previously stated, the Money Management Agreement has no such provision and Tyler Glass, who was sending said statements to Douby only to find them unopened, categorically denied that he, Ringel, his father or anyone else had asked for bank statements until April 24th, 2007 (Gx23, Paragraph 5, Tr.I, 174-175). If there had been such requests, one would expect to find substantiation either in writing or otherwise, but there is none. Indeed, Ringel, who testified that he and Douby's father were supposed to get statements (Tr. II, 167), never once asked for them during the entire season, saying, for reasons unexplained, that he didn't want to "rock the boat" (Tr. II, 179-180). Clearly, a single request, given Tyler Glass's concern over Douby's spending habits, would have produced results.

Both Glass and his son also denied that Douby ever said one word about any asserted "requests, complaints, and warnings" regarding dissatisfaction with Glass's services and there is no evidence in this voluminous record to support Douby's questionable assertions that he personally ever did so. If, in fact, the complaints were as alleged, one would also expect documentary evidence of some nature that they were made. Ringel, who readily agreed that Douby probably made no mention of any complaints during the playing year, testified that he had told Glass about not visiting Douby and the fact that Douby's bank card sometimes got stopped (Tr. II, 168-169). However, as set forth below, there are a number of reasons to question Ringel's testimony regarding any disputed aspect of this proceeding.

As to the management of Douby's finances, there is no evidence, except Ringel's undocumented assertions, that his bills were unpaid or that he was in arrears in any obligations. Both Douby and Ringel do assert that they discovered he had $400,000 in a checking account when they went to the bank on April 24th following Ringel's conversation with Miller the previous day. Given the fact that Douby, like all NBA players, was paid in 12 equal semi-monthly installments and that those installments, from which taxes were withheld, did not begin until November 15, 2006 and the further fact of Douby's expenditures and the payments to a realtor and contractors for the house he was building for his parents in North Carolina, it is unlikely that the figure was as high as claimed. But putting that aside, Glass's statement that everyone knew that the money was to accumulate to a point when they would speak to a financial advisor is uncontradicted in this Record.

When all this is considered, I am not persuaded that Douby had voiced a number of complaints that had gone unanswered and that as a result, he alone had decided, by the time the season had ended in mid-April that Glass would be terminated. If things were as bad as now claimed, there would have been more proof – messages, letters of complaint – than what has been presented. I am also not persuaded that Douby single-handedly decided to terminate Glass on April 22. I am mindful that the termination notice bears that date. Quite apart from the inconsistent testimony as to whose words they were and who composed, wrote or typed the notice and with whose aid, if the notice was written on that day and Douby was so anxious to rid himself of Glass, why was it not immediately delivered, either by fax or certified mail or both? Or hand delivered, since Ringel's home, where the notice was assertedly typed, was only 16 miles or so from Glass's office. Any of these methods would have been easy enough. All the right words were there and the location of Glass's office was surely known. If not then, why wasn't it delivered on the 24th, since it was assuredly in hand sitting in Douby's car when Douby was in Glass's office picking up of his bank statements after the visit to the bank? Could it be, instead, that it was not written on the 22nd, but sometime later, and that the decision was made by Ringel, Douby's long-time mentor and advisor, and Miller on the 23rd or the 24th?

If the decision was made on the 23rd or 24th, it is unnecessary to determine when the Miller/Douby SPAC was actually signed; the decision, if made or aided by Miller and Ringel before Glass's termination, is, in itself, interference. Here, of course, credibility is critical. On that score, there is nothing in this Record, despite assertions to the contrary, that adversely reflects on the veracity of Glass or his son or their conformity with accepted standards. The same cannot be said with respect to the defendants.

In 2000, the State of Florida determined that Miller had recruited and solicited a college athlete on behalf of his then sports management firm in July 1999 while, contrary to Florida law, he was unlicensed in the State (Gx25). In the same year he was sued by Agent Eric Fleisher, his former employer, for a breach of fiduciary duty by secretly signing some of Fleishers' clients, such as Kevin Garnett and Chauncey Billups, and then leaving the firm. In 2002, as reported in the press, a New York jury rendered a $4.6 million verdict in Fleisher's favor, with the matter settled while on appeal (Tr.II, 110-111).

Ringel not only accepted money from an agent in order to "baby-sit" Douby and keep other agents away from him (Tr.II, 153); he testified he would have accepted what had been offered even if he knew it was contrary to NCAA Rules or otherwise unprincipled (Tr. II, 211-213). He also, in my judgment, asked Glass to pay him to keep Douby from leaving. Beyond that, he made it clear that at some point "down the line" he would ask Miller to pay him as well (Tr.II, 191).

Though there is no direct evidence that Ringel was talking to Brantley or anyone else about Douby in those pre-April 23 phone calls, it is indeed strange, since he had not talked to Miller for almost a year and knew that Miller was angry about what had occurred in May 2006, that he would suddenly decide, shortly before April 24th, to call for his office's assistance with other players.

Quite apart from that, it can fairly be said that his testimony does much to mask the circumstances surrounding his admitted conversations with Miller. For example, Ringel's insistence, despite phone records to the contrary, that the "thing at the bank" happened four or five days before he and Douby had spoken to Miller i.e., no later than April 19, and that April 19th was also the day that Douby, whom he was with, called Glass to say, much to Ringel's surprise, that it was over (Tr.II, 176-179). So too, was his testimony that he didn't tell Miller on the 23rd that Douby was "thinking" of going in another direction, but told him that Douby "was going" in another direction because Douby had "already told Keith out" four days before (Tr.II, 185-186). If this testimony is credited everything falls in place; Douby tells Glass "out" on the 19th; the termination letter is prepared on the 22nd, then Miller is talked to on the 23rd and met with on the 24th. But we know that Douby did not make the call on the 19th as he and Ringel were going to a bank that day. It is exceedingly doubtful that, Douby, who was in Sacramento playing against the Lakers on the evening of the 18th (Gx28), was even in New Jersey on the 19th. Beyond that, we now know that the trip to the bank was the 24th and, as the phone records established, the call to Glass was on the 26th, all of which took place after the meeting with Miller.

Thus, there is little reason to believe the sequence of events posited by Ringel and Miller. There are too many inconsistencies, changes in testimony and undocumented assertions for it to be credited. There was no call on the 19th, the content of which surprised Ringel, and the nature of which was memorialized in a letter written on April 22. No such call was ever made. Could Ringel have been mistaken as to the date, was it really the 26th? If so, how could Ringel, having already met with Miller, have been surprised at that call's content (Gx7)?

The accounts just doesn't hang together. What does hang together is that Ringel, who had wanted Douby to sign with Miller in the first place (Gx24, Paragraph 8, Douby), had decided that it was time for this to happen; that he then talked to Miller to make sure that Miller would agree, and that the meeting of the 24th, in which Miller never asked if Glass had been terminated as he should have, was the time agreement was reached, with the signing not to take place until after a termination notice was served and at least 15 more days had passed.

It is also my judgment that this interference, initiated by Ringel and participated in by Miller, was done intentionally and with no justification or excuse. It cannot successfully be argued that what occurred was the "custom in the trade" or "sanctioned by the rules of the game" so as to condone what occurred. Players often change agents, but the responsible agent in whom a player expresses an interest makes certain that the player's present agent has been terminated before discussions begin. To not do so or, to not ascertain that the situation is in fact as described, by asking, for example, for proof of a termination notice' delivery, is not "right and just dealing under the circumstances." As the New Jersey Supreme Court also observed in *Printing-Mart Morristown v. Sharp Electronics Corp.*, 116 N.J.739, 757 (1989), "Not only must [a] defendant[']s motive and purpose be proper but so also must be the means." Here, the means did not meet that standard.

One might ask of the motives beyond what occurred. After all, even if Miller became Douby agent, Glass was still entitled to commissions for another year and additional commissions if the Kings picked up the third year of Douby's contract. As for Ringel, he was still receiving a portion of those commissions and just might receive nothing from Miller. Given this, why would Miller bother to attain the representation of Douby and what would Ringel gain if this occurred? It is not at all difficult to perceive the motives involved. It must be remembered that Miller wanted Douby as his client in 2006; he had put in considerable time and energy, acting in what he described as an important advisory role, and looking to represent a player who, in his judgment, had possibility enough to pursue. Yet, the player signed with someone else. As a result, Miller was clearly angry. Though Douby did not have the best of years during his rookie season, getting the player back when he had promise and getting him back from the agent who had taken him away when all had pointed to his signing of Douby was motive enough. Ringel, who, as Douby said, had always wanted him to go with Miller, said he wanted to repair his relationship with Miller in order to aid other players in whom he had an interest. Miller, he knew, also had more clients than Glass, some of star caliber, and could be in a position to do better for Douby and, by extension, better for Ringel in the years ahead. Ringel, who expected to be paid by Glass until Douby's existing player contract ran out and expected, at some point, to be paid by Miller, could wait.

Though the courts, in judging tortuous inference, do not define malice as requiring ill will or enmity, events following Glass's lawsuit cannot be disregarded. Though Douby wanted no part in it (Dx7, 79-80), Ringel, ostensibly because he couldn't get any records from Glass, called for an audit of Glass by the NBPA (Tr.II, 26-227), an audit that revealed no improprieties (Tr.I,247-248, Glass). A week after Ringel's deposition he e-mailed the father of an Italian player, Danilo Gallinari, that Glass and Miller were both trying to sign, a "father to father" memo suggesting that he "think hard" about agreeing to an agent such as Glass (Gx12). When asked how he obtained the Italian e-mail address of Gallinari's father, Ringel said he got it from the Internet, not Miller (Tr.II, 223-226).

When all of the above is considered, I am fully persuaded that Glass has established the tortuous interference he alleged. Inasmuch as the other matters is this proceeding may have an effect on the remaining aspects of Glass's claim, including damages, I will move to those matters, then return to the loss of prospective gain and damage questions.

Ringel v. Glass

As indicated above, Ringel, in addition to his answer to Glass's Complaint, filed a counter-claim (MxB). The gist of the claim is that Glass agreed to pay Ringel 25% of the commissions he received; that said payments ceased contrary to their oral agreement, and that said payments are due for the entire time Glass has received his commissions. Glass's response, as also indicated above, is that the agreement was made after his signing of Douby, not before as Ringel has alleged, and that the agreement was that said payments would be paid only so long as Douby continued him as his agent. Since the termination notice was filed on April 26, 2007, no payments were subsequently due.

There is no need to spend considerable time on this question. As with other aspects of this case, there is little reason to accept Ringel's version of events. Both Glass and Tyler Glass testified that the agreement was made on April 9, 2006, following Glass's signing of Douby, not before. In addition to establishing that Glass entered into the agreement reluctantly, they also testified that payments were to continue, in Glass's words, "long as [Douby] is with me." Obviously, "with me" can only mean as long as there is non-terminated agent/player relationship. That relationship ended, in accordance with the SPAC, following receipt of Douby's termination notice. I credit the testimony of Glass and his son and, since Glass was no longer Douby's agent after the payments came to an end, I find no basis for awarding Ringel further payments, particularly given the above described circumstances of Douby's departure. Thus, this claim, as the Award that follows provides, is denied.

Miller v. Glass

The circumstances of this claim require greater detail. On February 7, 2008, Miller and a player named Taquan Dean signed what Miller described as his "standard" European Player/Agent Contract. Unlike the SPACs referred to above, that Contract (MxK) was to "continue for two (2) years" and "continue thereafter from year to year until written notice delivered by/to either party thirty (30) days before the anniversary date hereof, when such termination shall be effective."

Miller's Complaint (MxJ), filed during the course of the Glass v. Miller suit, alleges that on July 17, 2008, Dean had signed a contract with a Spanish team, CB Baloncesto Murcia SAD (Murcia), for the 2008-2009 season, pursuant to which Miller was to receive $24,000 in commissions payable by the Team; that on March 13, 2009, Dean breached his contract with Miller by terminating the agency relationship before two years had passed; and that on April 20, 2009, Glass signed Dean to an agency contract while the Miller/Dean agency contract was still in force. The claim, damages from which assertedly arise, not from the 2008-2009 Dean/Murcia contract, but from a contract Dean signed with another club, Malaga, for the 2009-2010 and 2010-2011 seasons, is that Glass, who has represented players in Europe, knew or, in the exercise of reasonable care, should have known that Dean was represented by Miller under a European contract, and that he knew, or in the exercise of reasonable care, should have known that said contract was for two years and "did or should have made inquiry as to the status" of that contract, yet signed Dean. Since Glass either knew or, in the exercise of reasonable care, should have known that Miller had an agency contract with Dean, Miller asserts that Glass's actions "constituted a tortuous interference with [his] prospective economic advantage" (MxJ, Paragraph 112) and that, as a result, Glass owes him his share of the commissions due on the two-season Malaga contract.

Miller testified that in July 2009, after the end of the 2008-2009 season, Regino Olivares, his Spanish agent partner, had negotiated a contract on Dean's behalf with Malaga; that said contract (MxM), was for two years, for which he and Olivares were to receive commissions totaling $90,000, and that it was a "done deal" except for Dean's signature (Tr.III, 10-12).

Approximately four months before the July 10, 2009 date of this contract which Dean never signed, Miller had received a March 13,

2009 fax from Dean terminating their relationship. The fax (MxN and Gx17) reads:

> As per the term of my NBPA contract that I signed with you in 2008 please allow this letter to serve as my official termination of our contract. As such you are no longer authorized to act on my behalf.
>
> I thank you for your efforts.

On the same day, Dean sent a fax to his then club, Murcia, advising that Glass was his agent and the only person authorized to speak on his behalf concerning future employment (Gx17).

Miller testified that he knew of the termination notice and said he had told his Spanish partner it had been received, but that they still had the rights to Dean under his agent agreement. At this point, according to Miller, Olivares reached out to Dean to find out "what he would like him to do." (Tr.III, 30-33). As it turned out, the signed agreement with Malaga (MxQ & Gx18), also dated July 10, 2009, lists Glass as Dean's agent. For our purposes, the essential difference between the unsigned contract and the signed contract is that under the latter the second season is not guaranteed unless the club affirmatively exercises the option while, under the unsigned contract, the season is guaranteed unless the club opts out.

Glass's defense, which rests on his testimony and the certification of Taquan Dean, is that he acted in good faith; that he did not affirmatively seek to represent Dean and that Miller has simply failed to prove the requisite elements of tortuous interference.

In his certification (Gx15), executed earlier this year, Dean stated that he had tried to contact Glass several times in late 2008; that Glass did not respond, evidently because he had treated Glass disrespectfully some months before; that when he finally did reach Glass, with the aid of a friend, in early March 2009, Glass "curtly advised" he would not talk to him unless he was without current representation. Even though he then sent Miller the termination notice of March 13, 2009, advising Glass that he had done so, and Glass subsequently sent him an agent's agreement (Gx18), Dean stated he did not immediately sign it. Instead, he selected a European agent, apologizing to Glass when he did so and saying he "was sorry to do this to you again" (Gx15, Attachment 5). Thereafter, he terminated the European agent and finally executed the agreement with Glass on April 21, 2009.

Glass affirmed this chronology, saying he had been hesitant to talk to him because Dean had gone another way in the summer of 2008 (Tr.III, 36-41). When they finally did talk, Glass asked who he was represented by, and when Miller's name came up, Glass, knowing he was involved in a lawsuit, asked Dean what kind of contract he had signed. Dean's response was he had signed an NBPA contract with agent Bill Duffy when he left Louisville, then signed another one with Miller in 2008. At this point, Glass said he would not talk with him again until Dean convinced him that he had severed all ties with any of his representatives; that he was not "taking any risks" and that Dean would "have to clear the deck" (Tr.III, 41-44, 53). Shortly thereafter, Glass received copies of the notices Dean had sent to Miller and the Murcia club. Glass, accepting what Dean had told him more than once and having received copies of the termination notice, did not ask to see the contract Dean had signed in 2008 (Tr. III, 44-46, 68-69).

Though Glass then sent Dean an agency contract (Gx18) after their early March conversation, Dean did not sign it. Instead, on April 2 he told Glass he was going the "euro route," i.e., signing with Beo Basket, a European agent (Gx15, Attachment 5). Later, Dean changed his mind, with the agency agreement finally executed on April 21 (Tr. III, 48-52). Though Olivares, the European agent affiliated with Miller, subsequently tried to induce Dean to let him negotiate the contract with Malaga, Dean refused (Tr.III, 80-84). The contract ultimately signed, dated July 10, 2009, is, as stated above, for two years, with the second year guaranteed only if the Club exercised an option for the second season.

The Contentions In Brief

As stated, Miller contends that Glass, by acting as he did, committed tortious interference. Rather than relying on what Dean had told him, Glass, who, as evidenced by his own form of an agency contract for Europe (Gx18), had clients playing in Europe, should have gone further. At the least, particularly since he considered Dean somewhat unstable, Glass should have made some "attempt to determine the nature and extent, on his own, of Dean's contractual relationship with Miller." He should have known, inasmuch as Dean had gone another way in 2008 and his jumping from agent to agent, not to trust his word. Glass' failure to take that next step, to do a further investigation, is enough to subject him to liability for the commissions Miller would have earned.

According to Glass, what Miller forgets is that his claim rests on the doctrine of tortuous inference. Proof of that charge requires proof that what occurred was done maliciously, i.e., intentionally and without justification or excuse. According to Glass, there is no such proof. Unlike Miller in the other proceeding, Glass took affirmative steps to assure that Dean no longer had an agent even before he agreed to talk to him. When those talks occurred, Dean went through the history of his agency relationships while in the States; first with Duffy, then with Miller, assuring Glass that what he had signed was an "NBPA" contract, i.e., a SPAC. Then, when Glass asked if Dean had any other contracts with anyone else, Dean assured him he had not. Dean then terminated Miller in writing, providing evidence of that both to Glass and the club for which played. That behavior, in which Glass took no steps to become Dean's agent until those assurances were given, just do not show malice as used in the tortious interference doctrine. As a consequence, Glass contends that Miller's claim must be denied.

Discussion

I cannot agree, despite Miller's contention, that the "only issue" is whether Glass knew or should have known that Dean had a two-year contract with Miller. More is needed; i.e., whether the known facts constituted tortious interference. As the Parties agreed, it is not just that prospective advantage might exist; the critical question is whether there was intentional and willful interference with that advantage, the establishing of which, under the cited case law, includes evidence of malice or otherwise inexcusable conduct.

Applying these standards, there is no evidence that Glass sought to harm Miller. Indeed, he exercised caution in even talking to Dean until he received evidence that the Miller relationship had been terminated. This "taking no risks" behavior, undertaken when Glass was suing Miller for impermissible conduct, is strikingly different from Miller's behavior in which he never even asked for such evidence. It's true that Glass might have gone further, but the fact that he did not do so, does not, in my judgment, rise to the level of malice as that term is understood in this context. There was no deliberate plan engaged in by others to lure Dean into signing with Glass; Dean repeatedly sought Glass out only to be rebuffed on a number of occasions. Neither was there undue influence or molestation as described in *LaMorte Burns & Co. v Walters*, 167 N.J.285 (2001). Under all the circumstances, it is my judgment that the line between generally accepted standards of common morality and unacceptable and malicious behavior was not crossed, and that malice and tortious interference was not established Accordingly, Miller's claim against Glass is denied.

Glass v. Miller

Prospective Economic Advantage and Damages

The Contentions in Brief

Turning to the remaining issue in Glass v. Miller, Glass contends that absent Miller's conduct, he would have continued to represent Douby for a number of years. He concedes that even though he was terminated effective May 11, 2008, he continued to receive commissions under the SPAC and that those commissions were paid for the 2007-2008 and the 2008-2009 season and for the entire 2009-2010 year even though Douby was released during the course of that season. He contends, however, that he could have continued to represent Douby and is therefore entitled to commissions for the time Douby is playing in Turkey and, since Douby is uninjured and relatively young, for years beyond. He also contends that he should receive commissions on future endorsements. Further, he maintains that, if Miller and Ringel had not induced his termination, he would have continued to receive 4% of Douby's income under the Money Management Agreement and that they are liable for interference with that Agreement, amounting to at least $48,000 a year for the 2008-2009 and 2009-2010 seasons for a total of an additional $96,000.

Miller and Ringel contend that Glass suffered no damages. Glass did not contend that any endorsements were at hand and neither did Miller, particularly since Douby, following a short stint with Toronto during the 2009-2010 season, ended up playing in Turkey. There is therefore no proof that there was even prospective economic advantage with respect to endorsements, much less calculable damage in that regard. As to playing contracts, there is no evidence whatever that Douby could have done better than Miller in the Raptors deal or the contract with the Turkish club. Miller also argues that, given the vagaries of the sport, including the continued health and ability of the player, prospective economic advantage to the extent posited by Glass is speculative at best and thus immeasurable by any acceptable standard. As to the Money Management Agreement, Miller and Ringel contend they had nothing to do with its termination and received no benefits from its cancellation and should therefore not be held liable for any fees lost. Miller and Ringel, noting that Glass conceded he was not a financial advisor, also argue that the amount Glass charged Douby for the few services his son performed was unconscionable and should not be permitted.

Discussion

I must agree that Glass's estimate of damages regarding endorsements and playing contracts is purely speculative. There were no endorsements on the horizon at the time of his termination and events since then have demonstrated that the dimness of prospects in 2008 was quite accurate. I say the same with respect to playing contracts. Even if Glass stayed with Douby longer, and given the fluidity of movement in this field, that is not even a realistic certainty, there is no basis for determining, when comparing the client base of both agents that Glass could have done better. Since this uncertainty of prospective economic advantage is too fragile a foundation on which to reasonably fashion an award, I will not award damages on these aspects of Glass's claim.

The Money Management Agreement stands on a different plane, but even here there is firm reason to disagree with Glass' conclusion that the Agreement would continue as written. The evidence he presented affirms that May and June 2007 was the time all had agreed to look at the funds at hand, to interview financial advisors, which Glass did not purport to be, and to turn over aspects of management to the person they chose. Hence, it is safe to say that Glass and his son would not have subsequently performed all of the functions for which they were then being paid. It can therefore also be said with considerable certainty that the fee would have been adjusted by agreement of all concerned.

Despite Miller's contentions to the contrary, I am not persuaded that the original fee, given that Glass was receiving much less than 4% on Douby's salary, was indefensible. In rulings with which both agents should be familiar, charges for both commissions and money management, when agreed upon without coercion or deception, have been approved under the NBPA Regulations. However, it is safe to say that such fees would not have been charged in the future. Since the parties to a future arrangement did not in fact decide on the amount of those fees under the aforesaid changed circumstances, it cannot be said just what those fees would have been for the two seasons at issue. As a consequence, one must decide upon a reasonable estimate, taking equitable principles into consideration. My judgment is that such a fee would have been $20,000 for each season. The Award that follows therefore provides that this is the amount of damages for which Miller and Ringel are accountable.

The Undersigned, acting as the Arbitrator pursuant to the Agreement of the Parties and having duly heard their proofs and allegations, renders the following

AWARD

For the reasons set forth in the foregoing Opinion, the counterclaim of Jack Ringel against Keith Glass and KGG & Co, L.L.C., referenced in Docket No. L-5339-07, and the claim of Andrew Miller against Keith Glass, referenced in Docket No. L-2806-09, are denied.

For the reasons set forth in the foregoing Opinion, the claim of tortious interference brought by Keith Glass and KGG &

Co, L.L.C. against Andrew Miller, ASM Sports, Inc, and Jack Ringel, referenced in Docket No. L-5339-07, is sustained.

As a result of the conduct described in said Opinion, Keith Glass and KGG & Co., L.L.C. have sustained damages in the amount of $40,000, for which Andrew Miller, ASM Sports, Inc. and Jack Ringel are jointly and severally liable and which is to be paid forthwith.

George Nicolau, Arbitrator

ACKNOWLEDGMENT

On this 24th day of July, 2010, I, George Nicolau, a resident of New York, affirm, pursuant to Section 7507 of the Civil Practice Law and Rules of the State of New York that I have executed and issued the foregoing as my Opinion and Award in the above matter.

George Nicolau